Thomas Abel Brimage Spratt

Travels and Researches in Crete

Vol. I

Thomas Abel Brimage Spratt

Travels and Researches in Crete
Vol. I

ISBN/EAN: 9783337211479

Printed in Europe, USA, Canada, Australia, Japan

Cover: Foto ©Andreas Hilbeck / pixelio.de

More available books at **www.hansebooks.com**

TRAVELS AND RESEARCHES

IN

CRETE.

BY

CAPTAIN T. A. B. SPRATT, R.N., C.B., F.R.S.,

HONORARY MEMBER OF THE ARCHÆOLOGICAL INSTITUTES AT BERLIN AND ROME.

IN TWO VOLUMES.

VOL. I.

LONDON:

JOHN VAN VOORST, PATERNOSTER ROW.

MDCCCLXV.

TO

HIS ROYAL HIGHNESS

PRINCE ALFRED, K.G., K.T.

THESE VOLUMES

ARE, BY GRACIOUS PERMISSION,

DEDICATED,

WITH THE MOST PROFOUND AND DUTIFUL RESPECT,

BY

HIS ROYAL HIGHNESS'S

VERY HUMBLE SERVANT,

· THE AUTHOR.

CONTENTS OF VOL. I.

CHAPTER I.   PAGE

Mount Ida.—Ascent to the summit.—Its flora.—Its geological structure.—Devonshire Chough.—The Ibex.—A moving mountain.—Sunset view from the summit.—Comfortless night.—Stormy morning.—Return to the shepherds' cave.   5

CHAPTER II.

Descent from Ida.—Zones of vegetation.—Village of Vorus.—Native conferences.—Pashley's 'Travels'; its deficiencies.—Reflections on the Revolution for Independence.   20

CHAPTER III.

Gnossus and Gortyna.—Candia founded by the Saracens—enlarged by the Venetians.—Its fortifications.—The great Siege of Candia by the Turks.—Gallant defence and surrender.—Reflections on the siege.—Khania supplants Candia as the present capital of Crete.   26

CHAPTER IV.

Dapper's Plan of the Siege.—The Cemetery.—St. George's Gate.—Lepers at ditto.—Youthful leper.—Married lepers and child.—Neglect of the lepers.—Lepers' village.—Reflections.—Duc de Beaufort.—Pasha's tomb.—Turkish superstitions.—Sculptured sarcophagus at the St. George's Gate.....................................   37

vi CONTENTS.

CHAPTER V.

Mahomedans of Crete.—Greek the common language.—Close association of the creeds—its natural effects.—An enlightened pasha, intrigue against him.—Over-estimate of the Greek population.—Greek rising, and persecution of the Mahomedans.—The Sfakians—their dialect—its Hellenic connexion shown by the late Col. Leake 47

CHAPTER VI.

Gnossus—its site—its few remains at present—cause of this.— The Labyrinth.—Plutarch's account of the Minotaur and Labyrinth.—Ancient tombs at Gnossus—its ancient ports of Amnisus and Heracleion 58

CHAPTER VII.

Gnossus an early seat of Art and Learning before Greece.— Sculpture by Dædalus.—Subsequent celebrity of Cretan art.—Its coins remarkable for art and for their imperfect surface and form.—Eminent Cretan sculptors.—A Cretan Venus.—A Cretan head of Zeus.—Leonardo da Vinci's picture.. 68

CHAPTER VIII.

Mount Iuktas, the burial-place of Zeus; route to it.—Turkish Monastery.—Three dervishes.—View from Mount Iuktas. —Rhaucus.—Valley of Arkhanes—its hospitable inhabitants.—Tranquil nights; their treachery to the traveller. 77

CHAPTER IX.

Ancient cities of Lyttus and Lycastus.—Position of the latter at Astritzi.—Thenæ.—Plain of Pediada; ascent to the site of Lyttus from it.—The description of the site and its remains—its inscription—its coins. 89

CONTENTS. vii

CHAPTER X. PAGE

The Plain of Lasethe—its fertility and salubrity—it contained no ancient City, and therefore belonged to Lyttus.—Descent to Khersoneso.—Ruins of an ancient aqueduct and road from Lyttus to Khersoneso.—Nummulitic fossils.—Ruins of Khersoneso.—Vestiges of a church or cathedral.—Tessellated fountain at the port.—Ancient theatre.—A Freshwater deposit..................... 100

CHAPTER XI.

The Mirabella district and uplands.—The Carob- or Locust-tree flourishes in this district.—The nutritious properties of its fruit.—The food of St. John in the wilderness.—Malia Bay and village.—Ancient site on the coast of the bay.—Discovery of scales of gold.—Probable site of a temple to Britomartis.—Site of Miletus.—Extensive cavern near it.—The harbour and fortress of Spina Longa.. 109

CHAPTER XII.

The ruins of an early Cretan city upon the Isthmus of Spina Longa, and of Naxos over it.—The identity of the former with Olontion.—Its ruins.—Its ancient port at Kalokythia.—The ruins and whetstone-quarries of Naxos.—The quarries of Elunta.—The ancient Bishopric of Allyngus recognized here 121

CHAPTER XIII.

The routes between Mirabella and Spina Longa, and also to Kritza.—The upland basin of Lakonia.—A remarkable site over it.—The very early character of the ruins.—Identity with Olus and Olerus.—The Olerian Minerva, her celebrated temple and festival.—Wooden statue to Britomartis, by Dædalus.—Kritza the present capital of the Mirabella.—Its fine situation.—The site of Minoa identified at the head of the Gulf of Mirabella.—The few-

CONTENTS.

ness of its remains explained by a recent submergence of the eastern half of Crete 130

CHAPTER XIV.

The ancient port of Olus at St. Nikolo, not Minoa.—Ruins of a Venetian castle, and of the ancient town of Camara, at St. Nikolo.—A deep pool adjacent to its old port.—A copious source at Almyro, and legends connected with it.—The two other Cretan almyros, or brackish sources.—The singularity of their situations, and of the mountain-features over them, a result of uniform geological conditions.. 142

CHAPTER XV.

The Gulf of Mirabella, and the isthmus at its head.—Characteristic features, their influence upon the earliest inhabitants.—The Eteo-Cretes and Mount Dicte.—The northern route into the Sitia.—The ruins at Leopetra.—The ruined Venetian town and bay of Sitia.—The probable site of Etea 152

CHAPTER XVI.

Journey up the Valley of Sitia to Præsus.—The site a fine one, but vestiges few upon it.—Its ancient name still retained.—Dicte shown by Strabo to have been proximate to it.—Its site at Kopra Kephalo—Ancient cisterns and ruins.—Faithless wives in the Sitia, and easy divorce.—Cretan marriage ceremonies 163

CHAPTER XVII.

The upland plain and village of Kataleone.—Hospitality of a Turkish family.—The plain and village of Khadra.—Rebuilding a church.—A hospitable Greek couple.—Description of their habitation; its furniture, comforts, and condition.—The little tormentors of travellers.—Leave Khadra.—A Venetian villa.—Return to Sitia Bay   174

CONTENTS.

CHAPTER XVIII.

The north-east extremity of Crete.—The Yanisades Islands.—Cape Salmone, doubtful application of the name.—The Topler Monastery.—Eremopoli the ancient Etera.—Its description.—Probably also called Arsinoe.—Its convenient situation for Alexandrian traders.—Relics of a præ-ptolemaic age.—Numerous inscriptions.—Copper coins .. 188

CHAPTER XIX.

Corruption of ancient Cretan names.—The modern name of Lasethe derived from Lyttus, as Sidero from Etera.—The Necropolis of Etera.—Sepulchral vases.—Ancient tombs and tombstones.—Volcanic protrusions.—Palaio Kastron.—Middle-age stronghold.—Vestiges of a city at the time of Minos.—The ancient name not determined.—Inscription at the Topler Monastery.—A cairn.—Local winds .. 200

CHAPTER XX.

Sponge-divers on the coast of Crete.—Aristotle's knowledge of sponges derived from the ancient sponge-divers.—The temperature of the Mediterranean deeps. — The large adulteration of the sponge with fine sand.—Practice of diving by the young children of sponge-divers.—A fleet of sponge-fishers at work, their mode of operation.—The inconveniences and accidents they are subject to.—The shark's occasional appearance.—Account of a large shark near a sponge-bank 215

CHAPTER XXI.

The east coast of Crete.—Gorge of Karouba.—Zakro Bay.—Cyclopean remains.—The ancient Itanus.—Destruction of it and Præsus by the Hierapytnians.—The ancient name still applied to a neighbouring village.—The coins of Itanus.—The appropriate emblems upon them.—Site of the small town of Ampelus. — Routes to return to Ierapetra 232

CONTENTS.

CHAPTER XXII.

The Kouphonisi Islands.—Roman ruins.—Ancient statue.—
The Island of Ophiusa.—Cretan pirates in early times.—
Roman and Rhodian war against them.—The haunt of
Algerine pirates.—An English traveller taken by one.—
Captain Manias.—His piratical deeds as a Sfakiot chief-
tain.—His death in my service.—A character, but not a
type of the race.—A patriot's grave 241

CHAPTER XXIII.

Return to Ierapetra.—Its situation and natural facilities for
forming a good port.—Its importance in early Cretan
times.—Its three theatres.—its three harbours.—An inscription with the name of the city.—A lepers' village.—
Visit to the village.—The neglect of the lepers by the
Cretans.—The Chapel of the Holy Cross upon a Mountain.—Misdirection of mind and means.—Constant resort
of the sick to the ships for medical aid.—Their wants
and wounds attended to by the doctor.—The good physician's pleasures 253

CHAPTER XXIV.

Discovery of two sarcophagi.—Their purchase and removal to
the British Museum.—A ghost story.—Description of the
larger sarcophagus.—The situation in which the sarcophagi were found, not *in situ*.—Conjectures upon their
origin and original sites 274

CHAPTER XXV.

The village of Anatoli.—Valley of Myrto.—Village of Malia
within it.—Tournefort's "simpling" journey to it.—
Route from Girapetra to Arvi.—A giant's tomb.—Pashley's learned description of the conflict of Otos and

CONTENTS. xi

PAGE

Ephialtes, sons of a giant, against the god Ares.—Protrusion of porphyritic trap.—Site of the temple of Jupiter Arbius.—Cleft mountain over it.—The probable origin of the temple at its base.—Geological notice of the adjacent coast deposits.—Keraton Rock and Bay.—Vast number of olive-trees.—Route to Viano.—Viano the ancient Biennus. —Route towards the Messara.—Roman aqueduct.—A fighting Turk.—Tchifoot Kastelli 289

CHAPTER XXVI.

Tchifoot Kastelli.—The supposed site of Arkadia.—Pashley's erroneous views regarding its position.—Pliny's description of its fountains.—Tchifoot Kastelli proves to be only a middle-age fortress.—Probable origin of the name.— Return to the tent.—Information of other ruins.—Proceed to them.—Identify them as Arkadia.—Their description 310

CHAPTER XXVII.

The Messara plain.—Its two rivers.—Proceed to Panagia.— Mussulman hospitality.—The effects of the Greek movement against the Turks during the past year.—Disappointing visit to reported ruins over Panagia.—Search for the Homeric Rhytion.—Discover ruins at Rotas.— Identify the site as Rhytion.—Kastelli the ancient Stelæ. —Sudsuro the ancient Priansus.—Its situation.—Sudsuro Bay.—Rock chapel 327

CHAPTER XXVIII.

Rock grotto and chapel of Niketas.—Barbary corsair.—Miraculous escape of some Cretans from the pirates.—The flight of a Cretan virgin.—The river Sudsuro.—A waterfall.—The city of Lebena.—Temple of Æsculapius.—The ruins of the city 343

APPENDIX I.

On Cretan and modern Greek. (By Viscount Strangford.) .. 355

APPENDIX II.

The capture of a Protestant divine by an Algerine corsair, in the seventeenth century......................... 384

ILLUSTRATIONS TO VOLUME I.

	Page
VIEW OF THE TOWN OF CANDIA . . . *Frontispiece*.	
COIN OF GNOSSUS	5
VIEW FROM MOUNT IDA, LOOKING WEST . . . . *to face*	16
SCULPTURED DRAMATIC SCENE ON A SARCOPHAGUS AT CANDIA	46
A CRETAN VENUS . . . . *to face*	72
VIEW OF KHERSONESO . . . . ,,	106
VIEW OF THE SITE OF OLUNTION . . . . . . ,,	128
PLAN OF GOOLAS, THE ANCIENT OLUS	129
CYCLOPEAN HOUSE AT GOOLAS . . . . (*woodcut*)	141
VIEW OF EREMOPOLI, THE ANCIENT ETERA	193
VIEW OF PALAIO KASTRON	208
SPONGE-DIVERS AT WORK . . . . . . *to face*	222
VIEW OF IERAPETRA . . . . ,,	254
SCULPTURED SARCOPHAGUS—THE DISCOVERY OF ACHILLES AT THE COURT OF LYCOMEDES	279
ACHILLES LAMENTING THE LOSS OF PATROCLUS	281
PLAN OF SARCOPHAGUS-CHAMBER . . . . . (*woodcut*)	282
CLEFT MOUNTAIN OF ARVI	295
GROUND-PLAN OF ARKADIA . . *to face*	321
VIEW OF LEBENA	351
MAP—EASTERN PART OF CRETE . . *at the end*.	

INTRODUCTION.

HAVING in May 1851, been appointed to succeed my lamented Commander, the late Captain Graves, in the direction of the Mediterranean Survey, I took command of the 'Spitfire,' a paddle steamer, and proceeded in her first to Crete, to complete its general survey, which had been previously commenced by him.

I was joined by all the surveying-staff of Captain Graves, and by Lieutenant (now Commander) G. Johnstone as the executive officer, my former companions in the Survey; and by their able assistance the survey of Crete would have been brought to a conclusion in the end of the year 1853, but for its sudden interruption in the middle of the season, by my recall to prosecute surveys, which the prospective Russian war rendered more immediately necessary, in the waters of approach to Constantinople and the Black Sea. The Cretan charts were in consequence necessarily put aside until after the Crimean war, and until other surveys that resulted from that war, viz. at the Danube, &c., had been completed and published.

Several journeys were made by me through Crete, during the progress of its survey, in company with some of the officers or alone, either with the view to co-operate in parts of its detail, or to collect reliable information regarding the local names, population, and ancient cities, many of them being as yet undiscovered or undescribed, and in consequence having an important connexion with the completion of its geographical and topographical description. The results of the journeys are briefly thrown together in the following chapters.

The most gratifying part of an important work or task is when the director and responsible head of it has it in his power to do full justice to the zeal and ability of those whom he has had the good fortune to have under his command during its progress.

But the value of these detailed surveys will speak for themselves, and for the several officers whose names are now attached to them. And to the harmony that existed must be attributed, without doubt, a large share of those good results that followed.

For in such a special service, as in every expedition of enterprise and research, where the zeal, talent, and interest of every officer is required to be enlisted and maintained, under various trying circumstances that are incident to such services alone, the maintenance

INTRODUCTION. 3

of accord and good-fellowship is the key to their endurance and perseverance, and the consequent harmony and perfection of the work.

Labour, under such conditions and circumstances, becomes light and pleasant; and men then need no other stimulus than the sense of duty to urge them to the fullest energy and exertion. For then the higher feelings, emanating from a conviction of the important and enduring value of such labours to the general navigator and for the advancement of general knowledge and science, become better developed and more operative in all.

My acknowledgments are therefore here heartily given to all. But it is my special pleasure to refer to the labours of my old coadjutor and companion, Lieutenant (now Commander) Mansell, of the 'Firefly,' and also to Lieutenant Wilkinson, of H.M.S. 'Medina,' by both of whom the greater part of the coast-line and topographical detail has been obtained; and no less to Mr. (now Staff Commander) Stokes, the able master and observer, who has been also associated with me in the Levant Survey for many years; and to Lieutenant Brooker likewise, for his assistance in the surveys of Crete. And as all have now their names attached, in their appropriate places, to the several plans and charts of it to which they have contributed, that official recognition must be as gratifying to them, as it is to me thus prominently to mark, in this Introduction to a general description of the Island of Crete, my individual appreciation of their responsible labours.

But a work of purely local and limited research, with the aim of preserving a few topographical and antiquarian facts, and without dashing adventure or touching incidents, cannot be expected to excite much general interest. Yet as some few, perhaps, of the next generation as well as the present may find these records and facts of use to them as travellers or universal students, I am induced to give them for their advantage and appreciation, which is the most flattering result I can hope from my labours.

The map is a reduction of the Admiralty Charts of Crete, published from our Surveys.

To Viscount Strangford I am specially indebted for the translation of the modern Greek and Cretan vocabulary given in the Appendix, and published at Athens by M. Chourmouzes Byzantios in 1842.

To the Rev. Churchill Babington, of St. John's College, Cambridge, also, I am indebted for a learned Appendix upon the several new inscriptions that were found in the island.

I have to lament much delay both in the time of commencing and the completion of this book, through press of other duties; and its publication has been further deferred, through a long indisposition, and my absence from England.

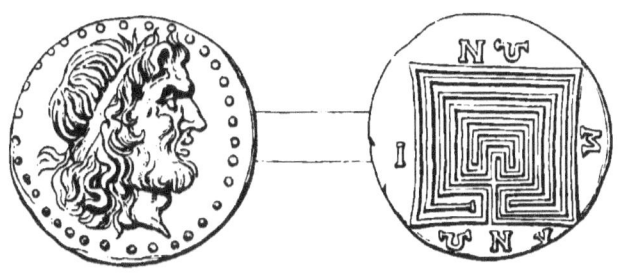

COIN OF GNOSSUS IN THE BRITISH MUSEUM.

CHAPTER I.

MOUNT IDA—ASCENT TO THE SUMMIT—ITS FLORA—ITS GEOLOGICAL STRUCTURE — DEVONSHIRE CHOUGH—THE IBEX—A MOVING MOUNTAIN—SUNSET VIEW FROM THE SUMMIT—COMFORTLESS NIGHT—STORMY MORNING—RETURN TO THE SHEPHERDS' CAVE.

It is now some few years ago that, on the last day of May, I found myself standing upon the summit of the Cretan Ida. The enthusiastic scholar will perhaps envy me this privilege, entertaining a sentiment of veneration for a spot so sacred in classical antiquity as the birthplace of Jupiter, according to the writings of some ancient authors who have treated of the mythology and traditions of the heroic ages.

The view from its summit, at 8200 feet above the

sea, over a great part of the length and breadth of this fine island is a magnificent one certainly; but I must undeceive the reader at once, by assuring him that it was no classical enthusiasm that carried me at this season to its snow-capped summit; I was there in furtherance of a scientific object only, viz. the obtaining the observations that were required for a complete triangulation over the southern islands of the Greek archipelago, and for the survey of Crete itself, in connexion with them.

To say that I felt no enthusiasm on the occasion would not be true. But mine unfortunately arose from no learned interest in the mythological features and faith of the men of the time of Minos. It had little to do with those who fed its fabled history with the story of the Minotaur, and the conquest of the beast by the Athenian Theseus.

The object of my mission had sufficient interest in itself to excite a feeling of enthusiasm, from an anticipation of its future utility, from the opportunity afforded me of studying some of the grander features of nature, and from the varied interests connected with the examination and exploration of a new field.

Besides, who has ever gained the region of snow, at a level of 8000 feet, with the sea, laving the shore, lying almost at his feet, or has attained any great elevation after great toil, without feeling the extreme pleasure of having his fatigue and exertion rewarded by the magnificence of the bird's-eye view obtained by his labours? Or who can prevent the mind from then soaring, like the eagle that hovers over the summit he is upon, as he first beholds the diminutive and now silent, but yet busy, world below, and thus feels the buoyant freedom of a temporary release from its vanities, intrigues, and bustle?

Enthusiasm is, however, hardly the appropriate term for one's feelings on such an occasion; for it is mixed with awe, with admiration, or with gratitude as the eye first reposes on the plunging descent beneath, upon the vast expanse and beautiful scene around, or reflectively peers into the ethereal space above.

We had halted, the previous night, at an upland plain more than 2500 feet below the summit, and four or five miles to the eastward of it, and a little below the margin of the now fast-receding snow, as the sun was nearly in the solstice.

The ascent from this upland basin or plain had occupied four hours and a half, following, as near as we could trace it, the brow of the main ridge leading to the summit, so as to avoid the depth of the snow in the hollows on either side, now sometimes treacherous from the sun's melting influence.

The quaint but celebrated French botanist and traveller, Tournefort, ascended the mountain a century and a half ago, in search of rare plants, but was not rewarded in accordance with his expectation, finding the mountain then comparatively bare and without flowers. The old mountain, however, is not barren of plants both rare and beautiful; for it has its alpine as well as its peculiar vegetation, like all isolated and all such greatly elevated mountains. The indefatigable botanist, however, was a month too late in the time of ascent, its flowering season having passed. At the time of our visit, on every bare patch of soil from which the snow had disappeared but a few days, and indeed I may say hours, there sprung up many beautiful varieties of bulbous plants, that flowered almost as soon as the snow disappeared from over them : one of these—a white-flowered variety of *Fritillaria tulipifolia*—not then in flower, I had afterwards the pleasure of seeing in bloom under the care of Mr. N. Ward, to whom several of the bulbs, which I had forwarded to my lamented friend Forbes, had been given, as well as to Sir William Hooker at Kew, where it also flowered. It was as white as a snowdrop and as delicate as a wax plant. The rest of the plants gathered on Ida were, as was to be expected, similar to those we had found on the summits of the Lycian Taurus about the same time of the year.

Dr. Pococke also ascended Mount Ida in the last century, and about thirty years later than Tournefort; but the learned Doctor's visit was in the month of August, when the vegetation was also gone from it. Both these celebrated travellers also ascended from the Monastery of Arkadia, at the north-west base of the mountain.

The upland basin in which we had bivouacked, and from which we now ascended on foot, was nearly two miles long, and from half a mile to a mile broad, with lesser plains at the same level in connexion with it. The natives called it Nida, Nidha, or *Netha*, which is evidently a corruption of the ancient name of the mountain, Ida, according to the modern Greek pronunciation. But the actual summit has for ages been called Psiloriti or Ypsiloriti ('Υψηλορείτιον).

This upland basin, in which we had halted as the highest point to which our sure-footed mules could carry us, was just now also green as the meadow, from the fresh spring grass and herbage upon its surface— the snow having been absorbed by its soil but a few days previous, under the warmth of the mid-May sun.

Our arrival, in fact, was with the earliest return of the shepherds and flocks that resort to its pasturage as the lowlands become parched by the heats of harvest-time, now in progress in the valleys below.

The verdant upland basin was as refreshing to the eye as the fine bracing air of so elevated a region was to the feelings; and its carpet of verdure was bespangled with patches of wild flowers, amongst which we were delighted to find the Buttercup of our own English meadows, or a species closely allied to it, that in some parts mellowed the verdure with its intermixed tints of gold*.

* A pretty little Clausilia gathered here was recognized by Dr. Pfeiffer to be a new land-shell, and named by him *Clausilia Idæa*.

GEOLOGICAL STRUCTURE.

The pasturage of Ida, according to ancient fable, had the peculiar property of gilding the teeth of the sheep that fed upon it; and I am told that the juices of its herbs or the pollen of its flowers certainly tinges them a little yellow at this season; hence may be seen the solution of the fable—that is, if the scholar can be reconciled to such a matter-of-fact explanation.

Mount Ida stands almost in the centre of Crete, and is insulated from the lesser ridges lying east and west of it. In one point of view—that is, from the north-west and west—it has a striking appearance, from its fine conical form and towering elevation; and on this account, as much as from its being the highest in the island by a few feet, it owed perhaps its repute amongst the ancients, and the fiction and fable which history and tradition have associated with it.

But when seen from the north and north-east, its long diameter is brought in view, and then it has not so noble and grand an aspect, having a long and undulating crest rising gradually, from its eastern extreme, towards the summit, which lies nearer its western. The south and south-west faces of the mountain are very steep, being the upraised side; and the uplifting agent, which was a mass of serpentine, has protruded or forced itself out there, forming a respectable mountain, but in comparison to Ida a mere hill at its foot; whilst on the north and north-east the face descends in a series of ridges and terraces, like so

GEOLOGICAL STRUCTURE. 11

many steps between the summit and base, and representing probably so many faults, dislocations, and upliftings of its strata. The substratum is mainly a mass of stratified limestone, with occasional interspersed beds of shale, which altogether attains a thickness of at least 5000 or 6000 feet. Between the serpentine at the south base and the upper limestones there also crops out a series of older or altered shales and limestone of probably 1000 feet in thickness. The precise geological age of this has not yet been demonstrated by fossil evidences; for although an English traveller in the island, of the last century, Dr. Varyard, describes some fossils found by him at the foot of Ida which would seem to correspond with Belemnites, and indeed calls them so, we did not in our ascent or descent find any fossils.

The summit is formed of thinly stratified grey limestone, which easily splits into large slabs, the whole dipping to the north-east at a small angle. With these slabs a small hovel, called a church, and dedicated to the Holy Cross (Agios Stauros), has been erected upon the summit, at the instigation of an old priest of Mylopotamo, in consequence of a command he is said to have received to that effect in a dream. But the only indication of its sacred character was our finding, within a small hole at its east end, a fragment of some earthen vessel, with a few pieces of charcoal and incense.

In my ascent to it I was accompanied by Colonel

Drummond Hay, late of the 42nd Regiment, who was then on leave and a guest of Captain Graves. He was a keen sportsman and a patient and earnest ornithologist; and his enthusiasm and interest in his favourite pursuit was brought to the highest pitch of delight on the evening of our arrival in the plain of Netha, by unexpectedly finding there a few of the true Devonshire Jackdaw or Chough (*Pyrrhocorax graculus*), of the skin of which he was deficient in his fine collection of British birds, owing to its peculiar limited location to the south-west of England, and whose list of birds observed by him in Crete is given in the Appendix to the 2nd volume. It was singular to find it here, when it had been so often sought for elsewhere by the indefatigable ornithologist. But, in selecting Crete for a location, it had instinctively resorted for breeding to an elevation of the mountain that possessed climatal conditions adapted to its nature.

When we reached the summit, the snow had melted from off the Chapel, as well as for several hundred yards along the crest of the peak on either side of it. Several bulbs were in flower upon these bare patches, which, with a few scattered tufts of a closely matted and prickly plant, that grew in the form of a sponge, and seldom larger than one, were all the vegetation that was capable of growing upon the bleak crest of Ida; and when we first sighted it, a group of Agrimia, a species of Ibex, that had been browsing upon the scanty pasture, were standing motionless upon its pinnacle. We had seen several others in the ascent, some forty in all; but they were too wary of any approach of man. They were not to be taken even by a Highland deer-stalker and keen sportsman like my friend and companion Drummond, but bounded away, as soon as we were perceived, over snow and steep, crag and precipice, until they had gained another commanding peak far out of reach of gun and rifle, and there again they watchfully grouped themselves with their ponderous and sabre-shaped horns curved in relief against the western sky. Crete and the uninhabited islet of Anti-Milo are the only islands of the archipelago in which the Ibex is found; and their introduction into the latter island must have been from Crete.

Several Hares were seen also during the ascent, all of which were started from their forms on the open snow—a spot their instinct seems to lead them to prefer during the day, from the bad lie of their scent upon it; and they seemed to be a smaller species than the Hare of the lowlands.

The summit of the mountain gained, the necessary observations for the distant triangulation were immediately commenced, but were only partially completed after several hours' trial at the theodolite, through the unfortunate and unexpected rising of a mist around us, or an occasional settling of a cloud upon the distant peaks. The important angles to the more distant islands usually visible from Ida could not, therefore, be taken satisfactorily; and it was so necessary and desirable to obtain them, if possible, after the time, labour, and expense incurred in ascending to the summit of the mountain with our instruments, that I felt it necessary to remain the night, hoping that at sunset or sunrise, as we had often experienced before, the clouds would temporarily descend or lift from the mountain-top and also from the summits of the distant islands.

One of the three muleteers who had accompanied us volunteered to remain, under the temptation of a sovereign offered as a reward to either, but not until much persuasion had been previously used by himself and the rest (one of whom was a shepherd from the plain of Netha) to induce me to return to the bivouack, as I was lightly clad and without food. But I gave no heed to their advice, as the day was calm and fine, although hazy, and the night could not be very severe, I thought, especially if my object was accomplished by my sunset view and observations.

When my other companions had left me, Marko and myself beguiled the time during which the mists intercepted the view, in gathering up by the roots a heap of the moist sandy tufts of shrub that grew around the hovel, hoping to raise a fire from them within it, should the night prove cold.

As the sun declined towards the west, I watched

A MOVING MOUNTAIN. 15

anxiously for the appearing of the distant mountains and islands; and as usual, as I had hoped, the clouds lifted from some of them, and thus a few of the more important were then observed. But the haze hung heavy upon the horizon in some directions, foreboding, with the white fleecy clouds, a coming Meltem, or northerly gale of summer.

And whilst scanning the horizon in all directions as the sun was low, I was surprised by the sudden appearance in the east of what seemed to be a well-defined mountain-top of some island in that direction, although no land was known to exist there. The phenomenon for a time puzzled me; for as plain as eye could see, and theodolite could observe, there was, to all appearance, far, far in the east a well-outlined and clearly defined conical mountain, that peered through the dark leaden haze hanging over the horizon there.

After a little pause, however, the theodolite was again directed to its well-marked summit; but on reading off the angle, it was seen to have changed positions. A moving mountain! The mystery was greater, until a little reflexion at once solved it: the phantom island was the actual shadow of the mountain I was standing upon, the haze being so dense in that direction as actually to receive a strong imprint of the outline of Mount Ida upon it; for when I turned the theodolite round 180° to the opposite quarter, it pointed directly to the sun, and the explanation was complete. I have never before or since observed a similar effect; and it will be seen, on consideration, that it can only occur upon a very high mountain, with a certain atmosphere, and only just before sunset or after sunrise, when the sun is of a sufficient height above the horizon to have light and strength enough to produce an opposing shadow upon an atmosphere or haze sufficiently dense, but yet not more intense in tint than the shadow itself.

The effect of this haze and windy-looking atmosphere upon the landscape, was also most gorgeous and attractive; and I sat watching its play of pink, purple, and golden hues, tinting the mountain-tops or lower landscape as the light faded, with intense admiration and pleasure, until, by the sudden disappearance of the orb behind its fiery screen in the west, the bright tints vanished, and all was grey. The day had declined; it had run its course; and the sober tint of age had fitly succeeded the brighter aspect of its glory, before darkness closed upon it, and night asserted its power.

I was captivated by this brilliant effect, and sketched the panoramic view of hill and dale, coast-line and bays, of this western half of Crete, as seen from my aërial position on Ida, which I here give to aid the reader's comprehension of my partial and imperfect attempt to describe it.

The chill of the evening, however, soon struck sen-

VIEW FROM MT IDA

sibly upon my nerves, and from my reverie I hastily retreated to the chapel or hovel, but then only to be made truly sensible of its dull, cheerless reality and shelter, and the comfortless night before me. But I had had my cup of enjoyment; and that never comes, in any shape, without some alloy in payment, either of toil, of anxiety, or of privation.

The wind rose as the night advanced; and as the hovel was built of loose stones, without mortar or soil, it blew through the apertures between, in a thousand little jets of cold piercing blasts that penetrated to the marrow of one's bones. It was in vain that Marko and myself tried to produce some warmth and blaze from the damp sponge-like tufts of shrub we had gathered. With his tobacco-pipe as blower, we puffed and puffed alternately for hours; but it only produced a smouldering smoke, and half suffocated us in the effort: they were too green, and too much saturated with the snow that had only recently been melted from them.

It was in vain, too, that we tried to quench thirst, by melting some lumps of snow we had stored for the purpose, upon large slabs of stone placed at an inclination over, or upon, the smouldering tufts; for what little did melt, and run off into the cup of my pocket-flask, was converted into gall for bitterness, by the smoke that had penetrated the snow during the process of heating and melting.

The night, however, passed in due time, as all nights of suffering and misery do—the sluggish hours as they pass away only appearing some ten times as long as they need or were wont, but when passed being soon forgot; for the birth of the new day brings its new pleasures and occupations of mind and body: and thus its dawn gladly found us moving to restore circulation and warmth. As soon as restored, therefore, and day had come, the eye was anxiously peering through the instrument towards some mountain or island whose angular direction I had hoped to observe.

This, also, was labour in vain, as the wind rendered the instrument too unsteady for correct vision or observation during the brief interval there was an opportunity of attempting it; for there soon ascended, from the valleys below, a white but dense vapour, whose playful masses curled, rolled, and mingled as it arose, like a turbulent and foaming sea. Some patches of fleeting mist, too, now and then shot up from it, as messengers of its approach; and rushed over the brow of the mountain, like steam from an engine in motion; and ere long, ere a few minutes more of watchfulness of its marvellous appearance and motions had passed, the whole cloud had come up, although to us it appeared as if we sank into it as into an abyss or ocean; and we were immediately enveloped in its gloom and mist.

I was too familiar with the meaning of a cloud upon

Ida at this hour and season, not to know that further observation would be hopeless, probably for several days. There was no alternative but to return, and be satisfied with what we had effected. Marko therefore shouldered the instruments, and I my books and the plants and wild flowers I had collected, and we worked our way back, bidding adieu to its bleak aspect with no reluctance, following, as often as we could, our footprints on the snow of the previous day, where our track had necessarily led across it. We frequently, however, lost them and followed the wrong ridge in the search, and had to retrace our steps, as we were often unable to see more than fifty yards before us. The cheering voices of our shepherd guides were at length heard when about halfway down—messengers of comfort, coming to our aid with clothing, food, and milk. Not long after noon, we had the satisfaction of reaching our bivouac in the Shepherds' Cave at Netha; and, in grateful remembrance of the comfortable night which followed in it, I here notice it, that the future traveller making the ascent of Mount Ida may know how well he can get lodged at this elevation, and how comfortable he can make himself with his rug and saddle-bags—provided, however, he previously sweeps and smokes out the manure and vermin from its interior.

CHAPTER II

DESCENT FROM IDA—ZONES OF VEGETATION—VILLAGE OF VORUS
—NATIVE CONFERENCES—PASHLEY'S 'TRAVELS'; ITS DEFI-
CIENCIES—REFLECTIONS ON THE REVOLUTION FOR INDE-
PENDENCE.

AT early dawn of the following day we were astir to prepare for the descent, under the escort of our famed Sfakiot guide and chief, Captain Manias, of whom I shall have further occasion to speak. As we returned by the road we ascended, I shall therefore here briefly notice the features we passed on our descent to the village of Vorus, on the southern flank of the mountain, as it will be of use to a traveller making the ascent from the same place.

After leaving the plain of Netha, Nidha, or Neda, by a short pass through a gap in the edge of the south face of this mountain-basin, we descend by an execrable road, for twenty minutes, over a bared and almost soilless part of the mountain-face, which during six months of the year is covered with snow. We then reach the skirts of a forest of ilex and maple, which at this zone of elevation (viz. about 5000 feet above the sea) belts the southern face of the mountain like a dark girdle, and occupies a breadth of nearly 1000 feet of altitude. The forest is dense in some parts, and is thus, from climatal influence, a vegetable zone peculiar to itself—forming a markedly distinct band between the alpine vegetation above, and the shrubs and plants of the lower regions and valleys, which next succeed it: sparingly at first, but afterwards, at 3500 feet above the sea (that is, about 2000 feet below the pass), we had around us the ordinary shrubs of the island, although somewhat stunted and sparse; and soon the wild olive took its place amongst them.

The descent to the village of Vorus occupied about two hours and a half, whilst the ascent required more than three hours and a half, and is, for the most part, a zigzag rocky track, a great portion of which is not practicable, or at least not advisable, to ride over, except upon the quietest and strongest mules of Crete. The Cretan mule is, however, generally a well-bred, surefooted, docile although somewhat shy animal; and the best are bred in the west part of the island, by the Sfakiots.

Tournefort ascended the mountain by its north-west face, and therefore did not visit the upland basin of Netha. There is a road to it also up the north side of the mountain, and from the large Greek village of Anoya, in the upper part of the Mylopotamo district—the inhabitants of Anoya being large sheep-farmers and shepherds, whose flocks pasture on the mountain.

It is very probable, however, that travellers will

not often, or at the present time especially, find guides to take them to the top of Ida by the way of the plain of Netha; for, in times of internal trouble, it has always been a place of retreat for many of the Christian inhabitants of the adjacent villages below. It is a mountain fortress given to them by nature; and before we had procured a guide to it from Vorus, a consultation seemed to be held regarding the propriety of showing us one of the ways to their mountain magazine and stronghold. The influence of Captain Manias's local repute and bland tongue, however, prevailed against the scruples of the villagers—who assembled in council regarding it—but not until after two and a half hours' detention before the guide was procured, and our necessary stock of provisions was obtained. The conference was held under some olive-trees just at the outskirts of the village, which is situated at the head of a long valley that leads from the plains or Valley of Gortyna to the narrow gap or col separating the hill of serpentine from the frizzled and distorted dark shales, schists, and semicrystalline limestone which underlie the great mass of grey horizontal strata of unfossiliferous limestone that rises from it to the crests of Ida.

These suburban conferences and open-air parliaments are often held amongst the mountain Cretans, either for some plan to evade the tax-gatherer or resist the authorities, or to settle some feud with a neighbouring village for blood-money or a victim; and they are characteristic of what the mountain Cretan always has been and still is, evidences of his high spirit and independent feelings. A knot of these Cretans in consultation, especially if composed of the Sfakiots or Therissots of the western part, presents a fine and interesting picture, from their tall, manly figure and carriage, and noble and generally handsome expression of features.

Thus, as my first introduction to the Island of Crete was by an early visit to the summit of Ida, I have thought that my introduction of the reader to the features and facts I have in the subsequent chapter attempted to depict, of localities left undescribed by Pashley, should also be with my bird's-eye view from its most elevated and classic mountain, so as to awaken at once such feelings and impressions as his previous readings and studies are capable of effecting within him, and to make amends for my deficiencies. The erudite but incomplete book of travels by Pashley, will no doubt do that much better with the classic traveller and scholar; and although we tread different paths in this respect, some may find my volume useful to them in the parts I shall dwell upon and describe, as a simple guide-book to an interesting island, and to a little-known, though interesting people.

I propose, then, to give a general description of the eastern half of Crete, as the part left unfinished by

Pashley; and to add a chapter or two on the western part, where discoveries of interest have been made by myself or the officers employed with me during the progress of the survey of Crete, either when conducted under the direction of the late Captain Graves or myself.

I have brought the reader, therefore, from the airy summit of Ida, down to the denser regions of ordinary life, and dissolved the spell or charm which its elevation, solitude, and grandeur of scene had cast upon the mind.

We shall in future, therefore, wade through a heavier atmosphere, and amidst the commoner scenes of life and strife, or amongst the humbler and less striking features of nature. But still man is present there—in prosperity, in misery, or in activity—and, in consequence, will give interest, sympathy, or life to the scene.

Sometimes, too, we shall be amidst the relics which tell of the power, wealth, and civilization of the past —of the cultivated race of Cretans twenty and thirty centuries ago—and sometimes amidst vestiges which too truly tell of a modern desolation, of a brutal strife, and of a barbarism that existed amongst the inhabitants of only a quarter of a century ago, the effects of which are still deeply visible and felt, keeping local civilization lagging far, far behind, through a spirit of hatred and of revenge, which some restless and violent spirits, and the memory of the past, too easily awaken.

Begun, no doubt, for a noble cause—for freedom, for liberty, but without being prepared for it, and without knowing freedom's best weapon and power— it was commenced, continued, and ended with needless and heedless barbarity and cruelty, both on the part of oppressed and oppressor. It became, in consequence, a war of retaliation between religions and races, and, by sword, famine, and diseases, half-depopulated the island, planting misery and sorrow in every feeling heart, and disease and poverty in almost every Cretan family, and thereby threw it back fully half a century in prosperity, in wealth, and civilization.

CHAPTER III.

GNOSSUS AND GORTYNA.—CANDIA FOUNDED BY THE SARACENS—
ENLARGED BY THE VENETIANS—ITS FORTIFICATIONS.—THE
GREAT SIEGE OF CANDIA BY THE TURKS—GALLANT DEFENCE,
AND SURRENDER—REFLECTIONS ON THE SIEGE.—KHANIA SUP-
PLANTS CANDIA AS THE PRESENT CAPITAL OF CRETE.

CRETE is divided by Mount Ida into two notable divisions, the eastern and the western. The roots and main branches of the mountain extend to the north and south coasts, and thus form a natural barrier across the island. Towards the north, an extended root projects the coast a little, along the Ægean shore, for an extent of several miles, and terminates abruptly over it—this branch or root enclosing within its bend the whole of the fine district and valley of Mylopotamo. To the south, the roots terminate more abruptly, and touch the Libyan Sea at the north-east angle of Messara Bay.

Gnossus, the famed capital of Crete in the time of its early and wise king Minos, stood amidst low ridges at a few miles from the north-east base of Mount Ida, and near the north coast, having its port of Amnisus on the Ægean shore. And Gortyna, its rival and the subsequent capital in the time of the Romans, ten centuries afterwards, stood at the south-east base of the mountain, on the margin of the extensive valley and plain of the Messara, which, from its fertility, was anciently called the granary of Crete, and had its ports of Metallus and Leben on the shores of the Libyan Sea.

After the conquest of Crete by the Saracens, about A.D. 820, the capital again returned to the north shore. They founded Candia on the site of Heraclea, the second and later seaport of Gnossus; and this town, until within a few years, has remained the capital of the island, and is still its largest city.

The Saracens retained possession of Crete for about 140 years, in spite of several efforts on the part of the Byzantine emperors to recover it from them. They were, however, eventually driven out by Nicephorus Phocas in 961.

At the division of the Eastern Empire by the Franks, Crete appears to have been given to Boniface, Duke of Montserrat, by Baldwin, in or about A.D. 1190, under the Genoese; and from him it passed by purchase to the Republic of Venice, on August 12th, 1204.

Candia, the name of the capital, became afterwards applied to the whole island by the European navigators and geographers, just as London is, amongst the mass of the Oriental population, now commonly understood by them to mean England, from being its principal place of trade and the principal place spoken of amongst past navigators and merchants. The Venetians too adopted it.

But, with the natives of Crete, the ancient name of the island has never been lost or changed; for Crete has been its local name since the days of Minos, by its entire population; and even the Turkish tongue has produced no other modification of it than Krit or Kirit, its natural pronunciation by a Turk, when written in the characters of their language.

The origin of the name of Candia is said by some authors to have been derived from the Arabic word Khandak (a trench), because the Saracens first entrenched themselves there after landing. It is a word now commonly applied, by the Greeks, to a stagnant canal, natural or artificial, and may have been locally applied to the then choked and stagnant port of Heracleon.

Recently it was commonly spoken of as the Megalo Kastron (the great fortress, or chief city); now the ancient name has been revived, and it is generally called Heracleon by the Greeks.

When Crete came into the hands of the Venetians, the town of Candia was about one-third of its present size, the inner wall of its fortifications of the time of the Genoese being still in parts traceable; and its old land gateway (which led to the south) was, until recently, the town-prison and guardhouse, and stood in the centre of the main street of the present city.

The Venetians not only greatly extended the limits of the town, but embellished it with eight large churches, several fountains, and some fine public buildings, of which latter the Armoury, in the main street, is still a handsome relic, of two stories, combining the Doric and Corinthian orders. And the large ruined church of St. Titus, over the eastern part of the fortifications, was, for such a town, of cathedral proportions and style of architecture: a handsome entrance and circular window over, and part of an elegant baptistry attached to it, are still standing.

But the wide and noble ditch surrounding the fortifications (and excavated out of the solid rock) which encompass three parts of the city, the fine bastions and high curtains connecting them, as also the several outworks constructed around the extended lines by the Venetians, are still monuments of their wealth, power, and skill.

Candia was consequently the best-fortified and finest city of its time in the Levant. Retiring from the shore upon gently rising land, it has a fine although not an imposing appearance from the sea,—few of its buildings or fortifications, except those near the sea-defences, being very conspicuous; for the houses of the upper part of the town, which the Venetians called New Candia, are mostly now, as in their time, of a single story.

On the east, the fortifications are flanked by a detached outwork, or fortified bourg, called St. Demetri, which is founded upon high ground, and partly excavated out of the natural rock.

The town-wall has seven bastions, named by the Venetians successively (beginning from the north-east bastion at the sandy bay near the port) Sabionera, Vittori, Giesu, Martinengo, Bethelem, Panigra, and St. Andrea at the north-west extreme and sea-shore; besides which there was a well-built castle upon the molehead that defended the port; ravelins and hornworks also fronted the angles of the counterscarp, and cavaliers surmounted the principal bastions.

The extent of these works was their greatest source of defect and weakness.

In April 1667, Candia was laid siege to by the Turks, under the Vizier Achmet, and was surrendered by the Venetians on September 18th, 1669, after a gallant defence of two years, three months, and twenty-seven days' duration. Its loss to Christendom at that time was deeply lamented throughout Catholic Europe. Succour was sent to it: but it came too late. At the eleventh hour, France, stirred by the call of the Pope for European aid, responded to the summons, and sent the Duc de Beaufort, with a gallant band of volunteers and soldiers, in nearly 100 ships, for its support. The Duc arrived off Candia on the 19th of June, and, heading a gallant sortie made a few days afterwards from the St. George's Gate, upon the

Turks' entrenchments between the Sabionera Bastion and Fort St. Demetri, was unfortunately killed; and the attack failed through a panic created amongst the new troops he had led forth, caused, it is said, by the explosion of one of the magazines they had taken from the Turks.

The gallant French admiral and duke, it is supposed, was blown to pieces by the explosion; for the body was never recovered.

The western face of the city, more particularly opposite the Bastion St. Andrea, was where the Turkish efforts and approaches, by numerous mines and entrenchments, were most vigorously pressed and most successful. A breach was consequently effected in the St. Andrea Bastion; and to prevent an assault upon it being successful, a sortie was made by the French and Italians in this quarter, at the same time that the Duc de Beaufort's party issued from the eastern gate.

It was the last hope of the Venetians; and it failing from the cause above assigned, Crete, with the fall of its capital, Candia, passed entirely into the possession of the Turks.

Thus fell the jewel of the Venetian Republic, in spite of its noble defence and the European sympathy for its preservation, and in spite of the succour which, by the instrumentality of the Pope, had been sent for its relief. The city, however, was surrendered a mere heap of ruins—and only when surrounded by a labyrinth of sappings, trenches, mines, and countermines that rendered it no longer tenable, and has made its siege, and gallant defence, one of the most memorable in modern history, and which the following particulars of the loss on both sides, and the expenditure by the Venetians, will more fully indicate the nature of, considering the time.

The Venetians had 30,000 killed and wounded; and the Turkish loss was 120,000. The Venetians exploded 1163 mines, and the Turks 462. The Venetians expended 50,000 tons of powder, and threw 48,170 bombs of all sizes, from 50 to 120 pounds weight, besides 100,960 grenades of brass and iron and 84,870 of glass, firing also 276,743 cannon-balls of different sizes.

Of the Turkish expenditure there is no knowledge; but against the Sabionera and St. Andrea Bastions they had erected batteries mounting 59 guns, capable of throwing shot from 50 to 100 pounds weight. In all, there were fifty-six assaults by the Turks, and the Venetians made eighty-six sorties.

The gallant defenders, under the Captain-General Fran. Morosini (who succeeded the noble Cornaro in the spring of 1669, after his death from the bursting of a shell), retired to their ships and country with honour; and the good faith observed by the Vizier Achmet during the twelve days granted for their embarkation, and the attention and respect shown by him towards Morosini at his departure, were equally honourable to the infidel victor.

Reflecting upon the circumstances of this memorable siege not quite two centuries ago, with that of Sevastopol so fresh in our memory, we see that the two were in direct contrast; for in the former it was the Turk besieging a Christian town which was supported by Christian Europe, in the latter it was Christian Europe besieging a Christian city in support of the Turk. Yet the principle of that war was right and just, and its result was the production of a great good; for the civilization of the East has been greatly advanced by it: moreover it was a war which no diplomacy could have averted. It was an event, evidently, ordered and devised for the drying up of the wide waters that flowed from the fountain of Mahomet; for the main spring, the vital source, of all that originated and supports Mahomedanism was thus checked when its followers from all parts—from Europe, Asia, Egypt, and Africa—willingly became banded with the Christian, in a common cause, in belligerent brotherhood. The follower of Islam then forgot his fanaticism under his enthusiasm, and the barriers which had previously confined the one, and kept out the other, gave way; and thus the flood of prejudice peculiar to the creed of fate is becoming slowly shallowed and absorbed, to the great benefit of the Mussulman themselves and the civilized world.

VOL. I.   D

At Candia, too, the besieging were not masters of the sea, as at Sevastopol; and consequently their investment was entirely confined to the land, whilst the besieged maintained their communications and support entirely by sea.

The plan of the Turks, at the siege of Candia, was evidently that of directing their main and patient attack, and approach, against the Sabionera and St. Andrea Bastions, at the north-east and north-west angles of the city, so as to cut off the besieged from their port, and from the sea; and therefore, as soon as Morosini saw this was imminent, and all hope of further succour gone, he wisely capitulated, to save the remnant that were left, and the defenceless city also from being sacked and burnt by an infuriated enemy. And when it was surrendered to the lieutenant of Achmet at the end of the time granted, he exclaimed with indignation and disgust, on viewing the heap of ruins he was to receive the charge of from Morosini, "Why, we have waited twelve days for a place that might have been taken in as many hours."

The Turks, on gaining possession of the city, took immediate steps to restore its defences and repair its breaches, and also its public buildings and churches, all of which were, excepting the Greek, converted into mosques. But their usual apathy and neglect during recent times, combined with occasional earthquakes (more particularly the severe one of 1856, which was felt throughout the East), have greatly damaged both fortifications and churches, seriously injuring also the public buildings as well as many of the habitations. The principal minarets were at the same time thrown down, and several of the galley-arches within the port fell in, so great were the shocks felt in Candia.

The piers enclosing the port are for the most part old moles, that formed the later seaport of Gnossus (Heracleon). It was, however, always too limited and too shallow to admit the larger and principal trading-vessels of the Venetians, which in consequence anchored within one of the two eastern bays that indent the southern shore of the Island of Standia, lying opposite to it. The bays of Standia were therefore the emporium or principal trading-port of Crete during its occupation by the Saracens and Venetians, as also during the Turkish occupation; and Candia remained its capital.

The rising of Greece against her oppressors, in 1821, aroused the patriots of Crete at the same time, who maintained the struggle, with varied fortune, against the forces of the Sultan and of Mehemet Ali, until the battle of Navarino liberated Greece, in 1828, when Crete was ceded to the powerful Viceroy of Egypt, for the part he had taken against it, and the governorship of the island was given to his able Albanian General Mustapha Pacha, who retained it for twenty years, and who deepened the old port of Candia by dredging, and rendered it available for trade.

But when the island passed back from Mehemet Ali to the Sultan again in 1841, after the fall of Acre, Khania was chosen as the seat of government, from its proximity to the Bay of Suda, and from possessing also a more capacious and convenient port within it, combined with the other cogent reasons— of policy, and local tranquillity.

The town of Candia is now therefore only the second city of Crete, although the largest, the most populous, and the most healthy. It is, however, a separate Sanjak under the Governor-general, who resides at Khania; and the subordinate Pashalic of Candia includes the whole of the division of the island lying eastward of the natural limits formed by Mount Ida. It contains about 13,000 inhabitants, Turks and Greeks, the former being the majority.

CHAPTER IV.

DAPPER'S PLAN OF THE SIEGE—THE CEMETERY—ST. GEORGE'S GATE — LEPERS AT DITTO — YOUTHFUL LEPER — MARRIED LEPERS AND CHILD—NEGLECT OF THE LEPERS—LEPERS' VILLAGE—REFLECTIONS—DUC DE BEAUFORT—PASHA'S TOMB—TURKISH SUPERSTITIONS—SCULPTURED SARCOPHAGUS AT THE ST. GEORGE'S GATE.

THE interest connected with the great siege of Candia and its defence will induce the traveller, no doubt, to visit the exterior as well as the interior of the town. Dapper gives, in his great work published thirty-three years after the siege, a very correct, elaborate, and interesting plan of the city, its fortifications and defences, as well as of the approaches of the Turks. This must have been derived from authentic Venetian documents and sources; and on inspecting the ground on the east as well as west sides of the city, its inequalities which yet remain, notwithstanding the subsequent cultivation of parts of it, induce one to trace in some of them the vestiges of these works, and thus mark the exact spots where many bloody contests occurred.

To the south of the city lies a large Turkish cemetery, which, unlike Turkish graveyards in general, is without a single cypress tree; it is, in consequence, a mere forest of tombstones, of interest only from containing many that fell in the great siege, and for the ancient fragments that may be found in it.

The eastern approach perhaps possesses the greater interest to the stranger, from its being here that the Duc de Beaufort fell. St. George's Gate, which leads to it from near the centre of the lines, was both strongly constructed and well defended; it opens from the parade-ground near the Turkish barracks. This gate being much higher than the ditch and valley lying close under it upon this side of the city, the covered way and approach has a considerable descent, and is thus well commanded by the lines above. After passing through this gate, the traveller is sure to encounter a group of miserable-looking objects lying by the wayside and imploring the charity of every passer-by. They are lepers—and in all stages of this terrible disease: on the opposite side of the valley is their village—the location to which all the lepers of the district are driven, and where they pass the rest of their days after the disease has been pronounced to exist upon them.

This day there were eleven lepers waiting at the St. George's Gate for the charity of passengers; and as they were an interesting group, I stopped to make some inquiries of them, which they freely answered. Ten of the group were ranged on the ground, under the angle of the high bastion, just without the gateway; the other, the eleventh, was apart from them, and an object of great commiseration from his disfigured condition and age, being nearly sixty. He had only been twelve years a leper, however; but his disease had been so rapid, that he was perfectly blind, and dreadfully swollen and disfigured in limbs and face, and hid his hands and feet in filthy bags of old rags, to hide their sores and deformities from the public, whose charity he solicited. He was seated in a small shed on the opposite side of the way, apart from his companions, from an apparent consciousness that he was almost too hideous to meet the eye of his fellow-man; and sad and singular it was to learn, that he had only been joined by his daughter about ten days previous. She, at the age of eighteen, and leaving a mother behind, had then, at the age of hope and promise, been driven from her village-home for ever, to be an outcast from friends and relations, in companionship, and with the stigma, of a leper! but yet just in time to become a comfort to her long outcast, and now helpless father, during his fast declining hours of misery. On first seeing her, although seated with the unmistakeable lepers, I could not believe she was one of them, being neatly dressed, of considerable beauty, though pale, and by no means overcast with melancholy, or indicating feelings of mental grief and depression at her new position and miserable prospects. I was induced therefore to ask her if she really was a leper; and she immediately showed me her hands, still delicate and fair, but with two of her fingers slightly bent and stiff. These unmistakeable symptoms, to those who know the early appearance of the disease, had only appeared on her about six months previously, when she was immediately placed under the surveillance of the matrons of the village, who then jealously watch any suspicious spots, from a general belief in its contagious nature. The signs of the foul spot or malady becoming more developed and evident during this time, together with the fact of her father being also a leper, were considered decisive. She was consequently now driven from her home, to become for ever the companion of corruption and misery; and, even on the tenth day of her exile, here she sat, compelled to seek alms on the public approach to a large city, and to meet the cold gaze and indifference of the passers-by. The healthy mind shudders, naturally, at the sight and contemplation of such a condition and future for one so young and attractive.

But perhaps even this change of scene was a relief from the sickening sights of the lepers' village; or perhaps she was buoyed up in spirit by the support and comfort she could now give to her helpless and dying parent. I could account for her apparent apathy from no other cause. " God tempers the wind to the shorn lamb"—a truth we so often realize; and surely these poor objects need that the sensibilities of the mind should be tempered under the helpless condition of advancing disease and corruption, and, what is worse, the cold neglect of their fellow-creatures. "To be put under the ground would be better than life," was, however, the feeling reply of one poor woman, with whom I had exchanged a few words at another gate.

By the side of the girl on the right hand were seated two lepers, man and wife, who had had a child, now six or seven months old, and lying in the arms of the latter, and which had been born to them after being married and residents in the lepers' village eight years! I learn from them that about seventy families compose this village, of which thirty-two are Turks, numbering in all 111 persons. What a life and reflections await these poor children on becoming conscious of their condition—burthens to society from their birth! for no employment can be sought for by them, as nothing from their tainted hands would obtain a sale, even if their stiffened fingers could be turned to hard work or handicraft.

It is with satisfaction, then, that I learn that the Turkish Government has recently shown some thought for these afflicted members of the community, by ordering half an oke of bread per diem to be given to every leper. This tardy charity is to them a great boon, and relieves the local government of this island from a great blot, and was given during the government of Vely Pacha.

Let us now, then, look at their village; for it is close at hand. And what are their habitations there? Why, they are chiefly the walled-up caves and tombs of the ancient Cretans—or the excavations made by the Turks, during the great siege, into the side of a ravine in the low ridge which bounds the valley east of the city, either for their magazines or for winter-quarters.

The lepers' village being only a distance of fifteen or twenty minutes' walk, it is therefore deserving of a visit, if it be only to learn a small lesson of the state of social feeling in this island at the present time, and to feel the sympathy that must be awakened at beholding such a community of outcasts, who are thus living in social degradation, purely because they are the neglected victims of a loathsome and erroneously supposed incurable disease. Yet, thus abandoned by the world and by friends, and doomed to a slow decay and corruption of body that eats away both the extremities and features, rendering them also helpless as well as disgusting from their disfigurement, they nevertheless intermarry in this state, and some of them even have children. For youth, and beauty too, as we have seen, are not spared: girls of great personal attractions are often driven from their village-homes and friends, to this community of sickening corruption, on the unclean spot appearing on them as an hereditary taint or sudden development of the disease (for which no good reason can be given, but that it is the result of unwholesome food and uncleanliness of person).

To suppress, then, some of the feelings which the sight of this scene has produced, let us return by the sandy shore at the mouth of the St. Demetri Valley, and, for a moment, enjoy the beauty of the blue Ægean Sea, and, in passing under the Sabionera Bastion on the way back, try to revive also some of the events of the great siege: for here the Turkish approaches had reached to the very foot of the works when the Venetians surrendered the place; and here also many severe contests between besiegers and besieged must have occurred, especially during the last sortie under the gallant Duc de Beaufort. But although there is no monument there, or tradition, to mark the spot where he fell, there is a white marble tomb close in front of the bastion, and of some interest in connexion with the siege, since it marks the grave of one Hassan Pasha, a general of the Turkish troops, who was killed there; and at a few feet from it, also, there is a rude unhewn black stone, apparently foreign to the island, that is said to mark the grave of a faithful Arab or Negro slave, who fell by his side in defending his master. Monuments to the faithful and brave have always an exciting interest—vibrating a chord of the heart that leaves salutary impressions and feelings, with all minds who love noble characters and deeds.

The superstitions amongst the lower class of Turks who now inhabit Candia seem, however, to have canonized the spirit of the Pasha and made him a Mahomedan saint; and the tomb, as well as the lantern which is always suspended over it, is decorated with votive ribbons and rags, for the cure of diseases or the salvation of the soul.

The bust of a Roman statue, at a fountain within the town, that is figured in Pashley, and which, according to Antonio Belli, a Venetian writer on Crete, came from Hierapetra, is similarly decorated and paid reverence to by some Turkish devotees every Friday (the Mussulman's sabbath), besides having a lamp with oil or incense set before it also. This is the only indication of image-worship which I have ever observed amongst Mahomedans; and I was informed that it is due to a belief amongst the superstitious, that it is the petrified remnant of the body of a sainted Ethiopian Mussulman who was killed in the war, and whose head and lower members were cut off by the Christians, but who is destined to rise to life when the Ghiaour are to be exterminated from the island.

This statue, and a sarcophagus just without the St. George's Gate, where it is used as a drinking-

SCULPTURED SARCOPHAGUS. 45

trough for cattle, are the only sculptured relics of the ancient Cretans that deserve notice in the town of Candia, although there are numerous fragments of columns, capitals, and architectural remains scattered amongst the buildings of the city. These, no doubt, were chiefly brought from Gnossus.

This sarcophagus has a curious group of four figures sculptured upon it, which have apparently a mythological or funereal association, and are, perhaps, a dramatic representation, which the antiquary may be able to explain: the tomb was therefore probably that of an author or actor of local celebrity. They are of fair execution, although much mutilated and very small in size; but being almost covered by the moss and slime that has formed by the stream of waste water flowing over the face of the sarcophagus, the sculpture is not easily observed, and will require to be well scrubbed and cleaned before more than the general form of the figures, can be seen by the passer-by. The first to the left seems to be a naked faun playing upon a pipe, and standing behind a robed and dignified sage, who seems addressing an emaciated figure or skeleton (probably intended to represent Death), next to which is a large tripod or stand supporting a shallow vessel containing various fruits, with a mystical box between the legs beneath it; on the other side of it stands a naked youth, apparently with an offering,—the whole having a kind of stage-screen of some drapery festooned behind them; the letters ΠΟΛΥ occur on the floor of the stage.

The old Venetian galley-arches at the port are also worth a visit as relics of Venice's naval glory and power in the east, although for the most part in ruins, several of them having fallen-in during the earthquake of 1856, which did such serious damage to the buildings within the city. In one of the vaults that remain standing, there is a singular fancy of the architect who built it, viz. an inverted arch over one of the side entrances. But the arch bears little of the superstructure, so to test the strength and durability of the idea—being beneath a well-made archway—and was therefore a mere fancy, as an architectural deviation from ordinary rules.

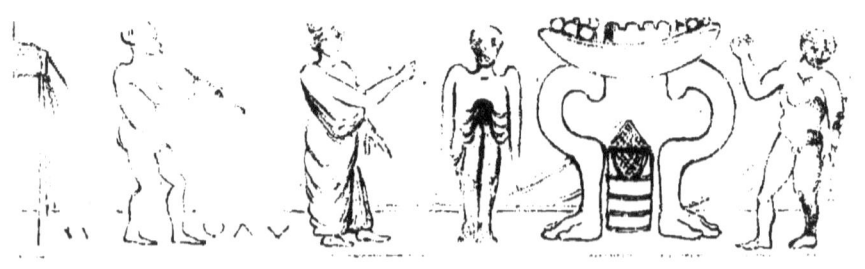

CHAPTER V.

MAHOMEDANS OF CRETE—GREEK THE COMMON LANGUAGE—CLOSE ASSOCIATION OF THE CREEDS—ITS NATURAL EFFECTS—AN ENLIGHTENED PASHA—INTRIGUE AGAINST HIM—OVER-ESTIMATE OF THE GREEK POPULATION—GREEK RISING, AND PERSECUTION OF THE MAHOMEDANS—THE SFAKIANS—THEIR DIALECT—ITS HELLENIC CONNEXION SHOWN BY THE LATE COL. LEAKE.

THE Mahomedan population of Crete amounts now to about one-third of the whole, and may be thus reckoned at between sixty and seventy thousand. Many of them are descended from Christian parents, whose forefathers, under intimidation, or interest, changed their religion in preference to their location and personal prospects, but not their language. Thus Greek is the universal tongue of Crete still.

Under these circumstances, and from the use of a common language, social communication between the Cretan Christians and Mahomedans is consequently more close than in any other part of the Turkish empire, intermarriage being not infrequent, in spite of the diversity of creed and the prejudices peculiar to the habits of each. The Cretans of both creeds, too, dress so much alike that the distinction is often not recognized by residents of long standing, or by Greeks of the neighbouring islands. High leather boots, brown or red, and often highly embroidered and laced, are the characteristic part of the dress of a Cretan, serving for buskin and hose, stockings being in general a useless article of dress to a Cretan peasant. A welldressed Cretan, in the costume worn on a festa, with his tight-fitting long boots of bright scarlet, and neatly embroidered jacket, is a picturesque figure; and much dandyism is sometimes displayed in the dress of the youthful and wealthy Cretan of the interior, but in the cities the European dress is fast supplanting it.

This close association of the two creeds, in Crete, was fast dissolving away the antipathies that had previously existed between them as a result of former oppression and the long desolating war which occurred between 1820 and 1828; but the revolutionary demonstration of the Greeks in 1859 has greatly interrupted it, and supplanted growing confidence by mistrust and hatred; and it is always found far more easy to pass from the former state to the latter, than to return to a state of mutual confidence and friendship. The evil and injury that resulted to the whole community, from this revolutionary movement, has been very great, by loss of trade, by loss of property, and by some loss of life through sickness, fright, and violence. It was begun without a justifiable cause, under the auspices of some foreign agents not interested in Turkish regeneration, mainly for the purpose of ridding the island of an enlightened native governor.

For, Greek being the common language of the island, Vely Pacha (who governed it at the end of the Crimean war, and was the son of its old ruler Mustapha Pacha) was induced by his enlightened views and local interest, amongst other improvements contemplated by him for the benefit of the whole community, to suggest the establishment of a public school for the instruction of the Turkish and Greek youths in general; and the building intended for it was completed nearly to its roof, when local opposition excited this demonstration throughout the island under false pretences. No doubt it was done under a feeling of mistaken and misguided patriotism; but it succeeded in putting an end to this liberal and enlightened project, and to the government of Vely Pacha also; and it has created a lasting spirit of intolerant prejudice against any improvements that may emanate from a Turkish governor.

That there has been and still is misgovernment to complain of here, as elsewhere throughout the Turkish empire, is patent; yet on the whole there are few people in the Levant at the present time more free and independent, or less taxed and oppressed, than the Greek community of Crete. But this misguided prejudice and infatuation, caused by pressure from without and party spirit within, easily led them into a mistaken view of their true interests, and brought to a standstill also several other social and civilizing improvements contemplated by Vely Pacha—such as the general introduction of mixed education, the construction of good roads, and the extension of the cure and sanitary treatment of the sick. They were blinded to the fact that the more the local resources and intelligence were developed by liberal cultivation, the more the patriotic hopes and interests of the Cretans must be advanced.

The population of Crete, from the best and most reliable information I could obtain, for the most part derived from local information and observation during the progress of the survey, I consider to be about 210,000, of whom one-third are Mussulman.

The total is estimated from the following data, viz. that there are in all about 800 villages only in which the number of families is more than five in each; in these the average, deduced from returns supplied by reliable local authority, and confirmed by my own personal observations over a great part of the island, is not more than about forty families for each village. This is rather above than under the average; and, reckoning each family at five persons, this will give 160,000 as the rural population.

The remaining 50,000 is made by reckoning the towns of Candia, Khania, and Retimo at 35,000, and the population scattered in monasteries, hamlets, and farms, as well as shepherds, at 15,000 more.

The population has, however, been estimated, in a

THE GREEK POPULATION. 51

work recently published at Athens by a Greek author, as over 300,000. This has been done by enumerating the villages at 1046, and averaging them all at fifty families each. But this exact number of villages has evidently been copied from a work more than a century and a half old, and is not derived from modern sources. A list of the names of all the villages is also given, to establish an apparent authority in the estimate and calculation. But I am enabled to state positively, from actual observation, that many of these villages no longer exist; and others are reduced to mere farms or hamlets, having only one or two families to represent them; yet they are included in the average of fifty families each!

Pashley made the population in 1834 about 130,000; and his opportunities and means of ascertaining the necessary information were very good, as it was done at a time when there were no motives for exaggerating or diminishing the real numbers of either religion or community.

The increase in the quarter of a century since has therefore been, according to our results, about one-third; but by the Greek authority it would be three-fifths or two-thirds, which is obviously an exaggeration, independent of the sources of error already pointed out.

The consequent enumeration of the Greek element at four-fifths and the Turks at only one-fifth of the entire population, by this Athenian work, is a misstatement of the facts, tending to the prejudice of both parties, by exciting the one to false hopes and fruitless demonstrations, and possibly the other to resort to harsher measures in support of authority; for a minority which is led to believe in, or is conscious of, its weakness will often, amongst uncivilized nations, resort to intimidation and terror, in order to maintain its authority against local disaffection.

The demonstration of 1859 against Vely Pacha, under Sfakian guidance and influence, thus suddenly put a check to the social fellowship between the Christians and Mahomedans that had previously existed; for it caused a great part of the Turkish community, under intimidation, to fly from their villages into their fortified towns just as their crops were ripening, being in consequence obliged to abandon them, as well as most of their stock, just at the beginning of harvest-time; and Vely Pacha was induced in consequence to call in the remainder, to prevent the revolutionary uprising being consummated by actual rupture and bloodshed.

Thus crowded within the fortresses and fortified towns at the hottest season, and many of the Turks being without sufficient food and resources for their families, sickness and want spread amongst them; and, becoming more and more irritated day by day under the growing misery of their starving wives and children, whilst their crops were spoiling through no fault of their own, it was with difficulty that open violence was prevented and order maintained in Candia—alarms or panics frequently occurring. Much credit is said to be due for this to our late highly respected Viceconsul, Signor Ittar, for his influence, exertions, and charity on that occasion, his house having also been filled in all parts with refugees for several weeks. For, in Candia, many Greeks had also fled to the towns with the Turks. Many, if not most, of the lowland Greek peasantry felt little interest in the uprising, well knowing that they would only suffer through it, by the loss of their trade and their property. It was the upland, the mountain patriots who originated and organized the demonstration, and who, for about two months, were in possession of the whole of the lowlands. They fed their beasts or themselves, for this time, upon the abandoned stock and crops of the Mahomedan, and afterwards upon that of their compatriots of the lowland villages, upon whom they quartered themselves. Mutual confidence was consequently destroyed, and the prosperity of the island seriously checked.

And thus has Cretan energy been too often misdirected under the guidance of mistaken patriotism on the part of its mountain-inhabitants and their chiefs, who, having less to lose, or being comparatively secure from losses and molestation within their mountain fastnesses, influence the lowlanders by the prestige of their name and the terror of their lawless deeds. The name of the Sfakiot is, in consequence, a by-word amongst the lowland Cretans, for talents perverted, and for unscrupulous intrigue, theft, and cruelty. Athletic and active, he stalks about the island from one extreme to the other, either as an itinerant merchant or pedlar, or political disturber, and is feared, but not respected. In stature, in activity, and hardihood, he is the counterpart of our Scotch Highlander, and in past days might have resembled him in other respects; but now, in respect to character and principles, he is the very reverse.

The blood of the Sfakians is undoubtedly the purest of all the Cretan race, its purity having been preserved by their mountain location and jealous clanship, that has maintained amongst them exclusive habits and manners, and a dialect, some of the peculiarities of which may have descended from the days of Minos, and probably prevented a close admixture with either Roman or Saracen, Italian or Turk, who have severally conquered them. Not so, however, with the lowland Cretans, who are naturally a mixed race, as may be seen by their features, their stature, and sometimes by their names, more particularly in the eastern part of the island, where the Venetians left a large sprinkling of colonists and Italian blood, to replace the original race, exhausted by plague or war in their time.

The learned seem to trace in the Sfakian dialect an affinity with the Doric; and it was the Dorians who, supplanting the early Cretans, colonized the western part of Crete. This dialect is more or less common also, among the peasantry, throughout the interior of the island; and as a native Cretan, M. Chourmouzes Byzantios, some years ago, in a brief notice of some parts of the island, published a vocabulary of the dialect of Crete, I have given it in the Appendix, for the benefit of the scholar and traveller.

Pashley says, in reference to the Sfakian dialect, " I cannot help again noticing the peculiarities of dialect which characterize all the Sfakians, especially the women, and some of which may be considered as traces of the old Cretan Doric" (vol. ii. p. 109).

" The frequent substitution of ρ for λ, and the formation with ξ of a greater number of aorists than is found elsewhere, are the most striking of these peculiarities, and are likewise the most interesting, since they are obviously derived from the old language of the island.

" Others will be observed, such as the frequent addition of the final ι at the end of past tenses and words, which are used by the Sfakians alone " (p. 192).

But there is a peculiarity in the provincial tongue of Crete that resembles the Tzaconic corruptions—viz. the frequent use of *ts* or *tz* as a prefix to the name of a place, or of an ancient city, and which was not recognized by me until I had heard it applied in the White Mountains over Khania, where, by a harsh pronunciation and fusion of the article with the substantive, *kampo*, a plain, and *embela*, a vineyard, became consequently *tzekampo* and *tsembela* in the mouth of a Therissot or any villager of that part of Crete. Hence I finally discovered that, as the name of Lakonia in the Morea has apparently been corrupted to *Tzaconia* by the vulgar tongue of its modern inhabitants, as shown by Colonel Leake, so the names of some of the ancient cities of Crete, more particularly those in the eastern part, have become changed in a similar manner—as *Hierapytna* to *Tzerapetra* (although it was written *Gerapetra* by the Venetians), and as *Itanus* into *Tzetana*, *Tsitana*, or even *Sitana*, &c.

The learned and lamented scholar Colonel Leake had pointed out, and given examples of, the peculiarity or purity of the Cretan dialect as compared with the other dialects of Greece, as early as 1814, in his ' Researches in Greece ' (p. 64), wherein he says, " The Cretan dialect seems to have adopted much fewer of its forms or phrases from the Italian than might have been expected, considering its long connexion with Venice. With the exception of some provincial words, it seems to be genuine Hellenic in a state of extreme corruption; or more nearly formed into a systematic modern language, bearing the same

THE CRETAN DIALECT. 57

relationship to Hellenic that Italian bears to Latin, than any of the other dialects of Greece."

Pashley's university studies, subsequently to this remark of the Colonel, must therefore have prepared him for the dialect and its Hellenic or Cretan Doric traces, although he seems surprised at its discovery by him in the Sfakian Mountains, and expresses astonishment that no one else has noticed it! whereas the Colonel had, long before, noticed that it was in Crete where the ancient dialect was supposed to be least corrupt, although it had been so long under the Venetians. This record of the fact is therefore due to the late Colonel Leake, that most amiable scholar and remarkable observer and traveller, whose loss I deplore as a sincere friend, but whose memory I revere as a great and good man, and whose reputation stands established with the learned, for the rare combination of modest pretensions with profound research.

CHAPTER VI.

GNOSSUS — ITS SITE — ITS FEW REMAINS AT PRESENT — CAUSE OF THIS—THE LABYRINTH—PLUTARCH'S ACCOUNT OF THE MINOTAUR AND LABYRINTH—ANCIENT TOMBS AT GNOSSUS— ITS ANCIENT PORTS OF AMNISUS AND HERACLEION.

GNOSSUS, the capital of Crete under Minos, was situated about two and a half miles to the south-east of the town of Candia.

Cramer writes of it as follows:—" Gnossus, the royal city of Crete, was first called Cæratus, as we learn from Strabo, which name attached also to the small river which flowed beneath its walls" (vol. iii. p. 476). Hesychius reports that this town bore likewise the appellation of Tritta; but it is to Minos that it was really indebted for its early importance and splendour. That monarch is said to have divided the island into three parts, in each of which he formed a large city; and fixing his residence at Gnossus, it became the capital of the kingdom. It was here that Dædalus cultivated his art, and planned the celebrated Labyrinth that contained the Minotaur, but of which no traces remained in the time of Diodorus.

It occupied no remarkable site; the spot was not characteristic for its strength, nor of striking appearance like the positions of the earliest Greek cities in general: it stood, for the most part, upon a low undulating plain between two parallel ravines, but terminating in two rather abrupt eminences on the south and west, one of which has still vestiges of the walls of a tower upon it, and gives its Italianized name to the small village of Fortezza lying over it, and apparently indicating the position of one of the exterior defences or towers of the city walls, but of a later time. On the north the site of the city was terminated by a lower and smooth-featured eminence,—the city having altogether a circuit of fully six miles in extent. It is bounded on the east by a narrow and rocky ravine, with a rivulet that intersects the white tertiary freestone and marls constituting the chief part of the undulating ridges lying southward of the town of Candia.

The hamlet of Makri Teikos, or Long Wall, is situated within the limits of the ancient city, by the side of the rivulet; and although the identity of the site is not to be disputed, as being that of the capital of Minos, which was also a fine city even in the time of Strabo, who, too, for a time resided in it, yet the only vestiges of Gnossus at the present time are some scattered foundations and a few detached masses of masonry of the Roman time. The entire surface is almost wholly cultivated and unfenced, but throughout indicates the remains of a dense city, from the vast quantity of stones and fragments of pottery that are intermixed with the soil.

This is all that at present remains of Gnossus. But in the time of the Venetians, Belli shows that there was still existing the remains of a curiously constructed theatre or circus; the plan of it, however, was not sufficiently distinct, to Belli, to be given in the manuscript, the relics of which have been recently published by Mr. Falkener in the 'Museum of Classical Antiquities.' The site of it is now recognizable in the centre of the tract; and the detached masses of masonry before noticed seem to be the very remains of the buttresses of its arches or vaults.

The cause of this great demolition and disappearance of its buildings and fragments is doubtless due to the recent rising up of so large and so well fortified a town as Candia near it; and within its fortifications, therefore, lie the chief relics of Gnossus. The old site is still resorted to, and dug over, for material for the construction or repair of any important building within Candia that may require it, extensive excavations being sometimes made in search of the foundations of its old walls or buildings in consequence.

Gnossus was celebrated for two monuments:— namely, the celebrated Labyrinth of Dædalus, which Diodorus the Sicilian says was built for the confinement of the fabled Minotaur; and, according to the same author, the Tomb of Idomeneus, the leader of the Cretan heroes who went to the Trojan war. The latter monument is not described, however; but I shall have to refer to it hereafter. And in regard to the former (the Labyrinth), it might seem to merit, to some minds, the same notice and the same credit that is due to many of the myths told of the ancients by the credulous Sicilian historian, in his recondite dissertations, from the mythology of the heroic times.

The Labyrinth of Crete is, however, now a household word with every scholar, having been noticed by most of the ancient authors who have treated of the fabled history of the Minotaur or of Crete. Homer is, however, silent upon it, unless the passage in the Iliad, book II., has reference to it, as some think. The early coins of Gnossus, indeed, represent it; but they cannot date further back than the 6th or 7th century B.C., if so early, and were consequently struck when only the tradition existed of such a labyrinth; and how vague even then was the idea of this labyrinth is shown by the varied representations of it upon these Cretan coins—some representing its passages in circular convolutions, others square, and also different in coins of different times:—

But Plutarch, in his Life of Theseus, gives a more natural explanation of the object of the Labyrinth than the story of the mythical Minotaur, and says it was a prison for the tributary youths of Athens;

and he gives also a common-sense view of the true origin of the fable of the Minotaur, in the story of the victory of Theseus over a general of Minos, named Taurus, but of whom he was jealous from his influence, and in consequence desirous of getting rid of. This notice of the site of Gnossus and its Labyrinth in these pages would be incomplete without giving the whole of the extract from Plutarch bearing upon it, since it has been overlooked, but particularly as it is derived from earlier authors, whom he quotes. It is as follows:—

"Not long after, there came the third time from Crete the collectors of the tribute, exacted on the following occasion. Androgeus being treacherously slain in Attica, a very fatal war was carried on against that country by Minos; and Divine vengeance laid it waste: for it was visited by famine and pestilence; and want of water increased their misery. The remedy that Apollo proposed was, that they should appease Minos and be reconciled to him, whereupon the wrath of Heaven would cease, and their calamities come to a period. In consequence of this, they sent ambassadors with their submission, and, as most writers agree, engaged themselves by treaty to send every ninth year a tribute of seven young men and as many virgins. When these were brought into Crete, the fabulous account informs us that they were destroyed by the Minotaur in the Labyrinth, or that, lost in its mazes

and unable to find the way out, they perished there.
The Minotaur was, Euripides tells us,

'A mingled form, prodigious to behold—
Half bull, half man!'

But Philochorus says, the Cretans deny this and will not allow the Labyrinth to have been anything but a prison which had no other inconvenience than this, that those who were confined there could not escape; and Minos having instituted games in honour of Androgeus, the prize for the victors was those youths who had been kept till that time in the Labyrinth. He that first won the prizes in the games was a person of great authority in the court of Minos, and general of his armies, named Taurus, who, being unmerciful and savage in his nature, treated the Athenian youths with great insolence and cruelty. And it is plain that Aristotle himself, in his account of the Bottiæan government, does not suppose that the young men were put to death by Minos, but that they lived, some of them to old age, in servile employment in Crete.

"But Hellanicus says that the youths and virgins which the city furnished were not chosen by lot, but that Minos came in person and selected them, and Theseus before the rest, upon these conditions, that the Athenians should furnish a vessel, and the young men embark and sail along with him, but carry no arms, and that, if they could kill the Minotaur, there should be an end of the tribute.

"When Theseus arrived in Crete, according to most historians and authors, Ariadne, falling in love with him, gave him a clue of thread, and instructed him how to pass with it through the intricacies of the Labyrinth. Thus assisted, he killed the Minotaur and then set sail, carrying off Ariadne, together with the young men. Pherecydes says that Theseus broke up the keels of the Cretan ships, to prevent their pursuit. But, as Demon has it, he killed Taurus, Minos's commander, who engaged him in the harbour just as he was ready to sail out. Again, according to Philochorus, when Minos celebrated the games in honour of his son, it was believed that Taurus would bear away the prizes in them as formerly; and every one grudged him that honour, for his excessive power and haughty behaviour were intolerable; and besides, he was accused of too great a familiarity with Pasiphaë: therefore, when Theseus desired the combat, Minos permitted it. In Crete it was the custom of the women, as well as the men, to see the games; and Ariadne, being present, was struck with the person of Theseus, and with his superior vigour and address in the wrestling-ring. Minos too was greatly delighted, especially when he saw Taurus vanquished and disgraced; and this induced him to give up the young men to Theseus, and to remit the tribute." (Life of Theseus.)

That there was, therefore, something of a labyrinth,

which might serve as a foundation for that which was attributed to the great master of art, Dædalus, is thus more than simply probable. "What, then, do we find in Crete to explain it? Is there a labyrinth of any kind?" is the natural inquiry. There is; yet not at Gnossus, but at Gortyna; and not a building, but a subterranean excavation resembling a quarry, or more properly the galleries of a mine, and penetrating horizontally, in labyrinthine courses, no one knows how far, into one of the roots of Mount Ida lying behind Gortyna, and in which I myself spent nearly two hours in tracing some of its courses, as far as they are now penetrable; for the Cretans have long since walled or stopped up its inner and unknown extremes, so as not to be lost in its inner intricacies.

And as this is not the Labyrinth of Gnossus, I shall defer a more detailed description of it until I come to speak of the City of Gortyna. "Where, then, was the Labyrinth of Gnossus?" will be the natural question still, as well as "Was there also one there in confirmation of the traditions?" And my answer is, that probably there was, and still exists, a similar subterranean quarry or labyrinth in the heart of the adjacent hills that surround the site of the capital of Minos; for the nature of the rock and disposition of the strata are somewhat similar to that in which the labyrinthic quarry of Gortyna is situated, being of the same geological formation, and the strata nearly horizontal also. And there is, in fact, an excavation in the side of the ridge overlooking the site of Gnossus, on the east side of the Makri Teikion rivulet, that is said by the natives to be the entrance to extensive catacombs, which, however, have become choked up by the falling in of its sides, and cannot be explored. The sides of the cavernous excavation have, indeed, several votive niches and tombs, and were first noticed, in Walpole's work, by Mr. Cockerel.

This entrance to the supposed Labyrinth or Catacombs of Gnossus has the same character as that of the entrance to the Labyrinth of Gortyna, excepting that the Gnossian excavations have been used as sepulchres, but whether originally or subsequently to Minos cannot be determined so as to identify it as the true Labyrinth, of which the tradition only has existed for twenty-five centuries.

Gnossus had two ports, viz. Amnisus and Heracleion. The former, a haven in the time of Minos, was said to have been situated opposite Dia (Cramer, vol. iii. p. 369). This undoubtedly points out its site at the mouth of the Kartero, to the north-west of the city, where a rocky point still affords some shelter against the prevailing north-west wind and sea, and where the river is also still deep within its natural bar, and would admit the craft of those days to be easily hauled into it. The bay, too, must have been somewhat deeper, and thus afforded more shelter, in the time of Minos than now, since it has been encroached upon by the alluvial plain, and shore, from the débris brought down by the river.

Pliny says that a city called Matium, as well as the river Amnisus, were both situated opposite Dia; and the site of a small town exists upon an eminence on the eastern side of the bay and plain. The vestiges of the city upon the eminence are now, however, insignificant, and chiefly of late date. Nevertheless this must have been the site of Matium, instead of its having been at Candia as Pashley argues with his usual learning; and as Matium as well as the port of Amnisus were also said by Pliny (whom he quotes in the discussion) to be opposite Dia, I do not hesitate to say that this fact defeats his reasoning; for it is only as thus identified in the river Kartero and the hill of Palaio Kastro, within the same bay, that the river Amnisus, as well as Matium, can be recognized as being both opposite to Dia. The other haven of Gnossus, viz. Heracleion, must therefore have been at Candia, where the vestiges of its old moles, upon which the Venetians formed the present port, clearly identify it; and therefore it cannot be Matium as Pashley supposes. Besides, Matium is not noticed as a port as well as city by any author.

CHAPTER VII.

GNOSSUS AN EARLY SEAT OF ART AND LEARNING BEFORE GREECE—
SCULPTURE BY DÆDALUS—SUBSEQUENT CELEBRITY OF CRETAN
ART—ITS COINS REMARKABLE FOR ART AND FOR THEIR IM-
PERFECT SURFACE AND FORM—EMINENT CRETAN SCULPTORS—
A CRETAN VENUS—A CRETAN HEAD OF ZEUS—LEONARDO DA
VINCI'S PICTURE.

HAVING in the previous chapters dwelt sufficiently upon what remains of Gnossus and its ancient ports, I am induced briefly to refer to its power under Minos, the wise founder of the city, and its influence also towards the development of art and social improvement in Greece, before I proceed with a brief description of its neighbouring cities and country. For at Gnossus, as the capital of the island, commerce, education, art, and social law seem to have attained a comparatively high state of advancement under its wise lawgiver and king, from the respect with which they were referred to by the earlier authors, who tell us that the Cretans under Minos were early trained to arms and hardships, and had to learn their letters, as well as certain pieces of music, as a necessary part of their education.

The laws of Crete, by Minos, were thus considered

to be the model of the more celebrated laws of Lycurgus. It was from Dædalus and his successors in Crete that Greece improved her art and taste; and even several centuries afterwards (B.C. 596) we find that the Athenians sent to Gnossus for its poet and sage, Epimenides, to purify their city, that, by his skill in the mystic rites and the learning peculiar to the age, he might free them from the plague they then suffered from, and which, they had learnt from the oracle they consulted, would not cease until it had been so purified.

Crete was thus apparently a school of art and learning in later times, as it had been in that of Minos; and in spite of its intestine troubles amongst rival republics into which it became divided after the Trojan war, and the bad character given of the Cretans at this time by Epimenides for lying and levity, Crete seems to have been still an early cradle for the arts and learning, forming the stepping-stone or link between the conventional condition of art in Egypt and its extension and purer cultivation and development in Greece, as the natural result of its situation, its naval power, and its command of the commerce of these seas at that time. For at the Trojan war it numbered nearly as many ships as the fleet brought by Agamemnon himself; and we are told that when Battus was ordered, by the oracle of Delphi, to colonize Cyrene with Greeks, he went first to Crete for a pilot for that dreaded coast of Libya, and obtained one from Itanus.

To Dædalus, the father of Cretan art under Minos, has also been attributed the origination of the first departure from the mummy-like, conventional, still-life form generally given to figures previous to his time, by separating their legs, and the consequent introduction of motion and action to the figure; and whether Dædalus was a man or a myth, as some assume, it was at Gnossus, according to the writings of all, that the school of art, under the mythical name, was planted and flourished. And it was even asserted that to his nephew and pupil, Talos, is due the invention of the saw, the plough, and potter's wheel (but that Dædalus slew him out of jealousy of the superior talent thus shown by his sister's son), and that his own son Icarus, on his attempted flight from Crete with wings that were attached only by wax, soaring too high, too near the sun, fell into the Icarian sea in consequence—as the poetic indication of the end of undue ambition and weakness. And as even a masterly picture is the more appreciated by the effect of the gilded frame that contains it, so does fiction in which there is some fragment of fact as well as moral give an appreciating interest to every tale, and to every scene connected with it.

The fact, then, that Gnossus was one of the earlier

seats for the development and cultivation of art, science, and education, and of social laws on the basis of liberty and equality of rights, will give its due interest to the locality and neighbourhood, without a compromise of any one's political opinions and creed in feeling it. For the art thus early planted in Crete was evidently retained long in the island, as we see by its coins; and from them we find that its school was peculiarly its own, both for excellence and taste; for there exists such a remarkably high style of pictorial art in the representations of animals, figures, and nature upon some of those coins that were struck by several of the cities of this part of Crete, as to be highly admired by all numismatists, although they are singularly deficient of the care and knowledge of form and surface necessary for the proper display of the high taste and school of art which they show to have existed in Crete down to a late period. But the following names have been noted by ancient authors, as eminent for sculpture in Crete:—viz., Chirisophus for a gilt statue of Apollo, time unknown; Chersiphron of Gnossus, B.C. 777; Dipœnus and Scyllis, B.C. 570: eminent sculptors in marble—Acestor of Gnossus, B.C. 450; Amphion of Gnossus, B.C. 430.

The general estimation of Cretan art by the ancients, and the many names of eminent sculptors that Crete has produced from the days of Dædalus, induce a feeling of regret, therefore, that no particular monument or statue has been mentioned by any author as worthy of special admiration. But this is nevertheless no criterion that it did not possess many fine works of art; for in the neighbouring island of Milo, between which and Crete there was doubtless anciently a close communication and family connexion, as now, there has been discovered within the last half-century that most justly celebrated statue the "Venus of Milo," undoubtedly the finest of the many representations of the goddess; but yet of the existence of this masterpiece nothing was known until it was accidentally found; and this little isle was the last to be suspected to be possessed of such a relic of ancient Greek art. The sculptor is consequently unknown, except from conjecture; but from its close proximity to Crete there is a possibility that, if it did not come from there, its design and style may have been derived from the Cretan school.

The Venus represented here is from Crete. It was found at Gnossus some few years ago, and came into my possession soon after.

It was discovered without the head, which was fortunately found afterwards some 200 yards from it; and the figure, when found, was so encrusted with a thick coating of carbonate of lime, as hard as the marble itself, that the merit of the little statuette was not fully seen. It is about 2 feet in height; but the top of the head was sliced off obliquely on the back

part, and evidently done subsequently to its finish, so as to make it fit into some niche or recess. By long, patient labour the incrustation was at length cleared off, and the polished surface of the figure restored without injury, except where previously worn; and then its great beauty, as a probable copy of some admired work of a great master, was made apparent.

As a nude Venus of exquisite delicacy and taste, some might be induced to consider it to be a copy of some unknown work of Praxiteles, of which he was said to have made many besides the celebrated Venus of Cnidus, the exact design and position of the hands of which, it seems, is not known with certainty; but one of its characteristics was the high finish of the back of the figure, so that it was placed in the centre of an open temple that it might be viewed all round: and such is also the characteristic of this little statuette; the back is strikingly beautiful.

There are apparently several bronze copies of it in the British and other Museums, which show that there existed somewhere a much-admired original as a statue or statuette of some great master. Although these copies differ in a slight degree, according to the ignorance or fancy of the local artist, the common attitude of all identifies them as intended for some reputed original somewhere. A copy in marble, but headless and of very inferior art, was also found amongst the Cyrene marbles.

In this statuette, the goddess is represented as having just come out of her bath, and in the act of tying up the sandal of her left foot; and although a very difficult attitude to represent, from the necessarily half-turned and bent position of the body and yet with the head erect, it is marvellously wrought notwithstanding*.

The style is of the attenuated school of figure peculiar to a certain early period of Greek art and taste. The perfect grace and easy *pose*, the modest and beautiful expression, and the different position given to the arm and hand, to that usual with all nude figures of Venus known to us, will naturally strike the admiration, and greatly enhance its appreciation as a work of the most chaste and delicate conception and beauty, and of the purest taste for the representation of so difficult a subject as that of the Creator's most perfect work, the human figure.

In contemplating any fine work of art from a master mind, we are led into various trains of reflection; and one naturally first desires to learn the name of the genius, and his history and birth, and then to dwell upon the labour of thought and time devoted to the conception of the subject, and its patient manipulation by the masterly brush or chisel

* The left arm of the Venus is wanting. It was thrown back to rest upon the pedestal the figure is leaning against, and, in consequence, is not missed in a front view.

until complete. And how often is it that, when so completed, the mind that has wrought it into perfection dwells least upon the beauty and excellence of his work, and, with the last dash of his poetic pen or brush, or the final touch of his chisel, casts aside the long labour of love, and sighs for a new conception, whilst we are never tired of admiring the great work and the genius of the man that made it.

It is more than possible that master minds will often have the same conception of design, with the same idea and aim. Thus the sculptor and painter may sometimes both produce the same expression of features, and design of form, for the same ideal subject.

There is no more common representation of Greek masterly conception than that of the head of Zeus, either upon ancient coins or of statues and statuettes, all of which are, no doubt, copies of the great statue of the god by Phidias.

Zeus was, however, of special veneration in Crete, which, as the isle of his birth, in ancient mythology, must have had many statues and statuettes of the god. One little head of Zeus, which I obtained in Crete, always impressed me with admiration, from the majesty, benignity, and serenity of its expression; and when contemplating it, I was struck with the impression that in it I recognized a striking similarity with the celebrated head of our Lord in Leonardo da

Vinci's "Last Supper," but with this difference, that his was a youthful representation of the Greek conception of the features of their God of gods, Zeus.

It is thus probable that to some admired head of the god, seen by him, Da Vinci owed the conception of that beautiful countenance—intended for the Saviour, and celebrated as the masterpiece of his almost perished picture at Milan.

It is, however, quite possible that the great painter's head was a conception of his own; yet I cannot but repeat that, from a study of the face and expression of this little head, it seems to me probable that Da Vinci's is a copy of that of the Greek Zeus as conceived in youth, or rather the commencement of manhood; whilst the Greek heads of Zeus naturally represent him in its maturity and strength, with a profuse beard to indicate it.

CHAPTER VIII.

MOUNT IUKTAS, THE BURIAL-PLACE OF ZEUS ; ROUTE TO IT—
TURKISH MONASTERY — THREE DERVISHES — VIEW FROM
MOUNT IUKTAS — RHAUCUS — VALLEY OF ARKHANES — ITS
HOSPITABLE INHABITANTS—TRANQUIL NIGHTS ; THEIR TREA-
CHERY TO THE TRAVELLER.

THERE will be a natural desire, with those who have been able to follow my reasonings and narrative thus far, to know something of the features of the locality, which favoured its selection by Minos. And the idea which a glance at the map naturally gives of the reason is, the convenience of its central position. But that does not appear to me to be its only or its chief reason ; for nature had otherwise favoured this central position of Crete, by its many fertile valleys and plains, its richness of soil, and its comparatively moderate elevation—thus combining facility of communication and a salubrity of atmosphere rarely found over so large a district in any other island.

This central part of Crete, which comprised several other cities of Minos, viz. Lyttus, Lycastus, Gortyna, and Phæstus, and has an area of twenty miles, is a hilly but low district that lies between the bases of the two central mountains of Crete, Ida and Lasethe or Lassete, which mountains are respectively over 8000 and 7000 feet in elevation, whilst this depressed or lower district intermediate between them is not more than 2500 feet in any part except one, namely, a conspicuous conical mount that rises nearly in its centre, at about six miles south of Candia, and called by the natives Iuktas.

Iuktas is traditionally supposed to have been a mountain that was held in great sanctity by the ancient Cretans, and even long after the Christian era; for it seems to have been regarded as the burial-place of the " God of men," of Jupiter himself; and the myths and mysteries of that superstition and religion, which Christianity finally swept away, long held this spot in special veneration. And although it is a mere hill, as compared with the lofty Ida that directly overlooks it, its form and its isolation amidst lower land give it a striking appearance from all sides, especially in the approach to Candia by sea, as will be seen in the view given in the frontispiece.

Pashley visited this mountain in 1838; and as I now thus tread upon the footsteps of a scholar who has described it and the few remains that he found there, and who regarded it as the site of the sepulchre, or rather states that it was anciently so regarded and venerated, I shall quote his enthusiastic words. " I now stand," says Pashley, " upon the spot on which

Zeus is supposed to be at rest from all celestial and terrestrial cares, and which was so celebrated for so many ages. The testimony of a long series of ancient and ecclesiastical authors proves fully and distinctly that the tomb remained an object of curiosity and veneration to the Cretans from an early period until after the age of Constantine."

The spot thus spoken of by the above traveller has some few Cyclopean foundations, at a small cavern situated upon the northern brow of the mountain, which has two summits, lying nearly north and south of each other, and nearly of equal elevation. They are distant about a mile apart; so that from the sea they appear as one sharp peak, but from east and west the hill has a saddle-backed form, bare, rugged, and grey (the characteristic colour of all cliffy and naked rocks of limestone), especially on its east and west faces. The hill is an insular mass of hippuritic limestone rising out of the surrounding strata of tertiary marls and whitish-yellow limestone.

As a spot, then, that seems to have been regarded by the Pagan worshippers, of a late as well as an early period, with something of the reverence that Mecca is held in by the Mahomedan, and Jerusalem by the Christian, I am induced to dwell upon the way to it, recommending a visit to the mountain by every traveller to this part of Crete, from its easy accessibility from the town of Candia, and the command of view he will obtain over the surrounding country, more than from the interest he perhaps will feel in the few old stones to be seen there, either of the supposed tomb of Jupiter or of the habitations for the priests that guarded its sanctity.

The way to the mountain, after leaving Candia, is through the half Turkish and half Greek village of Phortetsa, over Gnossus, whence can again be obtained a glance down upon the undulating ground under it to the east—the site of this once important and interesting old city. But now how different the aspect, to what it was then!—either green with the luxuriant crops of corn that year by year grow from the fertile soil that has accumulated upon its remains, or brown from the débris of stones and rubbish that form its surface when the crop is removed and the summer's sun has baked it. The remains of an old rough-paved Venetian road are occasionally met with as we ascend the brow of the ridge from Phortetsa, which our sagacious mules generally avoid by following a deep, well-trodden rut they have worn by its sides, to avoid its slipperiness and shock to their feet; for every stone seems turned the wrong side upwards.

In about an hour and three-quarters' ride from the town, we reach the foot of Mount Iuktas; but as it is not accessible from this point, our muleteer tells us we must proceed to the south extreme, and ascend to it from over the village of Arkhanes or Arkhanais;

to do which we turn towards a narrow valley that runs parallel to the eastern base of the mountain.

But, before reaching this valley, we passed near a somewhat substantial but solitary building upon the ridge-brow leading up to Iuktas from Phortetsa, and which my guides pointed out as being a Turkish monastery for a certain sect of dervishes, accompanying the communication with a muttering of some word of contempt, and with a curse upon the race. In turning off the road into a path that leads to the monastery, which, in spite of my guides' disinclination, I was desirous of approaching, we came suddenly upon three young dervishes, who were seated in a secluded position under a rock, and apparently where they could receive the full force of the sun's rays upon their features during a devotional reverie,—the principal object of which, however, seemed to be to enable them to obtain that tanning of their features and skin for which the mendicant dervish of the East is remarkable. It thus was apparently a part of their training or education for the obtaining a complexion of the skin, as a professional requisite to the exercise of their craft and calling; and I frequently observed afterwards, during my stay in Crete, one of the three so sitting at the hottest time of the day, under the hottest wall, in the hottest part of the town, with breast and face bared to the sun's bronzing influence, and with composed features, indicative of the most perfect absorption, and the most enthusiastic devotion of mind and aim; nothing distracted him. " Allah is great, and Mahomet is His prophet, and I am his devout disciple," seemed to be the all-absorbing sentiment on these occasions. And thus as the three young dervishes faced the mountain that had been so venerated in the days of Paganism, as well as the midday sun, the idea could hardly help arising in my mind, that the situation of the monastery might have been chosen from some tradition of its sacredness relative to the tomb of the God of gods.

Places of religious sanctity, of any time and people, always retain a certain special interest attached to them; and thus it is natural that the superstition of one creed should in some degree become absorbed in the superstitions of another that succeeds it, especially such as those of some of the sects of Mahomedan dervishes. Hence some are disposed to recognize in their religious dance a relic of the "Pyrrhic dance" of the Greeks. And this reminds me that the Pyrrhic dance was called the Cretan dance. So also the worship of Zeus and other deities has frequently been changed, in those localities, to that of the prophets or saints of the Greek church; and thus the chapel replaces the shrine, or the church the temple. And it appears from Pashley's researches in reference to the Tomb of Zeus, that it continued to be venerated in Crete until the Theodosian persecution of the heathens, in the fourth century, put a stop to the worship of the old deities by the Cretans.

Quitting then the Turkish monastery, we enter the narrow and stony ravine that leads to the open valley of Apano, or the upper Arkhanais, at the southern base of Mount Iuktas, pitching my tent near a small cottage, amidst the flourishing vineyards for which the Arkhanais district is somewhat noted from the quality of the wine they produce. The vines extend over the upper part of two valleys, called the upper and lower Arkhanais, and contain within them two scattered villages of the same name, their inhabitants being nearly all Christian, and amounting to nearly 300 families. The Venetians conveyed water to Candia from here by an aqueduct; and the fountain whence it came has an inscription to commemorate this public benefit to the town, by Morosini, its last proconsul, and defender, before its surrender to the Turks.

Mount Iuktas is easiest ascended from the head of the Arkhanais valley: for the southern summit of the mount has a Greek chapel upon it; and a mule-track, zigzag and steep, in consequence leads to it from the valley. We ascend the mount therefore by it, and enjoy the fine view its summit commands, more than having our curiosity gratified in seeing the old foundations and stones upon its northern brow which Pashley recognizes as the site of the sacred Tomb of

Zeus. But if a contrary opinion may be allowed to be entertained by any one, I should be disposed to think that the venerated spot was more probably where the chapel now stands, since it is the most commanding as well as highest point; and the sanctity which is still attached to it being derived from the pre-existence of an older chapel (the present being a recently restored one), seems to favour this view; while local tradition is as much in support of the latter site, instead of the Cyclopean remains on the slope of the northern summit; and some ancient fragments that belong to an early Greek building seem to indicate that it had a temple or tomb upon it.

The view the hill commands will be of interest to the antiquarian traveller also, since it overlooks the territories and sites of the two early Cretan cities of Rhaucus and Lycastus; the former of which I am induced to recognize in two remarkable craggy peaks which he will see about two miles to the south-west of Iuktas, called Khani Kastelli, as also Rocca. The abruptness of the rise surrounding these two peaks, with the connecting plateau between them, gives to the spot considerable natural strength and convenience for a city. The remains now upon it are mainly those of the middle-age Fortress of Temenos, which was built by the Greek emperor Nicephorus Phocas, in 961, after he had expelled the first Mahomedan settlers, the Saracens, from Crete.

Pashley, however, supposes Khani Kastelli to have been the small city of Thenæ; and that Rhouca was situated at or near Agios Myro, on the ridge near the foot of Ida.

I am induced, however, to believe that the name Rocca, sometimes applied to it, is a relic of its ancient name, and not simply an indication of its rocky character, as Pashley presumes. Local tradition also confirms my opinion, as does also the name of the neighbouring village of Roucani, as that has a still nearer resemblance to Rhaucus,—Roucani Kastelli (now abbreviated into Khani-Kastelli) meaning the Castle of Roucani, or of Rhaucus.

Rhaucus was at one time a city of some importance as a republic, since we find that the Gortynians gave to it the territory of the Lyctians after their destruction of that city by a surprise (Cramer, iii. 390). But it is curious to find upon its coins the emblems of a coast-city, which no author has supposed it to have been; for the trident and Poseidon are the legends upon the obverse and reverse of its coins: and these exist in silver and copper, and are large in size, but not numerous; indeed they are rather rare than common.

With this brief notice of Rhaucus, in support of its identification at Khani Kastelli, I will return to Arkhanais, and take Lycastus, the other city founded by Minos in this neighbourhood, in journeying eastward towards the more important city of Lyttus, or Lyctus, as sometimes written.

Arkhanais is one of those upland valleys or basins that nature has scattered here and there, as an oasis of fertility and richness, throughout the island. Possessing the charm of seclusion and of luxuriance, an imagined tranquillity and repose to all who live within them is the feeling that first strikes a stranger on beholding these retreats; more especially if he be wearied from his journey and the heat of a southern sun. For, the body wanting repose, as soon as it can obtain it, the mind of man often sympathizes in unison, and then lights his fancy with an imagined heaven of peace with all around him—but which, his experience of the world at other moments will teach him, is but vanity, and which, a closer association with the fifty or sixty families that chance to occupy the place shows him, will be sought for in vain. For little minds and large jealousies, little faults as well as large misrepresentations, will be found to have destroyed the existence of that supposed tranquillity where nature seems to have placed so many advantages to promote it.

We pitched our tent near a small Greek cottage upon one of these, at the invitation of the family who inhabited it, who deemed themselves honoured by our doing so, and by our accepting their hospitality in donations of fruit and eggs. A serene summer's evening brought many neighbours around our tent. Some smoked; some played with beads; and all talked— some in reference to the prospective crops, and others of the blight amongst the vineyards; but there was still a strong feeling and thought with all, that occasionally would break forth from the minds of the most earnest or the least discreet: it was that which ever rankles in the heart of a Cretan Greek, viz. the hope that they would be some day freed from the government of their present masters.

But, as I could not tell them a word regarding such a hope, silence was my best policy, although my sympathy in their naturally patriotic wish might have been strongly with them. A fair damsel, too, would sometimes lend her voice to the hope—that is, if she were married and her husband present; but even her efforts at feminine eloquence and persuasion, necessarily, failed to extort any such hope or opinion from me; and thus one by one the party stole away to their own domiciles, and we were at length alone in ours and to the stillness of the night that succeeded. For all nature was soon hushed in slumber and silence, excepting the melancholy and monotonous *too*, and the occasional *coo-coo-vaie* of the little Athenian Owl, that was perched upon a neighbouring olive-tree and thus repeating in the latter sounds, as the Cuckoo does with us, the very name he is commonly known by amongst the modern Greeks. How quiet is the serenity of a calm Levantine night in such a mountain retreat! and how enjoyable is this serenity! For the air then reigns still as death, and all nature seems hushed into repose and peace—not a breath moving a leaf to produce a rustle, and not a cloud in motion, or even visible, to obscure the tiniest little star to be seen by the naked eye. Such is its usual serenity in such a secluded valley.

The refreshing coolness of the atmosphere, too, after a hot day, adds to the enjoyment of such a night of serenity; and its enjoyableness must be experienced to be properly appreciated. But, alas! there is too often treachery in such enjoyment of an oriental night; for poison is too often generated during its stillness: malaria then rises from the reeking soil, but only to float a few feet above it; for, as it cannot be dissipated, it remains to displace the purer air there, as chloroform and some gases do when confined in a vessel, as Faraday and Brande have proved to us by the simple experiment of pouring some into a common teapot and putting a candle to its spout. The traveller's precaution, therefore, is this, not to allow himself to sleep, under such stillness, on the outside of his tent or lodging, *on any account*; for the germs of a malignant fever, or its modified type, ague, steal through such serenity and seclusion of scenery in the East, as the penalty of his enjoyment of it, through ignorance or neglect.

CHAPTER IX.

ANCIENT CITIES OF LYTTUS AND LYCASTUS—POSITION OF THE LATTER AT ASTRITZI—THENÆ—PLAIN OF PEDIADA; ASCENT TO THE SITE OF LYTTUS FROM IT—THE DESCRIPTION OF THE SITE AND ITS REMAINS—ITS INSCRIPTION—ITS COINS.

THE city next in importance to Gnossus and Gortyna, in this part of the island, was that of Lyctus or Lyttus. It was of very great antiquity, and is noticed in the Iliad, B. 647, along with Gnossus, Gortyna, Mylato, and Lycastos. "It subsequently received a Lacedemonian colony. At a still later period it was in frequent hostilities with the Gnossians, who, taking advantage of the absence of the Lyctians on a distant expedition, surprised Lyctus and destroyed it. The Lyctians were so disheartened by this calamity that they abandoned at once their ancient locality, and withdrew to Lampe, where they were kindly and hospitably received. Polybius on this occasion bears testimony to the great antiquity of Lyctus, and the superiority of the inhabitants in regard to moral character above the Cretans. It would appear from the same historian, that they afterwards recovered their city, with the aid of the Gortynians." (Cramer, vol. iii. p. 389.)

In the couplet from the 'Iliad' before referred to, regarding the early notice of Lyctus, there is mention also of a city of Lycastus, with Gnossus, Lyctus, and Gortyna, which city of Lycastus must in consequence be looked for in their neighbourhood. Strabo states that it was destroyed by the Gnossians, as Lyttus or Lyctus had been, and that it had entirely disappeared (vol. x. p. 479). But another author quoted by Cramer (Polybius) states that Lycastus was afterwards taken from the Gnossians by the Gortynians, who gave it to the neighbouring town of Rhaucus (vol. iii. p. 370).

This association enables us to identify its site more clearly now that Rhaucus has been identified (as I believe it indisputably to be) at Khani Kastelli; for the situation and territory of Lycastus must have been somewhere adjacent to the three cities of Gnossus, Lyttus, and Rhaucus: and to be so, it must have stood somewhere between them, or within the triangle formed by these three cities; for the sites of Gnossus and Lyttus have been long identified.

Thus Lycastus is identified by me at the ruins of a city now called Kastritzi or Astritzi, near the head of the Kartero valley, and near the western border of the upland plain of Pediada, which plain probably, in the Homeric time, in part belonged to it, since Lycastus was then evidently an important city of Crete. The modern name, too, of Astritzi or Kastritzi, although a diminutive of Kastron, the common name of a fort, may also be derived from Lycastus. And another point, indicative of the proximity of these three cities, is in the fact that Lyctus and Lycastus are family names in connexion with Minos, and were thus naturally given by him to the cities next in importance or proximate to Gnossus, his capital of Crete.

The route to Kastritzi, from our last tenting-ground at the foot of Mount Iuktas, lies to the south-east, across several low ridges and valleys, in each of which villages and hamlets are studded throughout, and indicate a district of some fertility and populousness.

A flat spur or ridge rises rather commandingly, at the head of the most eastern of these valleys, at about two hours' ride from the foot of Iuktas, and, although not very high, is naturally strong and inviting for the situation of an ancient city of the Homeric times.

Some few portions of its walls still remain, which are a mixture of Cyclopean and Hellenic, with square towers from 12 to 15 feet high, and very solid; and the foundations of almost the entire circuit can be traced round the margin of the hill for a distance of nearly a mile and a half. Within them are some foundations as vestiges of the habitations of the city, of both an early and middle-age character, and remains of terraces that supported them. Strabo, however, observes that Lycastus had disappeared in his time; and the passage may be used as an argument against the identity of these ancient walls with those of Lycastus. Yet I cannot but believe that it was the true position of this Homeric city, from the facts related, and in opposition to Pashley,—who placed it, as also Arcadia, on the east side of the Lasethe Mountains, and consequently far removed from the Rhaucian and Gnossian territory—which Lycastus evidently could not have been, to have become transferred to the inhabitants of the former by the Gortynians, as Polybius relates. Pashley is undoubtedly in error in respect to these two important cities of Lycastus and Arcadia, and especially, as I shall more fully show in a future chapter, in regard to the latter, as he is also in respect to Rhaucus, Matium, and Heracleion.

From Astritzi we proceed to Lyttus, across the large upland plain of the Pediada or Pethiada, lying directly between Lycastus and Lyttus. An hour's journey from Astritzi brings us to the small conical hill at the northern margin of the plain, upon which are well-preserved walls of an ancient fortress, called Saba or Sapa, and which I have presumed to be a small place called Thenæ, that was said to have stood near the Omphalian Plain, thus, also, recognizing this plain as the Pediadan Plain extending in front of it. There is mention of a temple of Thenæ, and also of the river Triton near it. At the village of Smavi, near Saba, the inscription No. 2, Plate I. of Inscriptions was procured,

PLAIN OF PEDIADA. 93

being a memorial tablet, by her parents, to Agatha-meris, who, from the objects represented upon it (a comb, plaited hair, and perfuming-vessel or soap-dish), seems to have been a lady hair-dresser. The Jews still show the trade of their deceased in a similar manner.

Its walls are purely Hellenic, and not Cyclopean, and are also in better preservation than those at Kastritzi; and this better preservation seems even more incompatible with Strabo's statement, of the total disappearance of Lycastus in his time, than the preservation of the walls of Kastritzi, identified as Lycastus, if it be conjectured that Lycastus might have been at Sapa. Strabo may, however, have only used the expression in reference to its habitations, or to its existence then as a habitable spot. Yet, as Strabo resided some time at Gnossus with his mother's relatives, who governed it, his words may seem on that account to deserve the more deferential consideration. I have, however, frequently observed elsewhere, at the sites of ancient cities which Strabo had mentioned as having been destroyed and no longer existing in his time, many remains and vestiges that enable them to be identified, although not existing as towns or habitable spots at the present time.

The upland plain of the Pediada is about four miles in diameter, and nearly 200 feet above the sea. It is bounded by gently rising hills on all sides but on the east, where they rise abruptly into the Lasethe

Mountains to a height of 7000 feet above the sea; and its northern part is naked and bleak, which seems to be caused by the force of the squalls that strike upon its surface from the north winds that prevail at certain seasons. The plain is, in consequence, comparatively treeless and naked near its north margin: and vegetation is stunted also upon the surface of the bordering hills from the same cause; and so much is its influence seen and felt here, that although I pitched my tent once at the foot of these hills, near the village of Apostoli, and near a few scrubby olives, we could not collect wood enough from the hills or plain to boil our tea-kettle, but were obliged to use, in lieu of wood, the sun-dried cow-dung collected from the bare plain adjacent.

This part of the Pediada Plain is in consequence left for the tillage of grain only, whilst the southern and central parts have fine vineyards and fruit-orchards near the villages situated there.

This fine upland of the Pediada must have been the principal territory of the Lyctians, or Lyttians, in the time of Minos; for the remains of this very ancient city exist upon the summit of a narrow but tortuous ridge, overlooking the plain upon its eastern margin, and just over the village of Xidhia or Xidhi, as it is variously pronounced by the native peasantry. The hill is an outlying and lower spur of the Lasethe, composed chiefly of friable shales and schists of a dark-brown, blue, and grey colour, that have a high inclination, dipping nearly vertically to the northwest, and appear to belong to the upper series of nummulite rocks existing in Crete.

In the ascent to the village of Xidhia, from the eastern margin of the plain, we meet with several very large Ilex oaks, growing upon the slopes of the ridge or in the sheltered ravines that descend it, the girths of some of which exceed any I had hitherto seen in Crete. It is not the Valonea oak, but a small and prickly-leafed kind, and with a small acorn like the acorns of the British oak, although with a much smaller leaf; and these acorns are gathered only to feed the village swine, their cups having apparently no commercial value for tanning, like those from the true Valonea.

The ascent to the village of Xidhia, from the Pediada Plain, occupied nearly three quarters of an hour, and we found the inhabitants all busy at their wine-presses; and the narrow, filthy lanes of approach to their several habitations were in consequence rendered more than usually filthy by the stream of refuse dregs of wine that ran from them like blood, and from the village pigs that wallowed in it. The gathering of the grapes is here fully a fortnight behind the time of the vintage in the plain of the Pediada, and also fully three weeks later than in the vineyards of the plains and valleys upon the coast.

Thus situated upon the summit of a western shoulder of the Lasethe, the city of Lyctus or Lyttus occupied a very commanding position; yet the hill has no striking form of outline or feature. The site is, however, a remarkable one; for it is at the point of junction or branching-off of numerous narrow ridges that descend from it to the south, west, and north, the sides of all of which are very abrupt, and their crests nowhere more than a few yards across; so that nearly every house and street required a terrace built to support it; and it was therefore a very difficult one to enclose within walls of a substantial and durable character, from the many ravines and ridges they had to cross, and from the steep and friable nature of the rock they had to be built upon. And the city being built upon the sides of these several ridges, its parts thus originally faced all points of the compass.

The fragments of the buildings of the old city have, in consequence of the abruptness of the site and the instability of their foundations, for the most part fallen into the valleys or ravines beneath, and become buried with débris, and soil accumulated upon them; nothing, consequently, remains standing or *in situ*, excepting a few facings of these old terraces, which are not very massive.

Amongst some accumulated fragments of the recent terracings to support the ground for the tillage of narrow patches of corn, there are scattered here and there several sculptured marbles and monumental bases or pedestals, some of which are inscribed, and supported statues of Roman emperors; and there are also several marble and even granite columns dispersed with them,—all indicative of the ruins of a city that was once rich and populous; for these granite columns are foreign to the island, most probably from Egypt, and thus have been transported from the coast a distance of seven or eight miles into the interior of Crete, and to embellish a city that was nearly 2500 feet above the sea.

On the summit of the ruins there lie also two marble statues near the small chapel. These are the chief relics of interest visible at Lyttus; for there are no vestiges of buildings *in situ*, nor any appearance of the great theatre which, according to Antonio Belli, existed at Lyttus in the time of the Venetian occupation of Crete. Several spots were suggestive of the possibility of a theatre having existed there; but the absence of remains, as also the greater diameter of the curve, at the heads of the several ravines is opposed to its probability, if any of them, from their forms suggesting it, be selected as the supposed site of this theatre.

The two statues here noticed are headless—one being a recently discovered statue of a draped female, the other the lower half of a colossal statue of Jupiter, known by an eagle sculptured behind the feet of the figure. Both are in white marble, but the latter appears the finest as a work of art.

There was also found, near the northern extremity of the city, a small square marble altar, upon two faces of which was sculptured a naked youth, or Cupid, having a torch in one hand, and a hare suspended by its hind legs in the other; rams' heads and festoons of grapes and leaves ornamented the other two sides and corner-pieces. The top of the altar-piece had a shallow hollow, like a baptismal font. The relief of the sculpture is low, but of fair art.

As some of the inscriptions copied from this site appear not to have been published, they are given in an appendix by the Rev. Churchill Babington. One of these, which I copied from over the door of a house in the village of Xidhia, is of great interest (although not readable), being probably one of the most early of all the inscriptions found in Crete. A duplicate copy by any future traveller, in correction of my own, would be very desirable, since a copy made at a different time of the day, and under a different light, might give a better chance for deciphering and reading it, and help the scholar in his puzzle.

The coins of Lyttus are not uncommon, and sometimes represent a bird, a prow, or a wild boar's head on the two faces, at others have the head of Pallas on the obverse, and ΛΥΤ to denote the city on the other side,—thus giving the true mode of spelling it as "Lyttus" in later times, instead of "Lyctus" as written by some of the early authors.

The coins of the Cretan city of Khersonesos—the seaport of Lyttus, and which evidently became the more important city of the two after the destruction of Lyttus—have also the same emblems, but with the letters **K E P** upon them, or combined thus in the monogram ⟨glyph⟩, so as to indicate for which city they were specially struck, and they show the close connexion as well as the once flourishing condition of both of these cities.

The hill upon which the city of Lyttus stood resembles, from its numerous branching ridges, the fibres that shoot off from the extremity of a great root —that root being represented by the single narrow ridge which springs out behind the city, and connects it with the bolder face of the Lasethe Mountain above it as the trunk or stem. This connecting ridge or neck divides the watershed or ravines that lead to the north and south coasts of Crete, by the Aposoleme Valley, the Pediada Plain, and the Valley of Ene; and there are the remains of an aqueduct upon this col or neck, that led from some distant part of the mountains of the Lasethe to Lyttus in its ancient and flourishing days.

CHAPTER X.

THE PLAIN OF LASETHE—ITS FERTILITY AND SALUBRITY—IT CONTAINED NO ANCIENT CITY, AND THEREFORE BELONGED TO LYTTUS—DESCENT TO KHERSONESO—RUINS OF AN ANCIENT AQUEDUCT AND ROAD FROM LYTTUS TO KHERSONESO—NUMMULITIC FOSSILS—RUINS OF KHERSONESO—VESTIGES OF A CHURCH OR CATHEDRAL—TESSELLATED FOUNTAIN AT THE PORT—ANCIENT THEATRE—A FRESHWATER DEPOSIT.

I HAVE noticed in the last chapter, that to the southeast of this ancient city of Lyttus there rise the Lasethe Mountains, the third in height in Crete, attaining an elevation of about 7000 feet, and therefore only 1000 feet less than Mount Ida.

Immediately under the summit, and due east of Lyttus, lies another very large mountain basin, also called Lasethe, which is at an elevation of about 3000 feet above the sea. It encloses a beautiful plain, which is extensively cultivated, and even populous, although so elevated, having no less than fifteen villages, besides several hamlets or farms, within it, the inhabitants of which enjoy a very temperate clime as compared with the rest of Crete, and great salubrity in consequence: the population at present is between 3000 and 4000 souls.

The ascent to the Lasethe Plain is by the coll or neck behind Lyttus, and thence by a zigzag road up the steep mountain-face out of which it springs. This remarkable upland basin has no outlet, being perfectly enclosed by mountains, and thus in appearance somewhat resembles a huge crater when viewed from the encircling summits above it.

Its rivers and torrents, consequently, have no visible connexion with the lower coast-streams, but, after uniting in one torrent-bed, the waters fall into a large cavern at the west extreme of the plain, and thus escape to the sea through the bowels of the mountains by what the Greeks call a katavothron, but to reappear, according to the native opinion, as the Aposoleme River, to the north-west, some seven or eight miles distant.

The villages of the Lasethe basin lie dotted around its margin upon small eminences and spurs that extend from the enclosing heights; and the habitations are for the most part surrounded by clusters of fruit-trees and some vines, the fruits being chiefly pears and apples, such as are natural to a very temperate region like Northern Europe; for the olive does not grow in it, from its elevation and aspect.

The impression which the view of this deeply embosomed plain must recall to the traveller, on first beholding it, is that of the "Happy Valley" of Rasselas; for a wall of mountains completely encloses it, and, on all sides, access to it is gained only by winding rugged paths. It thus forms a perfect oasis amidst the stern sterile hills that embosom it; and, enjoying a tempered climate more resembling that of Switzerland than of the populated parts of Crete in general, it is as salubrious as it is tranquil, and therefore an inviting retreat during summer from the great heats then existing in the lower valleys.

Thus the fruits of Europe, combined with the vine alone, flourish in this happy valley; for neither the olive nor the carob-tree can flourish in it, although indigenous and most productive in all the lower parts of this mountain. The inhabitants consequently have large flocks; but these are obliged to descend to the lowlands for pasturage in the winter season, when some of the inhabitants of its villages follow also, to avoid the severity of the winter.

The length of the valley of the Lasethe is about five miles, and its breadth about half its length. Its inhabitants are all Christians, having no Turkish resident but the Aga and his guard.

In early Cretan days the Lasethe, no doubt, formed part of the territory of Lyttus, as it possesses no ancient site of importance within it; for the whole plain has been examined and the topographical features surveyed by Lieut. Mansell, who found only some slight vestiges of a small fortress. It formed, therefore, the upland territory of Lyttus, whilst the lower plain of the Pediada under and to the west of it was its lowland territory, the city itself commanding the communication by the connecting ridge and the only accessible route between them.

This explains the reason of the selection of so unusual and so inconvenient a position for an early Greek city as that of Lyttus—upon the crest or backbone of a tortuous and narrow ridge composed of crumbling slaty rock, and with its sides so steep that it was difficult to find room for a single street or habitation without terracing it.

Descending from Lyttus, I proceeded by the valley of the Potamies to Khersoneso. At the point of junction of this valley with that leading direct from Lyttus, are some vestiges of an ancient aqueduct that spanned the valley at a high elevation, and must have been formed here of several lofty arches. It was built of small stones, bricks, and mortar, but faced with small blocks of limestone that were roughly squared and smoothed, and probably dates after the Roman conquest of Crete. But it was, from its height and extent, a great work.

As the aqueduct led to Khersoneso, it was necessary to be conducted at a high elevation, so as to cross the high intervening ridge just over Khersoneso itself. At the spot where the aqueduct crossed the Potamies rivulet the valley was very narrow; but the elevation of the aqueduct appears to have been here at least

200 feet above it, and some indications of buttresses and arches remain upon the sides of the valley, though not sufficient to show the number of tiers of arches which composed it, or of what date they probably were.

The road descending this valley is very bad, like most Cretan roads, from their rocky character; but the sure-footedness and strength of their fine breed of mules compensate in some degree for the absence of any artificial roads. There are, however, evidences here and there of a very broad paved road having once connected Lyttus with its emporium Khersoneso, and which followed nearly the same level as the aqueduct; and as the distance between them in a straight line is fully seven miles, and perhaps ten by its windings round the practicable ridges, these works of the aqueduct and ancient road are indicative of a period of great populousness, prosperity, and advanced civilization.

In the deep bed of the valley below the junction of the Lyttus and Potamies streamlets, I had an opportunity of examining some of the strata and fossils of the downcast series of rocks lying to the north-west of Lyttus, where beds of grey limestone are interstratified with dark shales, and contain two or three species of nummulitic fossils. Their dip here is much less than at Lyttus, although in the same direction. The limestones, however, are not uniform in thickness and continuous, but thin out, becoming replaced by shales and schistose strata of varying colour and compactness.

On reaching the pass which leads to Khersoneso, just over the modern village of the same name, we have a fine view of the Bay of Khersoneso, and of the ancient port of the city that stood upon the west shore of the bay. It is formed by a small peninsula and ancient mole that extended from it. Close under the cape forming the bay I beheld my ship awaiting my return; and in the little port there were two or three caiques, with their crew of Symiot sponge-divers lounging on shore, awaiting the abatement of a fresh north wind then blowing, for the continuance of their marvellous occupation in the depths of the sea,—some of whom dive to the depth of thirty fathoms, and upwards, for these luxurious and necessary articles of the toilet and hospital, and something of whose life and labours I shall hereafter describe.

Khersoneso attained such importance in early Christian times as to have been the see of a bishop, and therefore must have had a suitable church; consequently we find, upon the summit of the small point or peninsula by which the port is in part formed, the foundations of a large church, 112 feet long and 52 feet broad, with several columns that supported its roof lying upon the spot; and just under it, on the south side of the point, there is a small cave that is still used as a chapel, and dedicated to Hagia Paraskevi, or Holy Friday.

The site occupied by the city was low, sloping gently towards the port, and intersected by two or three shallow ravines. It is for the most part cultivated at present, and has few vestiges remaining visible but scattered fragments. There are the remains of a large cistern near the western entrance of the city, with an aqueduct leading from it; and near the port, there are the remains of a tessellated fountain in the shape of a shallow cone, so as to present four triangular sides of tessellated surface, each representing various figures, chiefly aquatic birds and fish, and fishing-scenes, such as naked fishermen with rod and line, a boat with two fishermen in it, one of whom has caught a fish, or a large eight-armed sepia or cuttlefish, which was no doubt as great a delicacy with the ancients as it is now with the modern Greeks.

The figures are rudely done, and in violation of every principle of perspective, although the bordering around each face of the font was elaborate and in good taste. As the waters of the fountain must have flowed over it originally, by being thus kept wet the colours of the varied marble were rendered bright and fresh, and better developed the scene represented.

The architects of our ornamental garden- or parkfountains might perhaps derive a hint from this

PORT AND SITE OF KHERSONESOS

rudely tessellated fountain of Khersoneso, to produce pictorial effect and variety in designs for the same object.

The only other ruin deserving notice at Khersoneso is that of a small theatre, 156 feet in diameter by my measurement: judging from its present form, it seems to have been a purely Roman theatre. But in the time of the Venetians it must have been in a much better state of preservation; for in the manuscript of Belli, published by Mr. Falkener, there is a very detailed plan of this theatre. Now, however, the foundation of the proscenium and a part of the wings and back alone remain; and the theatre appears to have been wholly built of small stones and mortar.

Pashley made a hasty visit to Khersoneso, but does not describe its remains. Dr. Pococke only heard of the ruins, but did not visit them. The above details are consequently the only description hitherto given of Khersoneso, a city which, by the traces now visible, had a circuit of between two and three miles. Strabo speaks of a temple to Britomartis there, of the site of which there is now no indication nor any vestiges. The accompanying view will better convey an idea of the situation of the city, and suffice for the general reader.

The district behind Khersoneso I found to be, probably, the most interesting for its geology in Crete. For the hills lying westward, and towards the point of Khersoneso, I found to be composed of both freshwater and marine deposits—the former lying in a sort of bay or hollow, between a portion of the marine tertiary and the limestones of the Hippurite or Nummulite series, and also overlying parts of the marine tertiary, so as to show its more recent origin.

Its position corresponds somewhat to that of the freshwater deposits at the east end of the island of Cos, and described in the Appendix to my 'Travels in Lycia,'—that is, lying within and upon a strip of the older marine tertiary strata so prevalent throughout the northern part of Crete. The Cos deposits contain numerous Pectens, oysters, and corals. The freshwater fossils of Khersoneso are identical with some of those found in Cos and Rhodes, and consist of Unios, Lymnæ, Paludinæ, and Planorbes, and thus contribute another fragment to the evidence for the existence of a freshwater lake over the Greek archipelago during the late Miocene or early Pleiocene age. (See Geological Appendix.)

CHAPTER XI.

THE MIRABELLA DISTRICT AND UPLANDS — THE CAROB- OR LOCUST-TREE FLOURISHES IN THIS DISTRICT—THE NUTRITIOUS PROPERTIES OF ITS FRUIT — THE FOOD OF ST. JOHN IN THE WILDERNESS — MALIA BAY AND VILLAGE—ANCIENT SITE ON THE COAST OF THE BAY—DISCOVERY OF SCALES OF GOLD—PROBABLE SITE OF A TEMPLE TO BRITOMARTIS— SITE OF MILETUS— EXTENSIVE CAVERN NEAR IT—THE HARBOUR AND FORTRESS OF SPINA LONGA.

THE district of the Mirabella, lying east of Lasethe, consists of a series of rugged ranges enclosing several upland plains and narrow depressed basins, like the great Lasethe Plain, but in miniature. All these valleys diminish in elevation as they approach the Gulf of Mirabella to the north-east, forming so many steps of ascent from it to the greater western basin and plain of the Lasethe, and, like it, are entirely enclosed. The principal of these is Khenurio Khorio, from a large village of that name within it.

Between the plains of Fournes and Mirabella, upon a high peak of the ridge dividing them, are vestiges of a small fortress, but which does not appear to belong to very early times, and seems to have been some middle-age stronghold, rather than either Roman or Greek.

In these lower valleys of the Mirabella district the olive flourishes, with the mulberry and other fruits. But the carob- or locust-tree is the tree that characterizes, and is the chief product of, the Mirabella, more particularly on the lower slopes of its mountains and valleys which border the coast. It, however, is not planted, as the olive, but cultivated where nature has accidentally reared it near the habitations or tilled ground, and it forms the principal wild shrub on these mountains. The carob is consequently the chief produce of the Mirabella, the fruit being also large and good.

The nutritious quality of the carob-pods, which are, singularly, produced in clusters from the gnarled and knotty parts of the stems of this stunted and slow-growing tree, is well known in South Europe; and they are a most valuable food for horses and cattle, as they contain a large quantity of saccharine matter. In some parts of the Levant they are, in consequence, even sold as a sweetmeat for children, who masticate the dry but raw pod with great gusto; and in Italy and Malta the sweet juice is expressed from the carob-pod to flavour the caramelli, instead of sugar, being preferred on account of the peculiar flavour it imparts to this confection.

It can be thus well understood how the sweet pulp of the pod of the carob and wild honey together could have afforded subsistence to St. John in the desert; and although true locust insects themselves have been supposed to have been the food upon which John subsisted, and no doubt are sometimes eaten by the Arabs of certain parts of Africa (for I myself have seen heaps of baked locusts sold in the market-place of Tunis during the time of a flight of these pests of the East), yet the sweet pulp of the carob-pod would form a more nutritious and palatable substitute for bread, and be also a more probable food, as the wild product of an uncultivated mountain or desert, than that of an insect subject to decay and putrify, which also is only procurable at one particular season, and to be preserved must be salted. But, as Biblical commentators have decided that it was the INSECT that St. John fed upon in the desert, I am doubtless at fault in showing the plausibility of the more common and vulgar opinion regarding the locust-tree, the mistake having arisen perhaps from the English name alone; for the word "arbau" of the Old Testament is translated "akris" (the insect) in the Septuagint Greek. The contemplation of the question, however, has its special interest still.

The open and wide bay extending eastward of Cape Khersoneso is also called Malia, and takes its name from a village situated upon a narrow slip of stony and undulating land which skirts the shore at the foot of the lower chain of the Lasethe mountains; and the neighbourhood is noticed for producing carobs of the finest quality.

The main road to the eastern harbour of Spina Longa and the Mirabella uplands lies over this plain, at no great distance from the coast. At about a mile to the north-east of the village, and a few hundred yards from the coast, are some vestiges of an ancient city which the natives call Sivadhi Hellenico. The site is upon a rugged piece of rising ground on the east side of a torrent-bed with a small cove at its mouth, where small boats could be sheltered when hauled ashore. The remains consist chiefly of some few foundations of ancient habitations, portions of cyclopean terraces or walls, and a massive platform about ninety-five feet square, formed of large slabs of limestone, which must have supported or been the approach to a temple. This latter, until a few years since, lay buried three or four feet beneath a reddish soil that had accumulated over it, when, a shepherd accidentally discovering a few thin plates or scales of gold in the surface-soil, the inhabitants of Malia, hoping that it indicated a mine of treasure beneath, laboured diligently for several weeks in excavating the locality, but were rewarded with a few ounces of the precious metal only, which was found in the form of scales or thin plates, that seemed to have covered some statue of baser material. Perhaps it was a statue to the goddess Britomartis (who, as shown by several authors, was anciently worshipped in this neighbourhood), and probably stood upon the platform without a covered building to enclose it.

About a mile to the east of these ruins is a narrow creek, at the mouth of a rocky gully or watercourse, which cuts through the stony plain extending from the foot of the mountains over Malia. As in this small inlet boats and coasting craft could find some shelter for trading in the summer season, and also security when hauled ashore in the winter, it must have been a port of this unknown site in ancient times, since it is used now for the exporting of oil and carobs from the district during fine weather; and when I visited it, some empty oil-casks were then lying on the shore, having been left there for filling, until the return of some coasting trader.

The creek is called Sisi, and at present the only building standing near it is a Greek chapel; but there are vestiges of some few other buildings, which appear, however, to be modern also. The natives, whom I found cultivating the adjacent ground, called it Hellenico Sisi, or Seese, implying that it was an ancient location as a port or fishing-hamlet of the district. The creek would afford excellent shelter as a retreat and hiding-place for six or eight row-galleys of past times.

At two miles further to the east of Seese is an open bay at the mouth of a valley which descends from the Mirabella, with a steep shingle-beach for its shore.

A small village, called Melato, stands upon a small eminence a little way up the valley. The similarity of the name induced Pashley to presume it to indicate the site and ruins of Miletus, mentioned by Homer with Lyttus and Lycastus.

Pashley only alludes to them in a note; but his map indicates that the ancient ruins he refers to as Miletus stood to the westward of the modern village of Melato, where, however, I could hear of none from the natives whom I met cultivating their fields at the mouth of the valley; but they pointed to a conical peak jutting off from the higher hills on the east side of the bay, and not far from the sea-shore, as the only true Hellenic site in the neighbourhood. But the only remains here visible were some old cisterns, some ancient terraces ranged round the side of the peak, and some collected heaps of stones on the sloping ground extending nearly to the sea from its base, and which seem to be the remains of ancient and rude habitations, such as might have been used by the inhabitants of an early city like that of Miletus. As Miletus was said to have been destroyed in the time of Strabo, greater remains can hardly be expected, perhaps, to identify it. This is probably the ancient city that Pashley heard of when passing through the district; for it is not clear from his remark that he visited the site he marks upon his map, and where I could hear of none now.

The Melato valley descends from the western basin of the Mirabella, which doubtless was the upland territory of Miletus, or this city, whatever was its ancient name.

But there are some ruins which I have before noticed as capping the summit of the ridge that separates the western plains of the Mirabella from the eastern ones. Pashley briefly refers to these ruins, and seems to have been more guided by the report of the natives regarding them than by a personal examination, from the opinion he has formed of their extent and antiquity; for he supposes them to represent Lycastus. But these ruins are purely those of a fortress of the middle ages or of the Roman times, and are built of small stones and mortar, and also are not more than 400 to 500 yards in extent.

But I have before ventured to differ from this learned traveller, by believing the Homeric city Lycastus to have been at Kastritza, to the west (instead of to the east) of Lyttus; for Lycastus was clearly in the neighbourhood of Rhoucus and Gnossos.

The Melato valley is noted for a capacious cavern that enters into the limestone-ridge bordering it on the east, and is celebrated in the local events of the Revolution, from having been made a retreat for a large number of the inhabitants of the Mirabella during that civil war in 1822.

Its principal entrance is about half a mile from the sea; and it is said to have another aperture at the east end of the bay, thirty or forty feet above the sea; but I was not able to visit them.

It is related of this cave, that several hundred Christians, having at one time during the Revolution retreated to it as usual when alarmed, were so closely beset by a band of Turks from Spina Longa, that, after many were killed or starved to death within it, the rest surrendered and were made slaves.

The natives of Melato, from whom I received this account, spoke of it with much reluctance in consequence; but when induced to do so, accompanied it with expressions of revengeful bitterness towards the Turks of Spina Longa, from the domestic afflictions which the reference to the subject even now awakened in their breasts. Of a civil war, especially amongst uncivilized peoples, such as that which spread over Crete, fanned more by the antipathies of religious bigotry and enthusiasm than those of race, it takes several generations to efface the effect, even under the most prudent governance of the mind against dwelling upon its memory or its traditions.

The village of Melato is wholly Christian, and contains about fifty families, who appear to be poor; but they have land about it, both on the hillside and valley, capable of profitable cultivation, although the ridges are steep. From it a mountain-road ascends to the long, narrow, and enclosed upland plain of the Mirabella, whence there is a fair road to Kritza, the principal village of the district, and also to Spina Longa, its principal port.

The port of Spina Longa is situated just within the cape, or headland, that forms the turning-point to the deep gulf or bay of Mirabella, the most notable flexure or indentation of the whole coast of Crete, and penetrating to the depth of nearly fourteen miles.

The cape turning into it, which is remarkably bold and wild, is picturesquely crowned by an old and rent tower or lighthouse of the Venetians; and the Ægean lashes almost incessantly with its angry surf and spray the worn rocks beneath, and with unusual force; for here the north and north-west winds blow for three parts of the year, and with double violence as compared with any other part of the neighbourhood. The south side of the cape, as far as the mouth of the inlet of Spina Longa, presents a high and rather picturesque steep, over which the hissing squalls descend during these winds like water falling from a cascade. The entrance to the port is consequently then difficult of access for a sailing vessel, and is somewhat unsafe also as an anchorage, unless the vessel anchoring within it moors with two or three anchors and cables, to secure herself against the force of these torrents of wind, which, both in summer and winter, rise as suddenly as violently. Moreover this inlet, although having four fathoms in its upper part, is barred a little within the entrance by a shallow bank of twelve feet, that extends directly across it. Thus in its upper part, where it is more capacious, the port is available for only small coasting craft, and in the outer part is very limited at its only anchorage for larger vessels.

Off the north end of the peninsula of Spina Longa, and close under the squally heights there rises abruptly from the sea a small but high and cliffy islet, upon which the Venetians built a strong fortress, serving both to defend the entrance to the anchorage behind it and also to be a secure garrison for the command and subjection of the natives of the Mirabella; for the Venetians, in spite of its inconvenience, made this the chief trading-port of the eastern part of Crete.

The fortress of Spina Longa was several times attacked by the Turks; but, being of the form and character of Gibraltar on a small scale, and, moreover, well fortified for the period, and also being wholly insulated, it remained in the hands of the Venetians long after the island of Crete had become subject to the Turks. Its fortifications are at present much fallen into decay; but it contains about eighty Turkish families, the town being situated on the western side of the rock, as the eastern face is quite precipitous, like that of Gibraltar. Its inhabitants are chiefly sailors, who carry on some trade in seven or eight schooners that belong to them, as well as possessing ten or twelve coasting feluccas, or caiques, for local trade, or for making summer voyages to the neighbouring islands for wood, grain, and melons, in their several seasons; for Crete, although so capable, does not produce sufficient of either to meet the consumption of its larger towns.

HYER[ys] BOND[ys] P[R] HOC HOS MIL[M] AFVN-
DAM[TIS] ER[E] GVB[RE] D.IOCOBO SORELLO CAR-
PENSI A.M.D.C.XXIX.

The above inscription is over the door of a church built by the Venetians at the south end of the town, but which is now used as a mosque; and there are some large cisterns at the north-east end of the town, that supply the garrison with water, of detestable odour and flavour from stagnation and neglect.

It is singular thus to find in Crete a community of Turks whose occupation is exclusively the sea! and some of them are excellent sailors. And I am told that a few years since they had a fine brig also, which they had the confidence to send with a cargo to England, as she was commanded by one of their most enterprising and skilful skippers, whose great repute and skill as a Levantine navigator had thus induced them to venture her on a voyage to our difficult seas and shores, where, unhappily, fate or fortune frowned upon their temerity; for both captain and crew and their fine vessel were lost together.

The trading ambition of the little community thus received a serious check in this loss, from which it is perhaps not likely to recover; for they have not ventured to build another to replace her. "Kismit" (*i.e.* Fate) settled it; so they are now content to trade at home, instead of venturing upon distant voyages.

A Mahomedan community of sailors and traders, on a barren rock adjacent to a fertile island, recalls to mind the community of Christian sailors and sponge-divers who inhabit the barren rocks of Castelorizzo, Symi, and Khalki, as well as others in the Levant.

The reason of such a location or occupation was perhaps in some degree identical, viz. the preferring to seek a livelihood from the sea to the risks and discord of a life in association with their neighbours the Christians of the Mirabella, and very probably from their knowing the deep-rooted hatred formerly felt against them, as participators in the tragic events connected with the cave of Melato, which rendered a return to their mountain-villages imprudent, if not impossible. Besides, they are also the appointed gunners to the island-fortress at the present time.

CHAPTER XII.

THE RUINS OF AN EARLY CRETAN CITY UPON THE ISTHMUS OF SPINA LONGA—AND OF NAXOS OVER IT—THE IDENTITY OF THE FORMER WITH OLONTION — ITS RUINS — ITS ANCIENT PORT AT KALOKYTHIA—THE RUINS AND WHETSTONE-QUARRIES OF NAXOS—THE QUARRIES OF ELUNTA—THE ANCIENT BISHOPRIC OF ALLYNGUS RECOGNIZED HERE.

THE harbour of Spina Longa is formed by a long peninsula, connected with Crete by a low and narrow isthmus at its south extreme, which is in one part only about 100 yards wide and hardly more than three feet above the sea. But this isthmus must have been in ancient times both much higher and much wider; for the ruins of an early Greek city exist upon it, and a large part of the city lies submerged beneath the sea on either side of the isthmus: and the subsidence must have amounted to six or eight feet, perhaps more, as there are no means of ascertaining the magnitude of these phenomena with such precision as that of elevations. The position thus chosen for an early Greek city, upon the neck of a low isthmus, is rather singular for the ancients; but still it was a much better one for the convenience of its local trade than that chosen by the Venetians upon the small islet at the stormy entrance of the shallow inlet of Spina Longa; for the adjacent bay of Kalokythia, on the east side of the peninsula, and sheltered mainly by the little island of that name which lies across the mouth of the bay, forms an excellently sheltered harbour at all times and seasons, and was its ancient port.

The identification of this city and the adjacent harbour with their ancient name has long been a difficulty with me; for, until recently, I supposed this city could be no other than Naxos, from its vicinity to some quarries for procuring a sharpening-stone known as the Turkey stone, for the sharpening of razors and fine tools, because, according to Dr. Cramer's showing, "there was a place called Naxos in Crete, celebrated for producing excellent whetstones;" and the identity seemed to be confirmed by the similarity of the names Oxah and Axos, which are now applied to a fortress upon a high crag just over the west side of the isthmus, and just over where the whetstones were anciently quarried although not so at present.

I have, however, recently come to the conclusion that these ruins upon the isthmus are those of Olontion of some authors, and that the latter is also the Soluntus mentioned in the anonymous 'Periplus' as a coast-town and port somewhere here. Previous commentators had supposed that Olus, Olontion, and Solus were meant for the same place; I shall, however, show that Olus was a distinct city. Soluntus is described in this document as a promontory and port with good water, at only sixty stadia from Khersoneso, whereas the actual distance between the latter place and Spina Longa is three times that given in the 'Periplus,' which is evidently an error of the original or some transcriber, as there is no intermediate promontory and port that can be mistaken for it but those of Spina Longa; and it is therefore the Soluntus of the author of the ' Periplus,' a modification of Olontion.

Its identity with Olontion is supported or confirmed more fully also from the name of the nearest village being Elunta, which name, I believe, really represents, and is only a slight corruption of the name of, the early Cretan city of Olontion, of which there exists a beautiful and very rare silver coin; but no record of its exact place in the island is given by any author.

The cultivated land adjacent to the site belongs also to the natives of Elunta, and not to the inhabitants of Spina Longa, who, moreover, call the ruins on the west side of the isthmus Messa Elunta, thus applying the name of their own village to a part of the ruins; but those on the east side of the isthmus are called by them Poro, although they are connected and part of the same old city, which circumstance is no doubt indicative of a passage through having existed since the old city was deserted.

A great part of the city, however, is submerged beneath the sea, or covered by salt-pans reclaimed from and on a level with it. These salt-pans are the revenue or pay of the Aga of Spina Longa.

The remains consist of several foundations of Hellenic habitations interspersed amidst heaps of building-stones and fragments of marble, which are scattered over the rising ground on either side of the low sandy neck forming the isthmus; and the city was defended on the east side by a massive Hellenic wall, which crossed from the shore of the inlet of Spina Longa to the cliffy coast over the Bay of Poro, this wall having five or six courses still remaining in some parts.

On the west side of the isthmus, the old boundary-wall is not recognizable, having been in all probability removed by the Venetians to build the fortress of Spina Longa, with most of the available remains of the city there. But there are traces of an aqueduct along the ground to the south of the salt-pans, which, the natives say, in ancient times went as far as the upland of Kritza, adding that there are traces of the aqueduct here and there on the intermediate hills, but that it was for the most part subterranean. That part of it now visible near the isthmus really does disappear in a subterranean cave or vault, which doubtless gave rise to the native tradition and opinion. But the fact of such an extent of tunnel ever having been made, as would be necessary even to pierce through the first ridge of mountains to the south of the ruins, may with reason be doubted; and I am inclined to believe the cave or vault was an ancient outlet of some source or spring whence the aqueduct was supplied, but which failed in later times—perhaps when the submergence of the part of the city which I have referred to took place; and thus, with the failure of this source, the destruction of part of the city, and the exposure of the indefensible part to pirates, it probably became early deserted.

I must here notice, however, that the passage in the 'Stadiasmus' referring to Soluntus is rather ambiguous; for there appears to be a word (denoting a cape, or port, or something) that is wanting, the original Greek word being in the genitive, which may be either the island or peninsula upon which the town of Soluntus in part stood. And as the Bay of Kalokythia, on the east side of the peninsula of Spina Longa, was no doubt the proper port of the Olontians, and not the long inlet of Spina Longa itself, this port, or the lesser islet that formed it, may be the port with good water alluded to, since it further states in the passage that this port was 20 stadia distant—meaning, no doubt, from the city or mainland of Crete—which is not far from the actual distance of the port of Kalokythia from the ruins; and I found that there are some ancient remains, such as ancient cisterns, quarries, and foundations of buildings, here and there existing upon the sides of the hills overlooking the port, which help to confirm this view, by showing that this must have been the principal harbour of the Olontians, and not the great Spina Longa inlet.

The high craggy peak and fortress of Oxah or Axos, lying to the south-west of the isthmus, seen in the accompanying view, and before noticed, has a long narrow summit, surrounded by precipices on every side, and leaving few places of access. The ruins upon it consist of two Hellenic towers, situated one at each end of the summit, and are thus placed, to serve as watch-towers as well as for defence, at the two points it was most easy or only practicable to approach. They were, therefore, not connected by walls.

On the narrow summit, intermediate between these towers, there are several ancient cisterns, and foundations of rude habitations, which appear to have been merely those of the labourers who worked an ancient whetstone-quarry in the steep face of the hill, beneath the ruins,—and hence its evident identity as "the place Naxos, celebrated for whetstones," and simply noticed, without any indication of the part of Crete in which it was situated. But from the similarity of the names Oxah and Axos now applied to it, and from this being also the principal place where whetstones are procured in the island, the identity is clear.

The trade in these whetstones is still carried on by the natives of the modern village of Elunta, at a price of about 4s. the cwt. But they are quarried from a more convenient spot, just above the village, where picturesque crags beetle over the narrow stony valley lying beneath, and continually contribute their rejected fragments and chippings to the already well-paved plain under them, that seems to the eye to be almost without soil in consequence. The natives, however, cultivate the valley; and when I saw it, on a November day, the young corn was showing a wonderful crop out of the apparently soilless pebble-fields within it, and some of the finest olive-trees and carobs I ever saw were flourishing in this same bed of stony fragments. The accompanying view will show the picturesque character of the scenery in the neighbourhood of Olontus, and whence the whetstones are procured, as also the nature of the position and the extent of the old city itself, and of the fortress of Oxah or Axos over it.

These whetstone-quarries exist in a rather thinly stratified calcareo-argillaceous rock, that belongs apparently to the Nummulitic series, and contains thin siliceous bands or strata of a very fine-grained and compact nature, that form these whetstones.

As there is notice of a bishopric called Allyngus in

Crete, but without any local record or tradition of its precise locality, and as I could not learn any tradition of it elsewhere, I imagined that its name might have been corrupted by some transcriber from that of this city of Oluntus, and thus became applied to this district, as in sound it somewhat approximates to the modern name Elunta, now applied to the site of Oluntus. I could learn nothing regarding its position, however, from the metropolitan of Crete. But on inquiry of the Bishop of Mirabella, although he said he had never heard of such a bishopric, and that all records relative to his see were lost in the revolution, yet he added there was a tradition with the old men of the Mirabella that this district, previous to receiving the name of Mirabella from the Venetians, was called "Kallinkus" or "Allinkus," a name that immediately seemed to me to be derived from Allyngus: hence, probably, this was its locality.

There are two roads leading from Spina Longa to the Mirabella. One, direct from the village of Elunta, ascends the steep and rocky ridges immediately over it; the other, much easier although a little longer, leads to the southward over the gap directly under Oxah, and crosses first a small upland basin south of it, then another to the westward, and leads then direct into the southern part of the Mirabella upland, where it joins the road to Kritza, and leads through the small marshy plain of Lakonia, between which and

PORO THE ANCIENT OLONTION

BISHOPRIC OF ALLYNGUS. 129

Kritza, however, there is a singular hill and ruined city upon it, of great antiquity and in a remarkably good state of preservation, and which I shall next describe, as it lies upon the route most convenient for a traveller to take in exploring the district. Moreover the site is very singular and interesting from its craterlike form. I made the accompanying sketch of the ground-plan of its position and character, and refer the reader to the following chapter for its description.

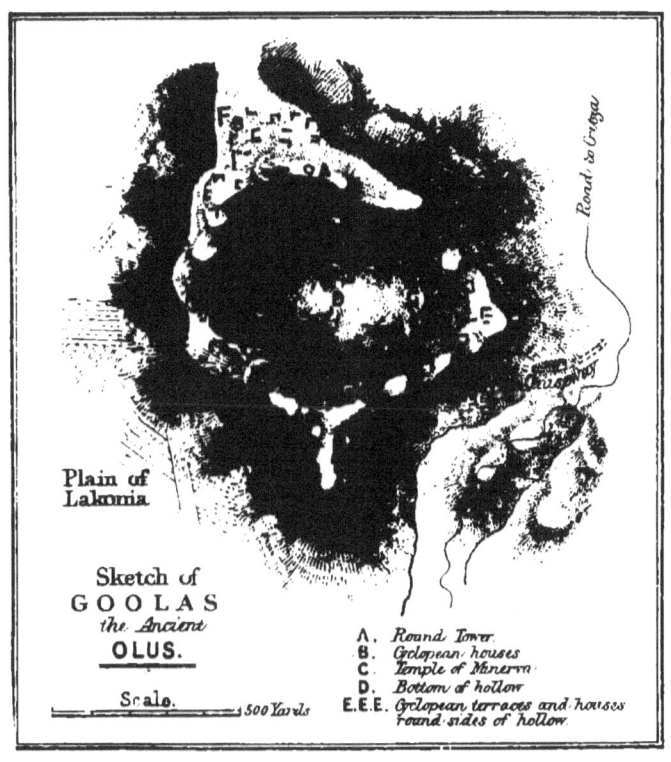

Sketch of GOOLAS the Ancient OLUS.
Scale. 500 Yards

A. Round Tower.
B. Cyclopean houses
C. Temple of Minerva
D. Bottom of hollow
E.E.E. Cyclopean terraces and houses round sides of hollow.

VOL. I.

CHAPTER XIII.

THE ROUTES BETWEEN MIRABELLA AND SPINA LONGA, AND ALSO TO KRITZA—THE UPLAND BASIN OF LAKONIA—A REMARKABLE SITE OVER IT—THE VERY EARLY CHARACTER OF THE RUINS—IDENTITY WITH OLUS AND OLERUS—THE OLERIAN MINERVA, HER CELEBRATED TEMPLE AND FESTIVAL—WOODEN STATUE TO BRITOMARTIS, BY DÆDALUS—KRITZA THE PRESENT CAPITAL OF THE MIRABELLA—ITS FINE SITUATION—THE SITE OF MINOA IDENTIFIED AT THE HEAD OF THE GULF OF MIRABELLA—THE FEWNESS OF ITS REMAINS EXPLAINED BY A RECENT SUBMERGENCE OF THE EASTERN HALF OF CRETE.

THE little upland plain of Lakonia recently mentioned, having no outlet or visible katavothron, as in the Lasethe, the melted snow and winter-rains which flood it remain spread over a large portion of this basin throughout the year, so as to prevent its being tilled, except around the margin, and thus render it marshy and unhealthy.

I ascended to this plain from the port of Agios Nikolo, in the Mirabella Gulf, where I had anchored my ship for the purpose. We entered the plain by a gap in the east side of the mountains which enclose it, after ascending a valley leading from St. Nikolo. Then passing by two farms and a grove of olive- and carob-trees on its margin, we reached, at the end of a mile and a half from the gap, the foot of a rugged double-crested hill. As we were now approaching it by the main road to Kritza, our guide pointed up to the two crags that surmount the hill, and said, to my surprise, that the old city was there; no vestiges of it, however, were visible from below.

The main road to Kritza and Ierapetra from the Mirabella here winds up its western side from the Lakonian plain, by a zigzag path for about a quarter of an hour, until a higher plateau or valley is reached. Here our guide, on reaching it, turned suddenly off the road and led us direct up the hill towards the crags, although it was steep and pathless. By this short cut to the goal of our aim, we soon came in sight of some massive Cyclopean ruins on the hillside; and shortly afterwards, at a little above them, we reached a gap between the two peaks that form its summit, and then discovered near it an ancient road, having a Cyclopean facing to support it, which led to the gap, from the eastern base of the hill and from the Kritza valley.

Its massive character and breadth at once showed that we were either upon a roadway leading to some important city of the earlier Cretan days, or a much-frequented way to some sacred spot on the mountain, such as that of a temple or oracle. As soon as the gap was reached by this road (and we had scrambled over some ruins of the same ancient character in getting to it), we were surprised to find ourselves upon the brink of a crater-like hollow, lying between the two peaks, and of an oval form, about 500 yards in diameter, and shaped like an amphitheatre, with a level area nearly 100 feet below the brink. It was terraced in its descent on all sides, by a series of half-natural and half-artificial terraces, somewhat representing also the steps of an amphitheatre, upon every one of which were the ruins of habitations of the earliest and rudest Cyclopean style. They were in some instances in a remarkable state of preservation, which, in fact, was the result of their massiveness and long neglect: for many had the large stone posterns to the doorways still erect; and these massive blocks, which were in single pieces, were the only stones that had been worked into anything approaching a rectangular form. But the mountain being composed of a highly stratified blue and grey limestone, the rock was easily split into large slabs, and thus facilitated the construction of houses and terraces in this style, and with some sort of uniformity also; and it sometimes led to the combination of the rude Cyclopean with the polygonal style, and also sometimes even passed into the Hellenic, with horizontal courses of blocks for short intervals, just as the splitting-up of the rocks seems to have favoured and suggested.

Only two buildings in the whole ruins (which consist of the remains of, I should think, at least 200 habitations) were formed entirely of close-fitting quadrangular blocks, like the pure Hellenic style. The ruins of a city more purely indicative of the early or heroic times I have never seen in such a remarkable state of preservation (nor one more singularly situated —occupying the hollow of a crater-like basin), where nearly every house can be traced out in its original length and breadth, the walls of many being still from six to ten feet high, and, as I before remarked, with their doorposts still erect. Some of the houses had two, and some three compartments, and varied from 10 to 20 feet in length; but the generality seem to have consisted of but one room, like the habitations of the poorer peasants of Crete at the present time, the door also often serving both for light and air to all compartments, one of which is shown at the end of this chapter.

Many of the houses had cisterns sunk in the solid rock, the sides of which were cemented by an exceedingly strong mottled concrete, formed of lime, small angular fragments of the limestone, and broken fragments of red brick or pottery—a very ancient style of cement for cisterns, as is well known to the antiquary: and this is the only indication of any brick, cement, or mortar being used throughout the entire city; for no Roman or middle-age remains are to be seen, to break the harmony of this unique Cretan city of the heroic times.

Pashley could not have visited it, or he would surely have given some note of its interesting character. Besides, his track, as laid down on his map, shows he did not ascend to it, but, hearing of the existence of ruins in the neighbourhood of Kritza, he concluded them to be those of Arkadia; and thus he led himself astray in respect to many other places. But there is clear evidence, both in its position and characteristics, to prove that it cannot be that city: for Arkadia cannot be satisfactorily identified unless the springs which belonged to it, and which were said to have dried up when it fell into the hands of an enemy, but flowed again when the city was retaken, are also identified; and certainly there are no traces whatever of springs upon this part of the mountain; neither could there have been any in ancient times, if we may judge from the labour and care bestowed upon the construction of the many cisterns existing there, and the somewhat insular position of the peak.

My guide, whose family are the proprietors of the ruins, tells me it is called Goolas. The name is so near to Olus that it cannot be doubted that these ruins are really those of that city—called also Olerus by a late author, and which city is mentioned as being noted for a festival celebrated to Minerva in early Cretan times, who was called in consequence the Olerian Minerva; and it is stated that it was situated in the neighbourhood of Hierapytna, and upon a hill

(Cramer, p. 391). Thus the mountain position of Goolas, the great antiquity of its ruins, and its being also the nearest ruined city to Hierapytna are combined evidences strongly supporting its identity with Olerus.

Having thus noticed the arguments bearing upon the verification of the name of this interesting city, I will further mention some more of its ruins which deserve notice; for the habitations above-mentioned, within the crater-like hollow, are but a portion of the remains of the city. There are many ruins of houses equally perfect. Indeed some of the finest specimens in the whole of these Cyclopean habitations are to be seen extending from the northern summit, down over the side of the peak for 200 or 300 yards or more; and this part seems to have been defended by a wall, and the summit surmounted also by a circular tower, as it was the most easy of approach by the connecting ridge which extends eastward.

I found fragments of pottery by no means plentiful amongst the ruins, indeed scarce. But near some of the habitations I observed some rude stone vessels, about a foot in diameter, that were no doubt used instead of earthenware for various domestic purposes, and some perhaps for pounding grain in lieu of grinding it.

Having mentioned that Olerus was noted for a festival to the Olerian Minerva, the question which

TEMPLE OF THE OLERIAN MINERVA.

naturally arises in the mind of the reader is, Where was the temple at which the festival was celebrated, if this be the city of Olus? I will now, therefore, describe what seems to me very probably the remains of this temple; for in a city so situated, and of so early a date and style, no building of very marked and finished architecture is necessary to identify it. On a long and broad terrace, of about 100 yards in length, which is a little above the level of the gap by which the city is entered, and within the hollow, there exist the ruins of a small building, that was formed entirely of large and closely fitting quadrangular blocks of limestone, and which is, in fact, the only one in the whole city that was so constructed.

Standing thus somewhat above and apart from the rest of the buildings of the city, with a well-built terrace for its support and approach, it certainly seems very probable that this was the very temple itself; and as it is also near the Cyclopean roadway leading up to the city, every circumstance tends to confirm the conjecture that Olus and its temple are thus identified; and as this temple, according to Strabo, had a statue to Britomartis, by Dædalus, in wood, thus accounting for the building being in compartments as well as the local celebrity of this early relic of the Cretan master and of the old city itself, the site and ruins are certainly the most remarkable in the island of Crete, and a traveller

KRITZA. 137

through the island will no doubt find much interest in its exploration.

Leaving the site and descending by the terraced road leading from the ruins, we follow a narrow plain running to the south-east, and in half an hour arrive at Kritza, the largest village of the Mirabella, picturesquely situated under some cliffy steeps, just where the valley begins to expand in its course towards the head of the Gulf of Mirabella, and where some fertilizing springs issue from beneath them.

The valley is well cultivated with olive-trees and vineyards, and confined by ridges covered with brushwood. But high above Kritza a grove of cypress and wild oak forms a dark line between it and the bald summits of the Lasethe Mountains, encircling them as a belt just below the snow-line.

The village of Kroustas is passed lower down, to the south, on the way to Ierapetra from Kritza; and another, called Kato Khorio, on the same route, stands on the boundary between the eparkhia of Mirabella and Ierapetra, or Gerapetra, and on either side of another rivulet descending from the Lasethe Mountains—the ravine and rivulet dividing the village. Strabo tells us that the town of Minoa stood immediately opposite to Hierapytna, where the island was reduced to the breadth of 60 stadia only. Thus the position of this ancient town cannot be mistaken.

Ptolemy seems to be the only other author who mentions this eastern Cretan city called Minoa (for there were evidently two of this name in Crete); and he also mentions its having a port.

In the south-west angle of the Gulf of Mirabella, and exactly at the position and distance in respect to Ierapetra mentioned by Strabo, we consequently find vestiges of an ancient city upon a small point of land jutting out from the centre of a sandy bay.

The river from the Kritza valley, south of Olus, flows into this bay on the west side of the point, and it contains a running stream all the year; but its embouchure being barred in summer by a small sand, the stream percolates through it into the sea.

The modern name of the spot is Istrona, which the natives state was also the former name of the village of Kato Khorio, but was changed some few years since. Onorio Belli, the author of the Venetian manuscript published by Mr. Falkener, mistook it for an ancient city of the same name, and was thus induced to place Minoa at Palaio Kastro, near to Cape Salmone, at the eastern extremity of the island; but the situation of the Minoa of Strabo is too well defined to be mistaken.

The fewness of the remains now found there is explained by Belli's statement, " that the city is at present entirely submerged by the sea, and that not far from Castel Mirabella there is another city overwhelmed by the sea in like manner." This latter remark no doubt applies to the submerged ruins of Olontion on the isthmus of Spina Longa.

All that remains of Minoa at present, consequently, are some few scattered heaps of stones, and foundations of ancient habitations, that are traceable near the low point jutting out from the centre of the plain of Kato Khorio.

In Belli's time these were more visible than at present; and upon the sides of the longer point, more to the eastward, there seems to have stood a small but pretty little monument or mausoleum in white marble. The blocks of which it was built are massive, and three or four of them remain, although half-buried in the sand. One of them is about 6 feet square, having one of its sides deeply carved with lozenge-shaped panels.

The rest of the city and its port are therefore either under the sea or more probably under the accumulations of sand and shingle brought into the bay by the adjacent river during its winter floods.

The three or four other Greek cities to which the name of Minoa has been given, I have observed, have, in part or wholly, stood upon peninsulas. This, then, is an exception according to the present features of the locality. It is probable, therefore, that the low point in the centre of the plain, upon which the city seems to have stood, was a small rocky peninsula originally; and although there has been a submergence of the coast that ought to have rendered the peninsular form of the point still more evident, or converted it into an island, yet that result has no doubt been overcome by the encroachment of the plain upon the sea, under the influence of the débris from the Kritza river—a change of feature precisely such as I many years since observed at the Minoa near Megara.

Bearing this in mind, it will explain how this Cretan Minoa could also have had a good port, as it was said to possess, although now without a trace remaining of it, from the physical changes resulting from the double effect of submergence and encroachment having obliterated it.

Over Minoa to the east is a sharp cliffy peak, which the natives call Palaion Kastron, indicative of some ancient ruin, and upon which there is now seen the remains of a circular tower, used no doubt, in the early times, as a look-out or signal-tower, to announce the appearance of pirates or a friendly sail; for it is now used by the local coast-guard for the same purpose, who lights his signal-fire at sunset when any vessel is in sight within the gulf, as a signal to the officials of the adjacent villages to be on the alert against pirates and smugglers.

Its basement is said to be Hellenic, being composed of large squared blocks, and doubtless was the watch- or signal-tower between Minoa Olontia and Olus in those early Cretan days when pirates possessed the seas. There does not appear to have been any other remains besides the tower, although it bears the name now of a palaion kastron, or old castle.

The notice of the submergence of these cities on the eastern part of Crete, by a Venetian author so long ago as 1586, as an explanation of the poverty of the remains then visible at the site of Minoa, is of considerable interest in connexion with the fact of a much greater movement having also materially affected the western half of the island, but by an elevation of the coast, instead of a subsidence: yet the fact and consequent result was not observed by this author, although amounting to more than 25 feet in some parts, and thus raising the old ports there into dry land—a description of each of which will be given in their places.

CYCLOPEAN HOUSE AT OLUS.

CHAPTER XIV.

THE ANCIENT PORT OF OLUS AT ST. NIKOLO, NOT MINOA—RUINS OF
A VENETIAN CASTLE, AND OF THE ANCIENT TOWN OF CAMARA,
AT ST. NIKOLO—A DEEP POOL ADJACENT TO ITS OLD PORT—A
COPIOUS SOURCE AT ALMYRO, AND LEGENDS CONNECTED WITH
IT—THE TWO OTHER CRETAN ALMYROS, OR BRACKISH SOURCES
—THE SINGULARITY OF THEIR SITUATIONS, AND OF THE MOUN-
TAIN-FEATURES OVER THEM, A RESULT OF UNIFORM GEOLO-
GICAL CONDITIONS.

MINOA, although situated at the mouth of the valley descending from Olus, could not have been its proper seaport; for there is one much nearer to Olus, which is formed by the shelter of two islands, and known as Port Agio Nikolo: it lies immediately to the east of Olus, between Minoa and Spina Longa.

St. Nikolo is at present the place of export for the chief produce of the Mirabella, from the convenience of reaching it by land; but the produce is generally transported thence to Spina Longa in coasting-craft, in consequence of the local laws prohibiting its export in foreign bottoms at any port but the inconvenient one of Spina Longa. The Venetians used it also as the chief trading-port of the Mirabella, Spina Longa being more a military or naval station. During our employment in this part I preferred the anchorage of St. Nikolo for my ship to that of Spina Longa. But the Bay of Poro, off the site of Olontion, is an anchorage for a fleet, especially as a shelter from the winter gales from the north-east and north.

The Venetians had a small town and fortress on the point which juts out to the south of the port of St. Nikolo, which they called Castel Mirabella, as indicating its trading importance in connexion with the province from which it took its name. The remains of this small castle or tower, and of the town that surrounds it, still exist; but there are no inhabitants at present, and the small inlet under it, to the north of the point, retains the name of Mandragio, which was no doubt first given it by the Venetians. But, besides these Venetian remains, there are some few marble fragments lying amongst these ruins, and some few remains of Cyclopean walls or terraces over the sea face of the hill, which give evidence also of its earlier occupation as a town and port of the district: it must therefore have been the port of Olus, as it is now of Kritza; and hence I am induced to think that these ruins must be those of Camara, mentioned in the 'Stadiasmus' and also by other authors; for Camara is the next town to Soluntus noticed in this anonymous 'Periplus,' and is stated to have been only fifteen stadia distant: the actual distance is thirty stadia, or three miles. But as the distances in the 'Periplus' are all much less than the truth on this coast, and as St. Nikolo is only about thirty stadia from Elunta (which I conceive to be the Olontion of early authors, but the Soluntus of the 'Periplus'), I conceive Camara to have stood at St. Nikolo; for there is no other spot on this coast where it could have stood, to accord in sequence of position, although not in distance.

And this view is in some degree strengthened by the statement of Ptolemy, who says Camara lay to the east of Olus; and besides he mentions it between Olus and Minoa. Thus, by its situation in reference to Olus, the supposition of Camara having been at St. Nikolo helps to reconcile the three, and thus to confirm the position I have assigned to Olus.

On the east side of the cove called the Mandragio of St. Nikolo is a small circular pool of brackish water, about 150 yards in diameter. It is separated from the sea by about twenty yards of low ground only; and yet this pool was found to have a depth of 210 feet in the centre—a depth which is not attained in the adjacent sea within two or three miles of the coast. But, in the traditions of the natives of the locality, it was said to be unfathomable, and to communicate with the lower regions of troubled spirits.

The sides of this hollow, beneath the surface of the pool, must constitute a precipitous funnel-shaped depression. Yet there is no appearance of its being a volcanic vent, or even the result of volcanic action, by any proximate igneous rocks being visible; and as it still has a small stream opening out of it into the sea, I think it was at one time the aperture of a larger source or subterranean river, which found its escape here from the heart of the mountains above; for there exists at Almyro, about a mile south of St. Nikolo, a copious source of brackish water that issues from the foot of a hill about half a mile from the sea, and forms a little river from its magnitude and strength. It is called Almyro, or Armyro, from the brackishness of the water; but it runs in a clear, limpid, and beautiful stream, turning some water-mills, and abounding with wild fowl.

The mountains immediately above the Almyro source are too steep and rocky for cultivation; but wild shrubs grow luxuriantly upon them. The limpid pool thus confined by the old and half-ruined mill-dam, and sheltered in so enclosed a glen from every breeze, reflects from its glassy surface, most distinctly, every form and tint the adjacent features of shrub, rock, or ruin present; and the stream when strongest, then cascading from the mill with a little ripple and foam, causes sometimes a misty vapour to rise over it, giving a picture of charming effect in the eye of an artist; but the superstitious and ignorant natives have created imagined visions out of these reflections and mists, that have given birth to various legendary tales and fireside marvels, from the earliest times to the present—one of them being, that Diana and her nymphs may often be seen sporting in this pool, as related by Onorio Belli (see Falkener's 'Museum of Antiquities').

This spring of brackish water so near the sea, and so copious as to form a deep stream that is navigable for boats up to the mill, is the third source of the same character and name on the north coast of the island; and as they are each similarly situated in respect to the configuration of the coast and the groups of mountains from whose base they issue, there is thus an indication of a like force having caused them, there being also none such on the south side of Crete; and this being the last of these, I shall, from their general interest, here notice them.

The first of the three is at the north-east base of the White Mountains, near the entrance to Suda, in the corner of Armyro Bay, and to the westward of Retimo. The second is the Armyro at the north-east base of Ida, a few miles westward of Candia, and also at the corner of the bay. The third is the Almyro (or Armyro) of Mirabella, at the north-east root of the Lasethe, and exactly in the same corner of that gulf also, like the others.

The pent-up waters of the mountain-torrents and streamlets, which disappear in the upland basins in katavothra, or through the soil, no doubt, in great part, find their escape by these great fountains; but whence their saline character is derived is not so easy to determine—viz., whether it is derived from the salt of the rock through which it percolates in some parts of its course, or whether from the proximate sea.

The former, however, seems the more probable; but their uniform position seems to imply a similarity or uniformity of inclination in the general mass of the strata composing these mountains, which are all apparently great masses of Hippurite limestone, with overlying Nummulite limestones and shales.

The position of the several sources leads to the conclusion that the mode in which these three mountain-masses were uphove must have been similar in all, viz. having had the uplifting effort greatest on the opposite side, because their internal filtering would naturally follow the general inclination or dip of the strata.

And it is of interest in a geological point of view, to perceive how this conclusion is verified on taking a comprehensive glance at the general character of the three principal mountains of the island. For on the opposite side to these three copious sources—that is, on the south-west or south side of the mountains— they are more abrupt, and have their higher crests nearest to the sea-coast on that side in consequence.

It is instructive also to perceive how remarkably the upheaving energy has in each mountain directed itself more generally towards the north-east, by the prolongation of each mountain into a well-marked promontory in that direction,—as Cape Malaxa, north-east of the White Mountains; Cape Dia, north-east of Ida; and Cape St. John, north-east of the Lasethe. For in each of these directions we find a series of level plateaux, or depressed basins, formed like a succession of steps in the scale of ascent, and each indicating, no doubt, the positions of great faults transverse to the line of greatest effort.

Thus the Suda Gulf, north-east of the White Mountains, with its centre sunk so remarkably to the depth of 120 fathoms, is just one of these basins, but submerged below the sea-level, within the headland of Maleka, which headland is the north-east prolongation of the mass of the White Mountains; and this mountain has also its upland plateau of Malaxa over the Suda Gulf, and of Theriso on the same side—besides several others nearer the top, that are above the line of vegetation.

Next, Mount Ida has its plain of Netha, or Nida, just below its snow-line of winter, also to the north-east of its summit, with a series of lesser plateaux descending to the large basin-like valley of Mylopotamo, which valley really represents the Suda Bay gulf in position, only being above the sea-level, instead of submerged beneath it like the Suda basin. For the knotty range of hills confining the Mylopotamo valley, and terminating to the north-east in the same manner, by the promontory of Cape Dia, represents also the Malaxa promontory and the serrated hill over it, since, if they were to subside a few hundred feet, we should have in the Mylopotamo Valley a gulf similar to that of Suda.

In the Lasethe Mountain also, the direction of the subterranean energy was exactly the same—that is, by the prolongation of a promontory or cape to the north-east; but being less powerful, as indicated by the less elevation of this mountain than of the others by an amount of upwards of 1000 feet, the promontory terminating it is less distant from the summit, and, the energy in that direction being also weaker, is represented by a succession of lower upland plains and basins, and more proximate to each other. Finally, the peninsula of Sitia also, which terminates the island of Crete to the north-east, shows that a similar, but still diminished, energy operated in the subterranean efforts that originally raised it; for its height and its most abrupt parts are all to the south-west, and the gradually descending peaks and their greatest prolongation are to the north-east also, and terminate at Cape Sidero, or Sidaro.

Thus, although the volcanic or upheaving energy has raised this island from the bed of the ocean by four distinct foci of eruptive efforts, there is a remarkable similarity of effect in them all; and thus the positions of the great fountains that spout forth at their bases, giving vent to the pent-up waters that penetrate the strata of the mountains from above, are in accordance with the phenomena presented in these mountain-features; and therefore I think the deep pool in the Bay of Mandragio, in the port of St. Nikolo, to be the result of one of these fountains, from which the greater portion of its original stream has been lost at some time long gone by, and transferred to the springs and source of the Armyro, not very distant from it. Sir Charles Lyell gives the following account of a similar result in Sicily, after an earthquake:—

" During the great earthquake of 1693, in Sicily, several thousand people were at once entombed in the ruins of caverns in limestone, at Sortino Vecchia; and at the same time a large stream, which had issued for ages from one of the grottos below that town, changed suddenly its subterranean course, and came out from the mouth of a cave lower down the valley, where no water had previously flowed. To this new point the ancient water-mills were transferred."

The neighbourhood of St. Nikolo affords some interest to the collecting naturalist, independent of the contemplation of its geological character and effects, in possessing an exceedingly beautiful and rare land-shell. It is a *Clausilia* of more than ordinary size,

A RARE LAND-SHELL. 151

and is ornamented with longitudinal plates or ridges, equidistant round each spire, but not in connexion as a continuous keel-like prominence.

Of this peculiar and interesting land-shell, which has a perfect little door for its narrow aperture, formed of a free plate of shell, there are several varieties peculiar to Crete, where, in number, size, and variety, the species seems also to have a maximum development as compared with neighbouring localities. The description of the six or seven that have been already identified as new by Dr. Pfeiffer will be given with the appendices to the second volume.

CHAPTER XV.

THE GULF OF MIRABELLA, AND THE ISTHMUS AT ITS HEAD—CHARACTERISTIC FEATURES, THEIR INFLUENCE UPON THE EARLIEST INHABITANTS — THE ETEO-CRETES AND MOUNT DICTE — THE NORTHERN ROUTE INTO THE SITIA — THE RUINS AT LEOPETRA—THE RUINED VENETIAN TOWN AND BAY OF SITIA—THE PROBABLE SITE OF ETEA.

THE Gulf of Mirabella is enclosed by picturesque mountains on both sides, being broken up into varied peaks and ridges, that are, for the most part, abrupt and bold; but it presents no cultivation that is visible whilst sailing up the bay, nor a single habitation on its shore; all looks wild and grand from the sea; Nature alone seems to reign around it, save and except the little speck of a fortress upon the islet of Spina Longa, near its entrance.

Two islands lie within the gulf—a small one, called Kumithia, near the head, and a larger one, called Psyra, near the outer part; but neither has been noticed by any ancient author, or contains inhabitants.

The isthmus at the head of the gulf is hilly, but low as compared with the land on either side. The hills are composed of limestone and shales, overlain in part by grey and whitish deposits of the tertiary period; and these appear to have been deposited between two great faults running transverse to the isthmus from sea to sea, and represented or indicated in the bold face of the mountains on either side.

But the eastern fault is more strongly indicated by the abruptness of the mountains which rise upon that side, forming a sort of natural barrier between the peninsula of Sitia and the western and larger division of the island of Crete.

Thus here the usual characteristic features of an isthmus and peninsula are preserved, viz. an elevated and bold barrier of mountains rising as a wall immediately over a comparatively narrow and rather low neck of land, so as to present a double difficulty to the means of communication from one side to the other.

For in such there is in general combined a somewhat narrow way of approach, that can in some degree be watched, overlooked, or commanded, with an abrupt and high chain of mountains, that forms a natural fortification or barrier that can be easily defended.

How greatly, in the early period of human history, such features have tended to separate peoples and to divide or confine races, I need not dwell upon; for every continent shows it.

This peninsula of Sitia, which contains an amount of territory as large as either of the important islands of Mitylene, Scio, or Rhodes, although constituting only a fifth part of Crete, presents the very features and character suitable for enabling a people or race to retain their original peculiarities longer than the aborigines of any of the other parts of the island, between which there was a more easy and free intercourse.

And the earlier authors of Cretan history do indeed refer to a people on the island who were exclusive or peculiar, under the name of the Eteo-Cretes, but whose exact location, even in the days of Strabo, was a point of archæological discussion. Modern commentators have therefore felt the difficulty of fixing upon its location, excepting that it was not in the western half of the island.

Strabo, however, says that Præsus was subject to the Eteo-Cretes, and that the Temple of the Dictæan Jupiter was there, and not near Ida, and derives the information from some early author or local traditions. But Strabo is himself evidently confused in reference to the exact position of the city of Præsus which was subject to the Eteo-Cretes; for he states just previously that Præsus bordered on the Lebena, a city undoubtedly in the centre of Crete. Hence by the name of Præsus he here probably intended to denote a city that existed near Gortyna in his time, called Priansus, and which may have had both names, thus giving rise to the confusion. But it is evident that there was another and more eastern town of the name of Præsus, and that it was only the one near Lebena that existed in the time of Strabo—the more eastern one having been destroyed by the Hierapytnians at an earlier period, and its exact site being now fully identified within the peninsula of Sitia, as I shall hereafter show.

Homer also makes the Eteo-Cretes distinct from the Grecian colonists; and others considered them as indigenous. Strabo*, however, quotes an author, Staphylus, for placing them on the *south* side of Crete, but without giving it as his own opinion; and it is difficult to find in the south of Crete a territory so peculiarly adapted to the requirements of an exclusive and peculiar people, such as the brave Eteo-Cretes are represented to have been.

Besides, Strabo himself places the earliest mythological traditions regarding the Mount Dicte, the supposed birthplace of Jupiter, in this very eastern peninsula of Sitia, and rejected the more generally received opinion that Ida, or some hill near it, was the honoured mountain upon which the king of gods and men was brought forth.

This view of Strabo, and that of the Eteo-Cretes being considered as the earliest inhabitants of Crete, have undoubtedly a connecting link, in spite of his statement that Præsus was near Lebena—an error which arose no doubt from his confounding the older

* B. x. c. iv.

Præsus of the Sitia with the then existing one near Lebena, but which latter place was undoubtedly the earlier Priansus.

Then let us enter the sacred peninsula in search of Mount Dicte—in search of Jupiter's traditional birthplace within it. To do which, the reader will return to the road that has been shown to him before as far as the village of Kato Khorio, near to the ancient Minoa; and thence he will be obliged to cross with us the ridge over it, and descend towards the south by the valley from Messalare, and passing several small hamlets and farms, or metokis (as in Crete all farms are called), he finally enters the olive-grove which shades the somewhat stony plain of Ierapetra, or Gerapetra, and sees the small walled town of that name on the edge of the Libyan Sea before him, but which town I will not stop to describe now; and as his back is therefore turned upon it, and he looks towards the high peninsula whose early history and interest I have touched upon, he will see the way to it apparently blocked by high mountains, but especially by a lofty square-headed but picturesque-sided peak, rising immediately from the head of the Ierapetra valley to a height of 4850 feet. This is the Effendi Vouno of the natives, or the Mountain of Our Lord (be he Turk or Christian, every one calls it so); and he will be inclined to think, perhaps, on hearing it so called, that the name may have arisen from some tradition of the early dedication of it to Zeus himself. I will not, however, stop here to inquire if it was Dicte, but proceed; for we must discuss the question when upon the site of the true Præsus of the Eteo-Cretes within the peninsula of Sitia.

The only roads into the Sitia from the isthmus of Ierapetra are one over the east coast of the Gulf of Mirabella, and the other from Ierapetra, which passes over the steep spurs bordering the south coast, and is considered the best of the two; but both are difficult and bad, and as defensible as Thermopylæ by natives with Spartan hearts and mothers.

Episcope is a pleasantly situated village, near the most eastern and lowest part of the connecting ridge which unites the Sitia mountains with the roots of Lasethe, and which runs along the northern side of the isthmus. Its name implies its having been the residence of the bishop of the province at some past and most likely early period; and it is noted both for the salubrity of its position and the fertility which surrounds it, being now enveloped in olive and fruit trees; so that the early bishops of Hierapetra, or Hierapytna, showed good taste and judgment in the selection of a retreat that was both pleasing and salubrious.

From Vasilike the northern road follows a valley opening into the Gulf of Mirabella to the north-east, to Kavousi, whence begins the ascent, and, by a difficult and rocky mule-path, the mountain barrier to the Sitia is surmounted through a pass.

This ridge being crossed, a semicircular basin, like a theatre, lies to the east and is open to the sea, but enclosed by high and steep mountains to the south, west, and east (the back of a branch of the Effendi Vouno), and intersected by narrow ridges and valleys descending to the north coast, which are composed of shales and limestones that are in parts much shattered and contorted in their strata, apparently by some great lateral pressure from the higher mountains that enclose them, and, as would appear, either during the uprising of the latter or the downcast of the former. There are several villages in this district. The first reached is called Lastro, and the last is Mulianah, of which there are two of the name: each has some charming spots of fertility and foliage near it; but the road is bad and tiresome.

No ancient site could be heard of in this district; but at the termination of the eastern ridge which confines it there are the remains of a small fortress and buildings crowning a high precipice over the coast, and called now Leopetra. The Venetians supposed it to be the ancient Assos—a town, however, which Pliny places inland, and by no author is it placed on the coast; I am therefore led to doubt the identity, and, although I had no opportunity of examining them myself, Mr. Stokes, the officer who did so, states his opinion that they are not very ancient, but rather appear to be of the middle age, and not Hellenic, there being nothing but the foundations of walls of a fortress built of small unhewn stones and mortar. Local tradition, however, asserts it to be an Hellenic city, but on such points it is often in error; at all events this seems to have been the capital of the Mulianah district at some early period, prior to the Venetians, and was a likely site for a city.

The mountain ridge which encloses the Mulianah district on the east separates it from a fertile but confined valley, called Skope, but which has several other villages within it besides Skope, each well supplied with water, and having productive fruit-gardens and vineyards near them. The fortress or town of Leopetra doubtless commanded both these districts at its period, whether Hellenic or middle-age, when feudal divisions and foreign enemies or pirates rendered such a stronghold necessary.

The valley of Sitia, running to the south of the bay of the same name, joins that of Skope, and is the most fertile and populous in the peninsula of Sitia.

The village of Episko Kephalo is at the junction of the two valleys, placed upon a low spur of the adjacent hills, so as to be some little above the malaria of the valley, in which, being well watered and well cultivated with fruit-trees and overhanging vines, fever is very prevalent in the autumn. Episko

Kephalo is the residence of the Aga of the province; and opposite to it is the village of Episkope, or Piskope, which name denotes the seat of the bishopric of Sitia in former times; now the bishopric is joined to that of Ierapetra, and the bishop in consequence generally resides at the latter place.

The Bay of Sitia, into which the valley of Sitia opens, is partially sheltered against the prevailing gales from the northward by the small point or promontory which juts out on the west side of the bay. The Venetians in consequence had a small fortress or fortified city upon the inner part of the point, just over the corner of the bay, which ranked next after Retimo in respect to size and population; but the difficulty of giving the needed support to this fortified town during the war with the Turks, from its outlying position, induced the Venetians to abandon it and demolish its walls soon after the breaking out of the last war; and it now remains a heap of ruins, almost as they left it, never having been restored or inhabited by the Turks since the island came into their possession.

Dapper gives a view of it, and shows that it was a fortress of some consequence, and contained three churches and a citadel, all of which are now easily recognizable.

Finding the bay convenient and safe as an anchorage at this season, I remained there in my ship for the autumn months of one season, up to the beginning of December, by anchoring her very near the shore, a few hundred yards to the north-east of the ruins of Sitia; for the wind very seldom blows to the eastward of north north-east, and being there under shelter from these points of the compass, we in consequence rode safely several gales from the northward during our stay: the security depends on being anchored within a couple of cables' length from the shore, where it is deep too.

An English yacht was lost here, however, having run into the bay during one of these gales and anchored too much to the eastward, by which she was exposed to the northerly swell from the open sea, and driven ashore in consequence.

Three good streams flow into the Bay of Sitia; and a deep well in the corner of the bay, adjacent to the ruined fortress, also yields a good supply of water close to the shore.

The name of Sitia seems to be identical with that of the ancient Etea, which stood somewhere in this part of Crete. There are no indications, however, of an ancient city having stood upon the same spot as the Venetian city, or upon this side of the valley; but on the east side of it, amongst the houses of the Turkish village of Petra, and on the hill over it, we found some detached remains of massive Cyclopean walls and terraces, that showed the position of a very early city of Crete, and which I think must have been then the capital of the district; probably it was the capital of Eteo-Crete, under the name of Eteo or Etea, which name is thus the origin of Setea in the true English spelling of it, but with the frequent Cretan prefix of the *ts* or *s* to those names that properly began with a vowel.

The ruins were discovered by accident, in making an evening's stroll up the valley—as the Greeks always spoke of a flat-topped hill, called Trapezonda, more to the east, as the only Hellenic site in the neighbourhood; but this Trapezonda proved to be a middle-age fortress, occupying one corner of the wide plateau existing on the summit of this hill; and as Petra was purely a Mahomedan village, having no Greek inhabitants, that fact may account for the ignorance of the Christians of the neighbourhood regarding the value of these remains.

The Christian inhabitants of the Sitia district have, however, at present a large intermixture of Italian blood in them, and undoubtedly very little of the Eteo-Cretes; for many of the Venetian soldiers stationed both here and at Spina Longa were encouraged by the Venetians to colonize and intermarry with the natives at the termination of their period of service, so as to increase the population of both Sitia and Mirabella; and thus the names of some are still retained both in the Mirabella and Sitia; but the present generation are Greeks in religion, and the family name of the renowned Dandolo still lives in the upper part of the Sitia valley.

CHAPTER XVI.

JOURNEY UP THE VALLEY OF SITIA TO PRÆSUS—THE SITE A FINE ONE, BUT VESTIGES FEW UPON IT—ITS ANCIENT NAME STILL RETAINED — DICTE SHOWN BY STRABO TO HAVE BEEN PROXIMATE TO IT—ITS SITE AT KOPRA KEPHALO—ANCIENT CISTERNS AND RUINS—FAITHLESS WIVES IN THE SITIA, AND EASY DIVORCE—CRETAN MARRIAGE CEREMONIES.

THE valley of Sitia penetrates towards the south more than half across this part of the island, and beyond the village of Episko Kephalo. It is confined between rocky cliffs of white tertiary strata and little cultivation, but overshaded in part by wild olive and plane trees, under which a pretty, refreshing rivulet murmurs along in its course, turning now and then a water-mill of some solitary inhabitant.

Procuring mules from Episko Kephalo, I started on an examination of the valley; and at a place called Berate, about two and a half miles up it, we saw Hellenic foundations near some ruined churches. Beyond it we were shown a cave in the side of the cliff, which here narrowly confined the valley, in which it was said a Turkish Aga of wealth retired with his family during the civil war for security, hoping in such a retreat to save them from their vigilant enemy; but plague then stalked through the land upon the heels of warfare, and found them out in their retreat, although the Greeks were unable to trace them, and thus the Aga and his family fell victims to the scourge together, and their bones became mingled with the stalagmite and dust of the floor of the cave; for there were none to bury them.

Beyond this, the villages and cultivation occupy the tops of the descending ridges or plateaux overlooking the valley, which near its head assumes the character of a gorge, from its abruptness and contraction; and here it divides into two branches, at a distance of five miles from the Bay of Sitia: the southern one approaching a low coll, or neck, which connects the eastern with the western group of mountains of the peninsula, the other enters a more lofty-sided but confined and very picturesque valley towards the east, and is surrounded by high rocky cliffs near its summit, as a natural barrier above, and is an inviting retreat for one tired of the world. A steep spur, extending from the southern hills, divides the two valleys, which we ascend; and on arriving near its summit, which is peaked and naturally terraced, at about 500 feet above the valley we find ourselves upon the old terraces of an ancient city.

Its principal remains visible are the ancient terraces that supported the buildings, and the scattered heaps of stone and pottery now lying between them, as there is nothing of the early building *in situ* remaining. Some of the terraces were supported by fine walls of polygonal masonry, and on the summit of the ridge are Hellenic foundations that probably supported a temple; for upon it are the ruins of a Christian church. This fine site commands a beautiful view down to the Bay of Sitia. The identity of the site is, therefore, based upon its still retaining the ancient name of Præsus nearly, being pronounced " Prasoos " by the natives.

In an ancient inscription found at Toplu or Topler Monastery, near Cape Sidero, and given by Pashley, a reference is made to this city, under the name of Praision. I procured two silver coins of Præsus at the village of Vavellos, which is situated just above it. They were found at the site, and represented the half-turned head and neck of a bull, with the head of Ceres on the obverse, but without letters. The legend, however, is in full upon some of its coins, and the name is written as in the inscription at the Topler Monastery.

This, then, was the Præsus of the Eteo-Cretes, previously referred to. And although Strabo evidently confounds the two distinct cities of Priansus and Præsus when referring to the true position of Dicte, as I have before shown, yet he is too precise to be mistaken in respect to the situation of the Dictæan Mountain being near the eastern extremity of the island, instead of the centre or southern part; for he says, "Instead of being near Ida, as Aratus alleges, Dicte is situated 1000 stadia from Ida, towards the rising sun, and it is only 100 stadia from the promontory Sammonium." And he says also, that the city Præsus, in association with it, "was distant 60 stadia from the sea between the promontory Sammonium and the Chersonesus, and that it was raised by the Hierapytnians," thus showing that Dicte was 40 stadia further from Sammonium, the north-eastern part of Crete, than the town of Præsus was. Strabo further distinguishes between the Dictæan and the Dictynnæan temple in Crete, which latter he places upon Mount Tityrus in the Cydonian territory, so as to clear up a confusion which seems to have crept into the writings of some authors before his time.

That the territory of the Eteo-Cretes and the Dictæan temple were in the eastern peninsula of Crete was thus the clear opinion of Strabo, although also brought into connexion with the Lebena, near Gortyna, by the mention of the Præsii near it.

Being, therefore, now upon the true site of Præsus, and about the distance from Sammonium at which Strabo places the Dictæan temple, I was induced to search for some vestiges of a temple upon some conspicuous mountain in the neighbourhood, such as would answer to that of the Dictæan Jupiter. And upon the crest of one of the crags over Prasoos, called both Agios Elias and Agios Stavro, from a small chapel upon it dedicated to both the Holy Prophet and the Cross, I found the foundations of some Hellenic building, which in all probability was an early temple of the city, but not the Dictæan; for I could not reconcile myself to the idea that the position was so commanding, or the remains there such, as to identify it as the site of the Dictæan Jupiter's temple. Although it overlooked a part of the Præsian valley to the north, its view to the south and east was limited by higher hills, and therefore it did not sufficiently accord with the idea of the position best suited; besides, it is nearer Sammonium than Præsus, which is contrary to Strabo's showing, who places the Dictæan temple at 100 stadia from Sammonium, and the city 60 stadia only.

The remains of most interest in this neighbourhood, therefore, as corresponding best to the distance and ideal view of the true position of the Dictæan temple, are those of two or three very ancient cisterns, with a few vestiges of buildings near them, which were found by Mr. Wilkinson upon the top of a mountain three or four miles to the westward of Præsus, called Kopra Kephalo, and immediately over the villages of Rhokaka and Mulianah.

This peak is about 3500 feet above the sea, and has a sharp bare summit, with a narrow backbone approaching from the east. The mountain is now destitute of vegetation, except of the most stunted nature. Although it is not the highest peak within the peninsula, yet it is the most commanding summit, overlooking the eastern and most cultivable, and therefore the most habitable part of the Præsian territory and Etean peninsula. It overlooks all, and is easily approachable from all; but towards the west the more rugged and abrupt character of the continuing but higher range extending towards Ierapetra, the Effendi Vouno, shuts out the view of and easy communication with that city.

A road ascends to Kopra Kephalo from Mulianah; but the most easy ascent is from Rhokaka, situated in a small elevated plain on the south side of it, and to the east of which is another elevated valley and village, called Daphne, with some others that are passed in going to it from Præsus; so that it was approachable on all sides. And thus, from the existence of the ancient cisterns on this high and bare summit of Kopra Kephalo, with the few foundations of buildings near them, the natural inference is, that it must have been a spot of some sanctity, to which the inhabitants were in the habit of resorting at certain times and seasons, and that the cisterns were consequently made to meet their greatest requirement, water, after the fatigue of the ascent, as it was not high enough to retain snow all the year, and had no natural springs.

The Greeks adopt the same plan now in connexion with many of the isolated monasteries or chapels that are perched upon the crest of some lofty peak, to which they are obliged to resort upon certain days in the year: a cistern in connexion with the chapel is essential.

The identity of the eastern city Præsus so near it, as shown by its remains and name, thus, I think, puts the identity of the Kopra Kephalo as the site of the Dictæan Jupiter's temple almost beyond doubt; and although some natives called the peak Kopra Kefalo, others also stated that the general name of the several peaks of that serrated mountain was Rikte, they thus retaining a name which almost accords with the very Dicte we are in search of. Diodorus Siculus mentions a town of Dicte as well as a temple, but of which there existed in his time only a few vestiges; and it is probable that these upon Kopra Kephalo are the vestiges he refers to as those indicative of a city as well as a temple of Dicte.

After exploring the site of Præsus, I proceeded to the village of Vavellos, the inhabitants of which are all Turks, except one, viz. a Spetziot, who, having been wrecked upon the coast some years ago, fell in love with, and married, an Eteo-Cretan maiden of his own religion, and settled in the district. The *sposa*, however, proved faithless, after the birth of a boy and a girl, and left him with these two children for another; and he now managed to gain a scanty living for them and himself by making cloths and sacks of goats' hair; and he gave us shelter in the hovel that contained his loom and habitation. His wife had since married her paramour, and lives in a neighbouring village. My guide on this occasion, who was from Piskopee, I afterwards learned was similarly situated, having also been left by his wife with one child, viz. a fine boy, to provide for. Infidelity and divorce thus seem to be both common in the Sitia of Crete, under the absolving powers of an easy or avaricious bishop. And in the Greek Church generally the sacred bond of matrimony is not very difficult to sever, divorces and re-marriages being permitted up to the fourth time; and where bribery is so large an element of what is necessary for the acquisition of church preferments and ecclesiastical privileges, it must naturally operate powerfully in the rearrangement of these sacred and social ties, under such latitude of episcopal remissions and reunions.

Cretan marriages are decided by the parents; but it is the part of the bridegroom, nevertheless, to ask for the bride. When the parents accept, they decide upon a day for the betrothing. On that day the bridegroom goes to the house with his relatives and the priest of the village, when the future bride makes her appearance with an offering of fruit and wine, which she first offers to the priest, next to the eldest of the party, and lastly to her betrothed, accompanied with a wish for a good and happy life to each. An exchange of rings then takes place, and they immediately separate.

Eight days before the marriage, the bridegroom invites his own relations and friends, and the parents of the bride their own; and the sponsors are named by the bridegroom, who are usually his godfathers.

The day before the marriage, the virgins assemble to garnish the bride's room, who cover the walls with new linen, and hang up, as a decoration, loaves of wheaten bread, as well as leaves of orange, lemon, and myrtle; and upon the pillow of the bed they put three crowns, formed of thorn, myrtle-, and orange-leaves,—all of which are significant: by the thorn is signified long life, and endurance under its cares; by the myrtle- and orange-leaves, that the love of the bride and bridegroom may be as sweet and lasting as the evergreens; and by the loaves of bread, plenty and peace.

The marriage-day arrived, at the appointed hour the bride and bridegroom proceed to the church, each held by the hands of their male and female friends, and the ceremony immediately begins; and when the priest says, in concluding the service, " Glory and honour to you who are crowned," they then throw cotton-seed and the leaves of the myrtle and orange upon the bride and bridegroom. This concluded, the salutes follow, by the parents of the bride first kissing the Bible, after that the bridegroom, and then the bride, putting upon her head, around her neck, or upon her shoulders handkerchiefs and other presents; the same is then done by the parents of the bridegroom, after by the sponsors, and lastly by the guests.

These salutes being over, they then proceed with the bride to the house of the bridegroom's mother, and, stopping at the door, ask her what she presents to her daughter-in-law, when the piece of land, house, or number of olive-trees is named. The bride then dips the little finger of her right hand in a pot of virgin honey, and makes four crosses on the door with it. After that they present her with a pomegranate, which she throws down upon the floor of the house, and thus scatters its ruby-coloured and gem-like fruit over it, by which is meant that the bride's house is desired to be filled with as many goods and chattels as the seed she thus scatters within it; and by the crosses of honey, that the bride's love is as holy, sweet, and strong as the symbol of her faith.

After these ceremonies are all finished with great exactitude, they enter the house, and the bride and bridegroom take their seat side by side upon the sofa at the end of the room, around whom sit the young virgins, singing songs in praise of the happy and honoured pair.

Dancing and feasting are then commenced, and

kept up the whole night, and also several following days and nights, sometimes for ten or even for twenty days, according to the wealth of the parties.

Marriage ceremonies in all countries have some interesting peculiarities, and doubtless these in Crete are in part derived from very early times—combining the poetic ideas of the primitive minds and races that early peopled this classic isle, with the stern and solemn ceremonies that seal the sacred bonds of matrimony between Christians.

Between Præsus and Rhokaka, upon a small rocky eminence, are the remains of a small fortress, with the ruins of a large church within it.

The natives called this fortress Hellenic; but it appeared to Mr. Wilkinson, who visited it, to be only a very insignificant middle-age ruin, and to have been used merely as a place of retreat, by the inhabitants of the neighbouring villages upon the slopes of the Dicte, when in danger of pirates.

The valley of Daphne passes to the south, and empties its winter torrents into the Libyan Sea, at a place called Kalo Nero, but receiving the appellation of "good water" from its medical more than its potable use.

CHAPTER XVII.

THE UPLAND PLAIN AND VILLAGE OF KATALEONE — HOSPITALITY OF A TURKISH FAMILY — THE PLAIN AND VILLAGE OF KHADRA — REBUILDING A CHURCH — A HOSPITABLE GREEK COUPLE — DESCRIPTION OF THEIR HABITATION; ITS FURNITURE, COMFORTS, AND CONDITION — THE LITTLE TORMENTORS OF TRAVELLERS — LEAVE KHADRA — A VENETIAN VILLA — RETURN TO SITIA BAY.

THE eastern part of Sitia, over Præsus, represents an elevated tableland, with a number of small plains or basins sunk within it in every part: some communicate with each other, but few have visible outlets for the escape of their winter streams. The largest is Khadra, the most western; the southern is Xero; and the northern Kataleone, with many small ones around and between them. The population within these plains is divided between Mussulmen and Christians.

I reached Kataleone from Præsus, after making an examination of the crag of Stavro. I found Kataleone a small village upon the upper edge of a naked plain, with more than half of its habitations in ruins, and particularly a well-built Venetian one that had stood adjacent to it. All this desolation was the result of the first years of the social war which raged from 1820 to 1826; and the few inhabitants now living here are Turks, the remnant that escaped, and consist of some six or eight families only.

It was their Sabbath when I arrived (Friday); but it was charitably presumed by the good wife of one of them, when she saw us arrive about mid-day, and who was then near her cottage-door, picking over some wheat for grinding, that we were wearied and wanted refreshment. Her husband, who was napping after his mid-day prayers, was therefore summoned, and we were speedily invited and welcomed by both, although all three of us were Christians, viz. muleteer, interpreter, and myself; and, without the least appearance of reserve or embarrassment on her part regarding her uncovered face, which, however, was not a very juvenile one, she went cheerfully to work, and soon set before us a meal of new honey in the comb, new cheese of delicious flavour, and snow-white bread, such as I had not seen before in any Cretan peasant's cottage. I found, on inquiry, that it is a peculiar wheat, grown only in the district; and it was said, indeed, that it would not produce so well, if cultivated in the coast-plains, as on these uplands, and that it degenerates there by both darkening in colour and losing flavour. Can this, then, be caused by the climate, from elevation, or chemically by the soil? So excellent did I find this wheaten flour, that I ordered a sack for my own use.

Having thus rested from the heat of the day, and

partaken of the hospitality of this family, I offered a present of money as payment, but it was refused without any hesitation, so that I at once saw that to press its acceptance would be hurtful to their feelings. Here, then, is a specimen of Cretan hospitality from a Mahomedan family, and such as the traveller will very often experience in this island.

The termination of the day's labour, in examining the several plains in the vicinity, brought me to the village of Khadra, which is situated upon the plain of that name, with those of Armeno and Pentelemona on the other side of it. Vineyards and groves of pear- and some other fruit-trees, grow in these uplands; but the olive is a stranger, as in the Lasethe, although the elevation is 1000 feet less than the Lasethe basin: this perhaps arises from the very high mountains which rise immediately over the latter to the south, and shelter it by checking the force of the north winds, whilst the plateau of Sitia is proverbially bleak from the strong northerly breezes that find a free escape over it.

As I entered Khadra I was soon sensible that it was almost wholly a Christian village, and, like Kataleone, half in ruins also; but there was a bustling activity going on with every male inhabitant present, twenty or thirty of whom were carrying stones to a particular building, whose walls were just rising a few feet above the ground. It was the rebuilding of one of the village churches after lying for upwards of thirty years in ruins. Old and young, priest and layman, were for the moment all builders and masons, under the guidance of a hired master, and were carrying large stones from some distant ruin, or bringing the mortar to cement them in their appropriate places. It was an interesting sight; for this half-hour's earnest individual labour at the close of the day was thus devoted to religion. Some were evidently past labouring for their own subsistence, yet they too carried their load, although with distress under the mere pebble they could bring; yet it was carried by some of threescore and ten or more, and was thrown into the general heap, as the widow cast her mite into the common receptacle. And who can say it was not recorded in heaven for good to their account! for the motive was good, although superstition or erroneous doctrine may have suddenly prompted it to avert the imagined displeasure of a St. Demetri or St. Nikolo. And it is in this way that many of the churches now found restored in the Cretan villages have been rebuilt; for in the revolution none escaped, and it will require another quarter of a century or more to restore Crete to its former wealth and beauty. Yet there are spirits that desire to renew those terrible scenes of desolation.

I had experienced the noonday hospitality of a

Turkish family, and now I will do justice to that of some friendly co-religionists, hospitable Greeks, who lodged me for the night; they were a young married couple, whose first child was not yet born, but nigh unto its birth, judging from the appearance of the good-looking hostess. The house was low and large compared to many others, but irregularly built, and consisted of two compartments, one for general use, the other for their mule and cows, with old stores and stock in one of its corners.

But the part inhabited was a specimen of primitive contentment:—a mud floor full of pits; a long bench on the inner side, half mud and half masonry, as the bedstead or couch; a fireplace in a niche; and a chimney just through the roof, with a broken water-jar as the chimney-pot; one low door, and a small window like a scuttle in the innermost part, served for ingress and light to the dwelling. As the room was low and wide, its roof was supported along the centre by two crooked trees ornamented with sacks, seeds, lamps, and earthen pottery, either stuck upon nails or upon some branches, but all black together like the roof above. Yet here was a tolerably well-to-do young Cretan's house of the eastern uplands; a more comfortless hovel one can hardly conceive amongst a race professing to possess some amount of civilization. What a contrast to the clean habitation of a Bulgarian or Wallachian peasant! where, upon a vast expanse of mud and clay, and simply out of that clay, with chopped straw and cowdung, the cleanest and neatest cottages are constructed; whilst here, where all is dry naturally, both soil and climate, and where they are surrounded by stone for lime, and abundance of fuel to make it, the peasant takes no pains to render his habitation much better than that compartment which is appropriated to his beast.

Is not this one of the many illustrations of the different effects resulting from the force of habit and example being made permanent by blind prejudice or indolence? or how can it be accounted for among an intelligent race such as the Cretans, that their habitations are so inferior to those in the neighbouring islands of Caso, Carpatho, and Rhodes, where the interior as well as exterior of the houses has an air of neatness as well as cleanness, as an evident necessity in connexion with the domestic requirements? The idea of order and arrangement of the various utensils for effect is also apparent in the latter islands; but in the Cretan villages it is wholly wanting. No whitewash is used for cleanness, dirt is hidden by darkness, and discomfort by apathy.

But, on the other hand, how often is the passion for cleanliness carried to excess when the mind is allowed no further expansion, and where the force of example has established it! He who has had a fidgetty, over-clean housekeeper, or lodged with an ever-washing

Dutch landlady, in a sort of perpetual swamp, will readily understand the idea.

In the one case it is torturing a habit or necessity into an inconvenience and nuisance, and in the other maintaining in perpetuity primitive discomfort and uncleanliness, simply because natural causes have not rendered the cleansing processes habitually necessary for health and comfort, as they have among the inhabitants of the swampy flats of Wallachia or the humid lowlands of Holland; and thus the benefit of a simple coating of whitewash is not considered or appreciated, either for cleanness or neatness, although so easily obtained and applied. But natural as well as artificial life is made up of such strange contrasts.

Moreover the upland Cretan's desire and hope is ever diverted into another direction than that of the improvement of his social comfort and condition; he sighs to shake off the hateful rule of the foreigner. Alas! he has so sighed and struggled for national independence ever since it was first lost to the Roman Martellus, and yet he is not convinced that it is more likely to be obtained by a development of moral improvement and influence, through civilization, than through petty intrigue, dogged apathy, or premature war.

But the sword of civilization is daily sharpening against continual misrule throughout the East, and, as a great diplomatist lately said, "it is knocking loudly at the gate of the Porte." Shall the Cretan, then, keep himself backward in the race by clinging to the ways and means that have already proved so fruitless, and prematurely fling a firebrand into the heap of inflammable element that surrounds him? and can he so soon forget the horrors of such a religious warfare as not long since crushed this heaven-blest land, and desire to renew it still, even before the pains and sufferings of that generation have passed quite away from memory—and that, too, where it may be said, "What Eastern people or nation is there who now enjoys so much freedom, and is so lightly taxed?" and, if the truth be spoken in spite of the promptings of personally interested and false friends and patriots, the answer will be, " Verily there are few!"

All that my kindly host and hostess of Khadra had to give was freely offered or given; and when I had finished my supper of simple bread and tea, which I carried with me, preferring it to their offered feast of fowl and eggs, then the villagers, having also by that time finished their frugal supper of boiled vegetables and oil, flocked to our habitation, and joined round the hearth to know my errand, and to draw inferences from my questions regarding names of places for insertion in the chart we were constructing for their future advantage, or respecting the way to some mountain, where observations were necessary from its summit.

Men and women thus, in a dense party, soon assembled; for it is a privilege of the East to enter unbidden any one's house, if curiosity, as on this occasion, furnishes the excuse as well as prompts the desire. And here I had a good opportunity of observing the very free intercourse between Turk and Greek families in this part of the island; for, to my surprise, I found that for more than an hour I had been sitting with the wife of a Turk of the village close by my side, who, with uncovered face, spun her cotton the whole time, and held a free conversation with men and women, to the number of between twenty and thirty, thus associated. At length they departed; and I arose also to prepare my bed in my own way, as I had preferred my own meal; for to work well a man must sleep well, and to sleep even at all, under the hospitality of a Cretan village's resident, one must have either a coat of mail for outside skin, or be buried in a sort of sack, or slung in a hammock, as partial aids to this requirement. I came, therefore, provided with both the latter, as I brought no tent, the season being advancing towards winter, and I expected to find it very cold at this elevation; for to hope for rest and sleep, unprovided against such companions as a Cretan's house contains, is out of the question, as I have often experienced when duty or the pleasure of travel has thrown me, as it too frequently has, into the company of legions of those tormentors of the human frame and mind, the fleas, and, alas! too, of those troubled spirits that haunt the long, long Levantine night, when they are present, with their trumpeting—a song that never ceases, but trumpets the louder the more they are thwarted and disappointed in their attack—and with snouts also that, in one's dozy, dreamy state of combat and resistance, the victim is led to compare to the bill of a snipe or the probe of a vampire which is endeavouring to bore into your flesh.

And then there is that other enemy of the thin-skinned man, the "B flat" (to use a delicate name often applied to distinguish it from the first-named, the " F sharp "), and yet an unmusical fellow, too, who steals upon you without sound, and generally without crawl or even touch that can be felt to warn you of his approach, but from some part of the clothes nearest you, under or over, as the case may be, probes or bites with head erect or bent backwards from his flat body, and with the mouth only just reaching you. Thus this cunning fellow, then and from there, sends the unfelt but yet penetrating probe into you, and sucks his full from the sweet veins he has reached, and, as a return for the nectar he has drawn, deposits an irritant something as a memento of his feast, that soon sets blood and skin in a blaze of fever and of certain torment for full forty-eight hours afterwards. And even through sheet or shirt the stealthy and silent " B flat," as also his trumpeting companion of the night, the mosquito, will bite and sting the tender-fleshed novice and traveller. At least they do so in the East, and Crete is no exception; for they dropped or hopped into my hammock from the floor and rafters of my hospitable Cretan's hovel at Khadra in dozens, and in desperation or delight as disappointment or success met their attacks. It is somewhere stated that the Hindoos, to surpass in charity the Mahomedans, who never destroy a maimed or sick animal, have established hospitals for animals of all kinds, and even for the creatures I have here named; and thus the poor native traveller who calls for a lodging or food is fed at this great house of charity on one condition only, viz. that he feeds the fleas, &c., in return, by sleeping for a night in the apartment especially kept for them. What dilettante repose they must enjoy, if they can feel! And surely the Levantine has a kindred charity when he revels in the myriads of fleas, &c., that are known to abound there. Oh, the penalty of research and travel in these lands! The feather-bed reader little knows how dearly the fruits are sometimes won.

The morning dawn consequently made me wish to be away from such enemies of rest and repose, my pellicle not being equal to its continuance or repetition; so with the rising sun I was off to the top of an adjacent mountain to rid myself of some of my friends, and to finish my observations for the topography of this part, after heartily thanking my host and hostess for their kindness and hospitality, although I had paid liberally for them in blood and coin.

A visit to a small Hellenic tower towards the northeast, and a peep into the enclosed plain of Xero, brought me by noon near a hamlet called Etea, at the western outlet of Khadra; and here I halted to examine a good-looking castellated Venetian villa, that had been erected by some wealthy, if not noble, proprietor of these lands. It has a vaulted basement, like a fortified tower, with well-constructed second and third stories above, and displays some architectural effect throughout. In the upper part were five windows in front; and in the lower, one on either side of a handsome entrance, approached by a flight of steps ascending from a paved courtyard, around which were the servants' dwellings and outhouses.

The arms of the proprietor (now, however, defaced) were sculptured on a large shield over the door, supported by carved figures and scrolls.

Here, then, was the castle of a Venetian proprietor, whose wealth was such as to enable him to construct a dwelling at the approach to his territory in a manner combining strength, luxury, and taste; and being situated just at the summit of the road and pass ascending from the lower ridges and valleys lying to the west, it was the guard and keep to his mountain retreat.

In the late revolution it was retained for some time

as the stronghold of the Turks, until, on surrender, they were driven into the towns, or made to leave the island; but many of the survivors have since returned to their ruined homesteads in these uplands.

As I could hear of no Hellenic ruins in them, I presume they were all the upland territory or property of Præsus, as the Lasethe was that of Lyctus, being somewhat similarly situated in respect to these two ancient cities; yet the name of Etea being still retained in the uplands of this peninsula, is of interest in connexion with its recognition as the territory of the Eteo-Cretes, and its modern corruption into Sitia.

Returning to Sitia Bay from Etea by the south-west side of the valley of Sitia, we fell upon traces of an ancient paved way soon after leaving Etea; we then crossed the valley to the elevated and prettily situated villages of Torlote, Apano Episkope, and Agia Marina. Each of these has rills of water, orange-, lemon-, and fig-groves near them; and they have tall poplars and spreading plane-trees also growing luxuriantly, for an abundant supply of water exists there. And with such fertility of soil it is not surprising that one of the family of a Dandolo was a proprietor here: for the village of Torlote belongs to the family that now retains that distinguished name amongst the present inhabitants.

In descending from this village, we came upon a stratum of white calcareous sandstone of the miocene tertiary period, which contained abundance of fossils, viz. Pectens and sea-eggs of large size, intermingled with masses of the nummulitic shell called the *Lenticulites complanatus*; and these being all Malta acquaintances also, I was enabled to identify the indurated tertiary of this valley as being of the same age as that of the Malta deposits. The strata dip from the enclosing limestone ridges at an angle of about 20°, and occur upon both sides of the valley as a zone flanking the older and higher mountains of the Hippurite limestone.

188

CHAPTER XVIII.

THE NORTH-EAST EXTREMITY OF CRETE—THE YANISADES ISLANDS
— CAPE SALMONE, DOUBTFUL APPLICATION OF THE NAME—
THE TOPLER MONASTERY — EREMOPOLI THE ANCIENT ETERA
—ITS DESCRIPTION—PROBABLY ALSO CALLED ARSINOE—ITS
CONVENIENT SITUATION FOR ALEXANDRIAN TRADERS — RE-
LICS OF A PRÆPTOLEMAIC AGE—NUMEROUS INSCRIPTIONS—
COPPER COINS.

THE north-east extremity of Crete extends towards the islands of Caso and Carpatho as a narrow promontory, formed of three distinct peninsulas, two of which are almost islands, and the terminal peninsula forms the present Cape Sidero or Sidaro.

Five or six miles to the west of Cape Sidero, and directly opposite the Sitia Bay, but seven miles distant from the latter, are the Yanisades Islands, four in number, all high and bold rocks of limestone. A long narrow channel separates the two southern islands; and although with too deep water to anchor in it, the channel is used as a shelter by coasting-craft that know it, such as the sponge-divers, and was used by the Barbary and Greek corsairs who frequented this neighbourhood in very recent times. A small drip of water exists in a cave there, which is sufficient for supplying a few men; and this has favoured the

THE YANISADES ISLANDS. 189

use of it as a hidden and favourable position for pouncing upon the passing trader.

This modern name of Yanisades now applied to them sufficiently shows that they are the Dionysiades Islands of the author of the 'Stadiasmus' and others; and both the port and water are actually mentioned by this anonymous hydrographer of the latter period of the Roman empire, whose minute details in regard to small, insignificant ports and bays, and indifferent water found in them, show that he was an experienced navigator himself, or derived the information contained in the "Periplus" from very good authority. The errors of transcribers, however, confuse his relative distances very frequently.

On turning Cape Sidero, to the south a fine bay opens, with two or three islands off it; and a small snug cove is also seen entering into the cape itself, forming an equally convenient retreat for a corsair or pirate of ancient days. The anonymous coast-describer evidently calls this headland Cape Salmone, as he mentions this port, and states that it had a temple to Minerva, the remains of which are apparently now seen at the head of it; for there is the basement of a small quadrangular building that is partly submerged beneath the sea, a single course of stones only appearing above the water, thus clearly showing a considerable subsidence of the coast here also, as at the Gulf of Mirabella. It was simply a square building of small dimensions, and much like the modern Greek chapel that stands upon the point over it, dedicated to St. Nikolo, in which there is a fragment of an inscribed block of limestone that evidently came from the earlier temple.

Pliny also indicates this north-east point as Salmone—stating that it had seven islands surrounding it, which is the number now to be identified in the four Yanisades on the north, the Elasa Island and two Grandes Islands on the south side of it.

But I think it probable, if not evident, that some authors, and more particularly St. Luke, when, in the 27th chapter of the Acts, he refers to the passing of Cape Salmone by the ship in which St. Paul was being sent a prisoner to Rome, must mean the promontory jutting out towards the east some seven miles to the south of Cape Sidero, and called Plaka; for Cape Sidero is, in truth, not the headland or point his ship would pass nearest to in coming from Cnidus; and this promontory south of Grandes Bay, called Plaka by the natives, is indeed now by some Levantine navigators called Cape Salmone, to distinguish it from Cape Sidero. There is also a little peak immediately over this point, that has a name bearing a close connexion with Sammonium (as the name of the eastern headland of Crete was sometimes written by some authors); for it is called Samothes—a name I received from the

APPLICATION OF THE NAME. 191

Hegumenos of the Topler Monastery in its vicinity, and therefore authentic.

Strabo, after speaking of Hierapytna, also says that the shores terminated in the promontory "Sammonium, looking towards Egypt and the isles of the Rhodians"—that is, Carpatho and Caso; therefore he must mean to apply the name to the entire eastern promontory, and not any particular part of it; otherwise Cape Plaka only, as looking more towards Egypt and the isles, is the cape most in accordance with his description. With this indication, therefore, that Cape Sidero is apparently the Cape Salmone of Pliny and the 'Stadiasmus,' but not of Strabo and St. Luke, but that the Salmone of the latter is Cape Plaka south of Cape Sidero, I leave the solution of the question to the antiquary and the scholar, who may feel that it deserves a learned dissertation or research in connexion with the voyage of the great Apostle.

Having thus touched upon some points of geographical and Biblical interest connected with this eastern extreme of Crete, I will invite the traveller or reader now to a journey with me, first, to the promontory, from Sitia Bay, along the shore of the latter, as the direct and only road to it; next to ascend to the plateau over the east extreme of the bay, as far as the solitary and mean-looking monastery situated upon it, the name of which is Topler, derived from the Turkish word Topler, because it once had guns for its defence against pirates; but the Greeks (perhaps, not liking the derivation of the above name) more generally call it To-Plu.

And then, if he can endure the torments of certain little unmentionables I have before alluded to, let him deposit his baggage with the hospitable Hegumenos of the monastery and visit the shores of Grandes Bay, for the sake of the associations connected with, and the ancient sites that are upon it; and now descending with me towards Cape Sidero, to the old site at Eremopoli, over the slopes of the heathery but treeless plateau which gives pasturage to the many flocks that this reputedly rich but dirty monastery possesses, he will soon perceive that all is wild and neglected over this far outlying land of the Cretans. The very name given to the site of the ruins we are approaching—Eremopoli, or "desert city"—too, implies it. And then, if he is fond of settling the ancient name of an old city that has not been whispered for centuries, and loves it for its classical geography, let him prove me right or wrong in simply suggesting to him whether these ruins may not be those of Etera, because it bears some resemblance to the name of the point of land upon which they are situated, viz. Cape Sidero, as a corruption from Etera, Eis ten Etera, into Sitera, and next Sidero; for Etera was the coast-city mentioned in the 'Stadiasmus' as situated next after Camerus, the position of which I have before noticed in the Gulf of Mirabella; yet it was placed in this document before, and not after Cape Salmone, which, therefore, is my stumblingblock in the knotty question, if Cape Sidero was really the Cape Salmone of the author of the 'Stadiasmus,' as, from the notice of a port and temple, it would seem to have been; but if Cape Plaka, then Etera comes before it, and agrees.

EREMOPOLI, THE ANCIENT ETERA.

Eremopoli is, however, worthy of a brief description, from its inscriptions, old churches, tombs, and ruins that are still to be stumbled over, amidst a few stunted palms—the greatest number, too, of this peculiar tree, that grow in any part of Crete. The next little valley, to the south of the ruins, is in consequence called Vaia or Palm Bay, from their number; but they are stunted from neglect, and not stately ornaments of the landscape as they usually are.

The view of the site given on the preceding page, in which the ruins are seen to extend over the hills and slopes which overlook two small bays, will render a brief description of them sufficient.

Over the southern bay the remains of Cyclopean walls of some extent are seen ascending the hills there, and they show the more ancient bounds of the city in that direction. The little insular hill separating the two bays, upon which the city stood, is worn into a precipice on its sea face, and seems to have been much encroached upon since ancient times; but its western face descends in artificially and naturally terraced slopes, which were occupied by many buildings, one having been an early church of some size, of which the front and the side posterns to its two doors are still erect.

The building itself was about seventy feet long and nearly fifty wide; but it was chiefly formed out of the fragments of some more ancient building; for two granite columns lie within, that must be of Egyptian origin; some fragments of a Doric capital in sandstone, and a pedestal in Parian marble, are also adjacent to it.

These probably came from a neighbouring temple,

which may have stood upon the north side of an isolated rocky eminence seen standing in the plain, at the west extreme of the city, where there is a fine specimen of an Hellenic wall, forming the face of a platform and built of massive blocks of grey limestone, of the third style: seven courses of stones still remain.

Between these two eminences there is a confusion of ruins, with fragments of columns of granite, marble, and sandstone, more or less buried under or lying amidst fallen masses of stone and mortar masonry and heaps of stones, the loose stones having been thus collected to admit of some crops of corn being raised upon the generally productive débris of an old city. From the ruins of two or three other Christian churches that exist, and other characteristic remains, it seems to have flourished shortly after the Christian era; but, from an early period in the middle ages until now, it appears to have remained entirely a deserted city.

This fact in some degree favours the view of its being the Etera of the author of the 'Stadiasmus,' since it was evidently the only coast-city flourishing about this time to the east of Camara, and no other author has mentioned it. The existence of granite columns, and the many palms growing there, however, seem to show an Egyptian connexion; and for this reason it might be Arsinoë also, as Colonel Leake suggested—a town assigned by some to Crete, but on doubtful evidence.

Now the time that the 'Stadiasmus' was written, although its author is unknown, was, I believe, just that of the most flourishing period of the Roman dominion in the East, and when the southern coast-cities of Crete, or those nearest to Alexandria, were the most important of the island also; for then Gnossus and Kydonia, on the north, had given way to Gortyna and Hierapytna on the south; and this city, whether Etera or Arsinoë, was most conveniently situated as a halfway call for the stream of trade then constant between Alexandria and Constantinople, and even between Alexandria and Rome, on the coasting system then only practicable with the navigator—often adopted now, on account of the prevailing northwest winds which blow between Egypt and Crete, but then still more necessary to follow, so that a recognized chain of headlands or anchorages might be available as a succession of stations upon the voyage, when the compass was an unknown guide to the mariner, and he always anchored at night when practicable.

Thus it was natural that a city of both the Ptolemaic and Roman times should have flourished at the eastern extreme of Crete, when Alexandria was the great mart of the East, and with so commodious and safe an anchorage as that afforded in Eremopoli Bay to shelter and invite the navigator during the prevalent northerly gales of summer, in which season alone trade was carried on, viz. between the first appearance of the Pleiades and their disappearance in the autumn.

But let me refer to some relics we fortunately found here, of a city dating from an older time than even the Ptolemaic, but which these relics show to have been still flourishing at that era.

The rude inscription No. 20 (Plate I. of inscriptions), of the earliest times, with letters reversed, and with a fish or dolphin upon an unwrought slab of limestone, is one of them, which seemed to have formed a headstone to an ancient tomb, being found amongst the tombs on the north side of the city. This is now in the Fitzwilliam Museum of Cambridge. Another but more modern headstone had pigment of red paint in the letters, which was still brilliant when the stone was dug up.

Inscription No. 19, however, is perhaps of most interest to the scholar; and this I copied from the end of a large square block of limestone that had formed part of the flooring of the large Christian church, and therefore was not *in situ*. It was only recently discovered, during some excavations there for square stones to repair the belfry of the Topler Monastery; and being found too large to be removed, it was covered again with soil by order of the hegumenos, to ensure its preservation.

The good people of the monastery were for a long time unwilling to tell me of this inscription, thinking it might reveal some hidden treasure which I alone could profit by. I had received various hints regarding it from the shepherds and priests, but, for a long time, none would show it to me. At length an intelligent young deacon of the monastery, less superstitious than the rest, took me to the spot; and on uncovering a foot or two of the soil with him, I found it; and as I found it covered, so I again left it, to show that it was only the inscription, and not the imagined gold within the stone, that I wanted, requesting at the same time that the stone might not be broken up for the purpose originally intended by them. Although inscriptions were so numerous here, coins were rare; at least the ground was too little worked to yield many; but a shepherd sold me four copper coins, of a singular type and rudely struck, but of considerable interest and importance in the question of the identity of the name, since I have no doubt that they belong to this city and represent the type of its ancient currency, and as they are inedited.

They represent a helmeted head of Pallas, like those of Itanus, on the obverse, and have a large open-rayed star on the reverse, the centre of the star being formed by a circle, in which there is, in all but one, a mere dot or obliterated letter, from the defect of the

COPPER COINS. 199

die: one of the four has the letter E distinct in the centre of the star; but this one had evidently been struck from a different die; it was apparently one of the first series from a new die, as it had a better finish as a work of art and was in a better state of preservation.

CHAPTER XIX.

CORRUPTION OF ANCIENT CRETAN NAMES—THE MODERN NAME OF LASETHE DERIVED FROM LYTTUS, AS SIDERO FROM ETERA—THE NECROPOLIS OF ETERA—SEPULCURAL VASES—ANCIENT TOMBS AND TOMBSTONES—VOLCANIC PROTRUSIONS—PALAIO KASTRON—MIDDLE-AGE STRONGHOLD—VESTIGES OF A CITY OF THE TIME OF MINOS—THE ANCIENT NAME NOT DETERMINED—INSCRIPTION AT THE TOPLER MONASTERY—A CAIRN—LOCAL WINDS.

I AM here induced to refer again to the frequent addition of the sound *ts* or *s* to Cretan proper names beginning with a vowel (such as Setera, considered as showing that the name of Sidero was derived from Etera), now that the coin above described seems to give additional evidence in favour of this view. The author of the 'Stadiasmus' seems to indicate the existence of this corruption of proper names as existing in his time, by his Soluntus for Oluntus, and Solus for Olus, as I have before shown. I found the prefix prevalent also in the upper districts of the White Mountains above Khania, in the west of Crete, and amongst the Sfakiots; thus *cambo*, a plain, is pronounced by them *secambo* or *tsecambo*; and *embale*, a vineyard, *sembale* or *tsembale*, &c. And thus as I have found it repeated in the eastern part of the island in the corruption of the names of two of the ancient cities in this part, viz. Etea as Setea, and Itanus, which is now undoubtedly represented by a village above it, called Sitanos or Tsitanos—and Ierapetra is also pronounced in the mouth of the peasant Tserapetra, although written Girapetra by the Venetians and others,—therefore, for the same reason, it is legitimate to conclude that the name of Cape Sidero identifies the proximate ruined city of Eremopoli as the Etera of the time of the 'Stadiasmus,' whatever it may have been previously—Arsinoë or Sammonium.

And further to extend the proof, I trace in a similar manner Lasethe, the name of the upland plain and mountain over Lyttus, to be really a corruption of the name of this city that stood upon its slope; for although this may at first appear far-fetched, yet it becomes more simple and evident by taking up the still more diverse name of the village which now occupies the ancient site of Lyttus, viz. Xithia (or Xeethe as it is pronounced, Xidhi as the scholar would write it). For that name is really the connecting link between Lyttus and Lasethe, as on a little reflection I discovered, and in this way:—To Lyttus was first applied the usual prefix of the *s* or *ts* as a vulgar corruption, by which it became Tselyttus, or Tselytti (the people of Lyttus), and from that it was changed easily into Tselethe, which in the vulgar mouth would be pronounced Xelethe, and then was finally abbreviated into Xeethe, now applied to the modern village that occupies the ancient site of Lyttus, and which is therefore its modern representative in name as well as position.

This, then, seems to me to have been the course of the vulgar corruption of Lyttus into Xeethe; and thus far it had no doubt proceeded when the Venetians came into possession of the island. Now followed the Venetian or Italian addition of the *la* to it when applied to the upland territory and mountain over the village; hence La Xeethe became Lasethe (as it is now pronounced and spelt), the modern name of the upland basin and mountain above the village.

Now, as the site of Lyttus is too well identified, by its ruins and the inscriptions found upon it, to be disputed, here is a proof of the importance or value to be sometimes attached, in the identification of the site of an ancient city, to an apparently far-fetched similarity of name.

As Ariadne gave the thread to her lover Theseus, I offer the scholar this clue to guide him through the maze of difficulty and conjecture in which I found the ancient geography of Eastern Crete, and still perhaps leave a large portion of it as a dilettante study for him in his closet, where his learning and his books will better enable him to penetrate the labyrinth and gratify a passing hour thereby; and I wish him better success with this mental puzzle and amusement.

And to add to his interest regarding this ancient city of Etera, I will here detail some facts connected with the mode of burial of its inhabitants, as revealed through opening a few tombs and funeral jars found on the top of the rising ground over the northern bay, where was situated the sole necropolis of the city. On one occasion, when strolling over it with Dr. Willcox, trying to pick up what seemed to be the broken handle of an ancient jar that appeared on the surface, we found that it was not a fragment, but that there was the jar entire, although somewhat cracked; and it was still more interesting to discover that it contained the bones of a child. This led to the discovery of several others near it, two or three being very large and standing fully four feet high; and in all of these were found the bones of children. In one of the larger jars the Doctor found that there were parts of the jaw and teeth of two children from seven to eight years of age; and in each jar was an earthen bottle or cup, of very common light-coloured pottery, and of very simple form: of these, only one was ornamented—a sort of lamp-shaped article, but with a wider opening in the centre than usual with ancient lamps; the design was simply rings and dots of a black pigment.

Besides the pottery, there were found in the jars about a dozen shells of the genus *Cyprœa*, a Mediterranean species, of about an inch in length; but no coins were found in any of them. May not these shells, then, have been the substitute for coin made use of by the people who in early times inhabited this city? for the ancients are known to have employed them as money before metal was stamped for that purpose. As, therefore, from their number, it seems probable that they were deposited here as coin, we may reasonably infer that the tomb and jars in which they were found belonged to some of the earliest inhabitants.

These jars were found in all cases lying on their sides, with a flat slab of slate or stone placed against their mouth; and most of them were within a few inches of the surface, from the little soil there, and were partially or wholly crushed in consequence. They were of all sizes, from that necessary for mere infants, to that for children of eight or ten years of age.

The tombs for adults were also scattered about adjacent to where the jars were found, wherever the surface of the hill could be excavated sufficiently deep without being obstructed by rock; and they were regular built graves, yet not more than one or two feet under the surface anywhere, from the difficulty, no doubt, of excavating deeply into the native rock that underlies the thin surface-soil still covering the ridge.

These graves were either formed of simple rough slaty slabs of the natural rock, placed erect round the sides and covering the top, or they were built of square and close-fitting blocks of sandstone; and it was also observed that these tombs were placed in two directions, viz. some north and south, and others east and west. In nearly all some relics of bones were found, with amphoræ and very plain pottery. One had the skeleton still in an almost perfect state, with an amphora and cup placed between its legs: and some black matted fibrous substance, like coarse moss or hair, but much coarser, was found at its feet, but its nature I have not yet determined; probably it was a sponge.

This description of an insignificant, out-of-the-way, but yet interesting city from its evident associations with Crete's early customs and days, will doubtless more than suffice the reader or traveller; so I will now proceed southward to another Palaio Kastron, in the south part of Grandes Bay, across the brown slaty or gravelly ridges that intervene between Eremopoli and the valley opening into that bay. A solitary ride, however, it will be: no inhabitants will be seen, and no living thing, save fox, hare, and partridge; and they abound, for it has long been abandoned as the haunt of corsairs.

Then, if the traveller has any taste for learning something of the rocks he treads on in the way, or the origin and cause of the strata being so variously lifted and tilted, in the several features of mountain and hill which surround him, into elevated grey crags here, or smooth dark-brown ridges there, he can divert his mind on the way by contemplating them. For, in the effort to throw off and uplift these superficial series of stratified rocks and slaty beds, nature's hidden caldron within the earth's crust boiled over, and an igneous jet of trap burst through the mass, tinging with purple, red, and white the shales and schists which came in contact with it, and thus frizzled, contorted, and overturned them as they were being uplifted or folded by the protruding mass of molten rock. An instance of this protrusion he will pass on his left near Vaia Bay, and another at two miles south of Eremopoli, where a narrow valley has been cleft through the hills bordering the coast, through which the torrents that in winter descend from the slopes and ridges of the Topler-Monastery plateau find their outlet, and above the mouth of which there is an interesting display of upturned strata.

Then, as he crosses the intervening ridge that overlooks the Bay of Palaio Kastron, where was another ancient city that will require a few words, he will see to the south of it a fringe of grey cliffs bounding his view in that direction, running nearly east and west, and forming the northern face of the Samothe plateau, upon which is the little peak of that name. That line of cliff is the face of an old fault made in these old-looking rocks when so lifted and shook by the volcanic agents we have before noticed. And if he looks also back upon the hills north of Eremopoli (or Palaiopoli, as that desert city is sometimes called), he will see something of a lesser line of steeps as a fault that seems to correspond with the southern one in time of disturbance and elevation.

The intermediate depressed district behind the old cities of Eremopoli and Palaio Kastron, then being so much lower, constitutes the part that was subject under the movement to an amount of lateral pressure that has, together with the volcanic protrusion here and there forced through the dark strata, crumpled and scorched them into various forms and hues, and in some cases appears to have completely inverted them, which the geological traveller, if he has time for a closer examination, will see in the cliffs and ridge bordering the shore near the before-noticed valley.

A quarter of an hour's ride will bring us to the top of the ridge that overlooks Grandes Bay. I therefore add a sketch (see next page) of the Palaio Kastron hill and the bay on its first coming in sight, as it will aid the reader in understanding an imperfect description.

He sees on the margin of the bay to the south-east the high conical hill upon which the Palaio Kastron or old fortress stood; and he sees also behind it the Grandes islets, and beyond them Cape Plaka—a flattish but high point or prominence of the coast, that I have before noticed as the probable promontory of Salmone mentioned in St. Luke's account of the voyage of St. Paul, previously to his reaching Fair Havens in Crete (Acts, xxvii.).

PALAIO KASTRON.

I will set the reader down, therefore, to dwell upon the scene, to contemplate the insular position and striking form, and speculate on the origin of the hill of Palaio Kastron; and doubtless, as his mind has just been dwelling upon volcanic rocks, he will say, " And here too is another volcanic protrusion, a perfect basaltic or trap-like peak that has recently risen, or that subsequent denudation has left thus isolated and divested of its once-enveloping strata." But this will be only a passing thought, and erroneous, that hill being a result of a geological operation of another character, of an origin long subsequent to the previous —of long duration, nevertheless, both in the progress of formation and in that of subsequent degradation: it is a fragment of a marine tertiary, probably of the miocene period, and consists of nearly horizontal beds of gravels, sands, and sandstones in its lower parts, but is surmounted by a crust of limestone as a capping, that forms the fringe of cliff seen around its crest. Through the hardness of this upper stratum its level top has been retained; and this, being spacious enough to hold a small fortress, invited some middle-age Cretan to make it his stronghold against the bold corsairs who then frequented these seas—or perhaps the chief of the corsairs himself.

But the older Cretans were before him still, and had an earlier fortress there also, or, at all events, had a town on the base of the hill and level ground below it, as well as around the little bay south of it, where there are remains of rude habitations of the early style of construction.

In the ride down to visit them, some other remains will be seen on the bay to the north of the Palaio Kastron and about a mile from it, consisting of the walls of another small fortified town, apparently of an intermediate time, viz. between the rude and early and the middle age, being formed of squared stones as in the better Greek period. The foundations of these walls may be traced for a great part of their circuit on the west side of a low, flat-topped hill, more in the middle of the bay, and near the centre of the view here given. The former city was most probably one of Homer's hundred cities that composed the Cretan community under Minos, its early king and lawgiver, and the latter, perhaps, a later city, when divided into republics; for the two could hardly have been contemporary, and so near.

I was shown some ancient tombs that had been dug out of the side of the Palaio Kastron hill by the natives of the neighbouring hamlet of Angathe. I saw the fragments of one that had been recently opened, which was formed of large and thick slabs of terra cotta, rudely ornamented; and some other fragments visible seem to indicate that, in this city, entire coffins or sarcophagi were formed of this material. A very curious terra-cotta figure was obtained from one by a lay priest of a neighbouring farm; it seems to be of Phœnician origin, and to indicate a Phœnician settlement or a place of call in their trading-voyages between the eastern and western worlds. The other remains are insignificant.

There is a fragment of a sitting figure, of colossal size and very white Parian marble, on the beach under the Palaio Kastron. The figure was draped; but the sea having probably washed it for ages, since it fell down to the shore from the top of a gravel cliff undermined by the waves, the surface of the statue is so worn as to render it valueless, and its character and probable age indeterminable.

These remains, however, show that a town of some note stood here as well as at Eremopoli. Thus there were three cities at this extremity of Crete, where now there are but a few cottages and a farming monastery. But what was the name of this site? for I have only ventured to suggest it to be Sammonium or Grammonium in the map of Crete, without a single argument to offer in proof, except that such names have been noticed by ancient authors as those of a Cretan city or Cretan cities in this part.

As, in returning hence to the Topler Monastery, we shall ascend over some gravel ridges soon after quitting the cultivation around the hamlet or metoki of Kuremeno, in the valley behind Palaio Kastron, we can now conclude our geological view of the district by pointing out that the isolated peak of Palaio Kastron is a fragment of the same tertiary group of deposits that once filled the whole of the intervening basins and valleys, and covered the lower part of the slaty ridges which now appear without them; but, by denudation, when the sea stood at higher levels than at present, or rather when the land of Crete itself stood at a lower elevation, those deposits were carried away, and the Palaio Kastron hill thus insulated.

But there is a relic of more interest still (a mere remnant, however, of a deposit of a different origin and time) upon the present shore to the south of Palaio Kastron, viz. a fragment of a freshwater deposit, with fossils to identify it as being so, although it is now just at the sea-level, and overlain apparently by marine strata that must belong to a later period. Yet there is sufficient to enable us to state that here, as on the opposite coast of Rhodes, there exist detached fragments of the bed of the old archipelago freshwater-lake period, of which those noticed at Khersoneso are portions; and its position here also leads to the supposition that it had a wider extent over the eastern basin of the Mediterranean.

The Topler Monastery has nothing to recommend it to the attention of the traveller, except a long inscription on a slab which is let into the floor of a chapel adjacent to it, and which was noticed by Pashley, who has given a copy in his work. A more correct copy was desirable; but, as it consisted of eighty-three lines of close and small although well-cut letters, many of which are now not very legible, a labour of eight or ten hours upon the flat of one's stomach was necessary to effect it. (See Appendix by the Rev. Churchill Babington.) The inscription probably came from Eremopoli; it is a decree, and is interesting although imperfect, as it mentions the names of several of the eastern cities of Crete.

A school is attached to this monastery, at which about thirty lads of the district receive gratuitous education, which is its best recommendation. Thus a sprinkling of instruction is being sown broadcast here and there amongst the peasantry of Crete by the several monasteries existing through it; but it is only a sprinkling, as they are often too inconveniently far from the villages to be available.

In returning to Sitia, the traveller will perhaps follow a road which a short distance from the monastery brings him to some masses of rock that stand up by the wayside, to which his attention may be attracted by a heap of loose stones being piled upon the top of and against them, and by his muleteer, if a Greek, picking up one and tossing it on the top of the heap as he passes it, muttering something as he does so. Hence the accumulation of this cairn or pile; but many fall back into the path again from want of space for lodgment upon the rock, yet only to be again and again cast up with an anathema for the soul of a certain Turkish Aga, who in the revolution took the monastery, polluted it by sword and fire, but afterwards fell at this spot when compelled to retire before the superior numbers of the Christian reinforcements. Thus we have here an instance of a monument raised to commemorate a curse, instead of to the honour of a man, as more frequently occurs.

The east end of Crete is noted for the prevalence of the north north-west and north-west winds, which blow there for more than half the year, but with much less force than at the Cape St. John (or Agios Johannes) of Spina Longa, and are therefore less inconvenient for the mariner. They prevail nearly all the summer, and correspond to the trade or summer wind which at the same time blows over Egypt and down the Red Sea. The wind is fresh only during the day, like a sea-breeze, and generally dies at night; and whether it blows a regular "meltem" (that is, a northerly summer gale) or only an ordinary sea-breeze in the adjacent part of the archipelago, it has the same direction here. By its strength, however, and the state of the atmosphere, the experienced local seaman knows which, and consequently knows the weather he will encounter if he ventures to proceed to the northward, amongst the islands of the archipelago. The former condition is indicated by a more hazy sky, which is his warning to remain; with the sea-breeze the air is more cool, but humid, when a sailing-vessel may proceed with a prospect of being able to contend against it and the southerly current then usually found running through the Caso and Cretan channel from the archipelago.

CHAPTER XX.

SPONGE-DIVERS ON THE COAST OF CRETE—ARISTOTLE'S KNOW-
LEDGE OF SPONGES DERIVED FROM THE ANCIENT SPONGE-
DIVERS—THE TEMPERATURE OF THE MEDITERRANEAN DEEPS
—THE LARGE ADULTERATION OF THE SPONGE WITH FINE
SAND—PRACTICE OF DIVING BY THE YOUNG CHILDREN OF
SPONGE-DIVERS—A FLEET OF SPONGE-FISHERS AT WORK, THEIR
MODE OF OPERATION—THE INCONVENIENCES AND ACCIDENTS
THEY ARE SUBJECT TO—THE SHARK'S OCCASIONAL APPEAR-
ANCE—ACCOUNT OF A LARGE SHARK NEAR A SPONGE-BANK.

THE east coast of Crete is noted for the quantity and very fine quality of the sponges which grow in its waters, and it is in consequence annually frequented by from 50 to 100 boats, with seven or eight sponge-divers in each, who are chiefly from the islands of Symi, Calymno, or Khalki; and they frequently visited the north-east coast during our stay there, and excited much interest among us in their occupation. Of the many varied ways by which man labours to procure his bread, there is none perhaps so interesting and extraordinary as that of the sponge-diver; and when the luxurious fair use the sponge at their toilet, or the gentleman at his morning ablutions and bath, little do they know or think of the hard and peculiar trials and exertions some fellow-creature has gone through before he was enabled to procure for their gratification this valuable and peculiar marine production. And as little, perhaps, have they ever troubled themselves with the discussions that have arisen among philosophers, since the days of Aristotle, as to whether the sponge is an animal or a vegetable. Its now well-ascertained but fitful circulation of the sea-water through its pores seems at length to have led many *savants* of natural history to conclude that it really is an animal. Yet this fact is all that can be advanced, viz. that it has a spasmodic inspiration and rejection of sea-water; and, except being covered with a slimy, viscous coating, of a bluish-black colour above, and dirty white beneath, the sponge is of the same shape and size when cleansed and fit for use as when living,—the mode of cleansing it being simply to squeeze and wash the sponge two or three times in the sea and dry it in the sun for a few hours, until all gelatinous matter is extracted from it.

When a reflective mood comes over a man as he sits enjoying the sight of his parlour fire, he is apt to think, *then*, of the means by which the coal he sees sparkling in the grate is procured from the recesses of the earth, and he shudders perhaps as he thinks of the thousands who are at that moment labouring in the bowels of the earth, from 1000 to 2000 feet below its surface, in the midst of darkness, dirt, and danger. But when he handles the soft sponge that so gratefully moistens his body, he has no conception of the hardships and dangers that beset the man that procured it for him from the depths of the sea, in all probability between 100 and 200 feet below its surface, and by actually diving for it! Marvellous as it may appear, yet such is the fact, that man's power of versatility is so great that he can be brought to endure suspended respiration and to sustain the pressures experienced during a dive to depths of twenty or thirty fathoms; nay, I have been assured that in some few instances he has been known to reach forty fathoms without the aid of any diving-apparatus save a flat stone carried in his hands to facilitate his descent. I have myself known many instances of divers going down to depths of from twenty to thirty fathoms; and I knew a family of three brothers, belonging to the island of Symi, who were called by their compatriots (and known to all the sponge-diving fraternity as) the Sarandaki, or the *Forties*, from their reputed capability of diving to that enormous depth. They were known to me more than twenty years ago, and for several years after; but only one of the three survives, and he is now employed in the Arsenal at Constantinople as the government diver. One of the other two lost his life whilst diving off the coast of Syria, either by a fit of apoplexy or by a fish, as the body was never recovered. Now it is evident that nothing but a most severe training from a very early age, and the possession of great powers of endurance as well as courage, could enable any one to perform feats so extraordinary as this; and when it is considered that at the depth of twenty fathoms the pressure of the water upon the body is 50 lbs. to the square inch, and at thirty fathoms 75 lbs., or about that of five atmospheres, and thus at every dive to those depths the body passes through these great pressures with inflated lungs, and in scarcely more than the time that it takes to write the fact, the full extent of the trial to the lungs, heart, and mental powers of the diver, to maintain self-possession and suspended respiration, can be better appreciated, and the marvellousness of the feat becomes the more striking.

I have in many instances timed the diver's stay under water, and found it to range from 90 to 120 seconds, and have no doubt that the most enduring diver could stay from 10 to 20 seconds longer; for when diving in the greater depths, and sponges are plentiful, they often remain, under the excitement of work and the prospect of profit, until they feel the sensations of drowning commence, or, as they express it, until they feel that they are "falling asleep."

The sponge is known to have been an article of commerce in the days of Aristotle, and probably long before; for it was used by the ancients in their helmets and boots as a cushion and absorbent of the moisture from the head and feet. Thus there must have been sponge-divers then; for Aristotle relates that the finest sponges came only from the greater depths, and accounts for it from the temperature remaining more constant there—a very interesting evidence of the knowledge of this great philosopher; for the range, permanency, and fluctuation of temperature in the depths of the sea is comparatively a very modern subject of inquiry; yet this great philosopher and master mind had in some degree understood it. And it is, I think, an evidence of the great depth to which the divers then went for the sponge, as now, because it was from them that he learned the fact: they were the thermometers that told it, from the sensations experienced by their bodies when diving in those depths.

The temperatures of the Mediterranean basins have a speciality or peculiarity in their conditions, from the insulated or detached character of the basins themselves. Thus I have found that below 100 fathoms the temperature is nearly always permanent, and stands at about (or perhaps a little above) the average annual atmospheric temperature of the locality, namely, from 54° to 58°, according to the part, and that it is between fifty fathoms and the surface that the temperature is most variable. This the diver's experience would enable him to describe, without reference to any comparative quantity or standard measure; for the length of the diver's stay under water, and the depths he can go, greatly depend upon the temperature of the water.

But I am disposed to give a different or another reason, besides permanency of temperature, for the deeper waters being the most favourable for the growth of the finer sponges. I think it arises also from the greater tranquillity and clearness of the water, as much as from the more permanent temperature of those depths; for their natural habitat seems to be where there is a firm basis, such as rock, to attach themselves to, and where little mud or sand exists to render the water impure and turbid under the agitation of storms and currents. It may surprise the reader to be informed that the quantity of fine sand he finds in a new sponge has not been enclosed there by the animal or vegetable during its growth, but is an adulteration practised by the agents and merchants who purchase the sponge from the divers, in order to increase its weight and their profit. I have seen, in the islands of Symi, Calymno, and Khalki, as well as elsewhere, the recently arrived cargoes of several sponge-boats undergoing the process of adulteration before packing. The sand having been imported from some spot known to yield it of the fineness requisite for the purpose, is mixed with water, in which there is a little gelatine or gum, to enable the sponges to take up and retain it the better, and without being detectable afterwards; the sponges are then well kneaded in it, so as to fill up their minute pores; they are then dried in the sun, and packed very closely together in goat's-hair sacks, of an open texture, that the sand, as it becomes detached from the sponges by the motion of their transit, may escape, and prevent detection by the European trader.

In this way a hundredweight of sponges in their dry state will be so sanded as to weigh more than a ton, before they are packed for exportation to Europe. The local merchants understand the process, and charge accordingly; and thus they have hitherto derived the chief profit, whilst the poor diver hardly obtains more than a scanty living for all his risks and hardships, and is in general in debt to the local trader; for, being idle all the winter, through having no other occupation, he is in consequence too frequently brought into the power of the local trader as a money-lender, and, through habits of drunkenness and gambling following upon idleness, becomes his perpetual debtor. The sponge-fishers are thus a degraded class of the Greek community, and chiefly belong to those islands where there is no produce or trade—barren rocks in comparison to the generality, but comparatively healthy localities; and as they are there almost free from the Turkish rule, they are more independent than in the larger islands or the towns on the coast of Asia Minor. This comparative liberty induces them to prefer their native rock to another; and necessity obliges them to seek their bread from the sea, as the island is incapable of affording it. Hence they seem to have followed the occupation of sponge-divers from generation to generation for many centuries.

A visit to the ports of one of these islands presents at certain seasons an interesting scene of the aquatic gambols of the young divers, who, from two to ten years of age, sport in the sea as if it were their natural element; for, in the summer months, when the grown-up are all absent, and the children and aged only left, the mothers seem to send their infants to the water as soon as they can walk, as a duck does her brood, and they are very soon expert enough to dive in two, three, and five fathoms.

At the first commencement of the diving-season the diver suffers much, and cannot easily dive at greater depths than twelve and fifteen fathoms for a few days; the eyes, nose, and ears then bleed freely under the pressure and consequent congestion of the vessels.

The sponge-fishing is chiefly carried on in neatly rigged but small caïques or half-decked boats from eight to ten tons' burthen, that contain from seven to nine men in each, and are very handy little craft, very good sea-boats, and fine models, that seem to have been the original of the famed yacht the 'Ame-

SPONGE DIVERS AT WORK

rica.' They go to work in companies of half a dozen to twenty or thirty boats for mutual support and protection; and when the weather is favourable, and they are in working condition, each diver will dive fifteen, and even twenty times a day, in as many fathoms.

They are obliged to be particular in their diet during the diving-season, making no meal until evening, and sustaining their strength by an occasional pipe and a small cup of coffee once or twice during the day.

It is to behold one of the most interesting sights possible, to be in the midst of a fleet of these sponge-boats when the men are at work on their fishing-ground; for they are like a flight of mosquitoes, or rather of butterflies flitting from flower to flower, as they move from one spot to another, anchoring for a few minutes only whilst a few dives are made, then hoisting their numerous and well-handled sails to shift a few yards further in the direction desired, and then anchoring again and diving, as long as the weather is favourable and sponges are procurable. The same ground is thus often worked over and over year after year; but they say that a rest of two or three years is necessary to ensure a good crop of full-grown sponges upon the same spot.

The accompanying sketch was taken from a group to whom I had indicated some new patches of rocks which I had just discovered, at depths of 15 and 20 fathoms, previously unknown to them. In a few minutes the whole party were actively diving there; and, the ground being new to them, they made a great harvest in a few hours. Being exposed so much in the sun whilst diving, they look, when stripped, a different race of men from the Greeks in general, in consequence of the bright copper-colour of their skins and their lean figures. The mode of operation preparatory to a dive is very peculiar and interesting: the sketch in some degree represents this also. The diver whose turn it is takes his seat on the deck of the vessel, at either the bow or stern, and, placing by his side a large flat slab of marble weighing about 25 lbs., to which is attached a rope of the proper length and thickness ($1\frac{1}{2}$ inch), he then strips, and is left by his companions to prepare himself. This seems to consist in devoting a certain time to clearing the passages of his lungs by expectoration, and highly inflating them afterwards, thus oxidizing his blood very highly by a repetition of deep inspirations. The operation lasts from five to ten minutes or more, according to the depth; and during it the operator is never interfered with by his companions, and seldom speaks or is spoken to; he is simply watched by two of them, but at a little distance, and they never venture to urge him or to distract him in any way during the process. It seems to a spectator as if the diver were going through a sort of mysterious ceremony or incantation. When, from some sensation known only to himself after these repeated long-drawn and heavy inspirations, he deems the fitting moment to have arrived, he seizes the slab of marble, and, after crossing himself and uttering a prayer, plunges with it like a returning dolphin into the sea and rapidly descends. The stone is always held during the descent directly in front of the head, at arm's length, and so as to offer as little resistance as possible; and by varying its inclination, it acts likewise as a rudder, causing the descent to be more or less vertical, as desired by the diver.

As soon as he reaches the bottom, he places the stone under his arm to keep himself down, and then walks about upon the rock, or crawls under its ledges, stuffing the sponges into a netted-bag with a hooped mouth, which is strung round his neck to receive them; but he holds firmly to the stone or rope all the while, as his safeguard for returning and for making the known signal at the time he desires it.

Now let us notice the proceedings of his companions in the boat floating some twenty or thirty fathoms above him. The two men who were nearest to him previously to his making the dive, but who systematically seem to place themselves so as to prevent him from conceiving the idea of being impatiently watched by them whilst undergoing the preparation, spring to their feet as soon as he disappears, and rush to the rope, which one of them then holds in his hand, veering it out or shortening it in as the diver moves about upon the bottom; and as soon as the signal indicative of his wish to return is felt, they commence hauling up the rope with great energy and earnestness, and in a way calculated to ensure the greatest expedition of ascent, since the overstay of a few seconds may be a point of life or death to the diver. The hauling up is thus effected:—The assistant who has hold of the rope, awaiting the signal, first reaches down with both hands as low as he can, and, there grasping the rope, with a great bodily effort raises it up to nearly arm's length over his head; the second assistant is then prepared to make his grasp as low down as he can reach, and does the same, and so on the two alternately, and, by a fathom or more at a time and with great rapidity, bring the anxious diver to the surface. A heavy blow from his nostrils, to expel the water and exhausted air, indicates to his comrades that he is conscious and breathes. A word or two is then spoken by one of his companions to encourage him, if he seems much distressed, as is often the case; and the hearing of the voice is said by them to be a great support at the moment of their greatest state of exhaustion. A few seconds' rest at the surface, and then the diver returns into the boat to recover, generally putting on an under garment or jacket, to assist the restoration of the animal heat he has lost, and to prevent the loss of more by the too rapid evaporation of the water from his body. Such is the trying life of a Levantine sponge-diver; and doubtless there are very few of us who have any idea of what a fellow-creature has suffered in procuring that little article which has become a necessity of our toilet-table and the luxury of our morning ablutions.

The number of sponge-divers, who depend on it for a livelihood, is probably about 3000 in all, almost all of them inhabitants of the five or six south-eastern islands of the archipelago, viz. Symi, Rhodes, Khalki, Tilo, Kalymno, and Astropalea: there are a few, also, at Lero and Castelorizzo; but they chiefly belong to the most barren of these two islands. It is curious that there are none in the neighbouring islands of Carpatho and Caso; and although the former is a singularly formed and comparatively barren island, the male population are all house-builders and masons, not sailors, and consequently pass the summer season in various localities, far and near, building and repairing houses; whilst the inhabitants of the still more barren island of Caso, between it and Crete, are all ship-builders and sailors, none sponge-divers, and, next to those of Syra, build the greatest number and the finest of the ships used by the Greeks.

Notwithstanding the number of divers thus dispersed over the Levant and along the African coast and Syria during four months of the year, viz. from the middle of June to the middle of October, engaged in the sponge-fishing, the deaths from drowning or accident are very few, averaging not more than five or six annually; and the cases which occur from the attacks of sharks or other fish are said to be rare: yet the apprehension of such danger always exists, and for this reason they say that the younger divers would dive best, and in the deepest waters, if they had the same courage as those who are older and experienced; but, by the time the required confidence has been attained, their physical powers are often diminished by premature age from the nature of the work. One of their greatest annoyances arises from a very little Actinia, which stings their hands and bodies, and is therefore called by them the *Vromo* (or the *stinging*): it is not larger than a halfpenny, and is of a pale orange-colour; and as the animal often clings to the roots of sponges, they suffer much from the irritation that follows: although it does not seem to blister, it causes a swelling, and prevents their working for several days. When an officer was about to take one into his hands, the crew all loudly called out in alarm to prevent his doing so; I was therefore not disposed to try its effect.

The shark is an enemy that appears sometimes amongst them, and when seen produces much alarm, suspending their operations at the time; for it is a fact that some sharks in the Mediterranean reach a considerable size, and attack men in the sea. An instance is on record of one having been caught at Alexandria that contained the half of a man, and of another that a few years since attacked and took down one of our own soldiers at Corfu; and when I was employed upon the coast of Africa about two years since, the largest shark ever observed by any one on board was seen by all hands. The ship was at anchor off Cape Tanoob, about 100 miles west of Alexandria, in 12 fathoms' water, and upon a clean sandy bottom, when the word was suddenly passed that a shark was in sight. We had only recently passed through a fleet of sponge-boats at work a few miles from the spot, and upon the very bank he was now steering for; but, attracted by the ship, he quietly sailed round and round, reconnoitring us, at a distance of about a quarter of a mile, until at length he was induced to approach pretty close, within 30 or 40 yards of the ship's quarter, and to poise himself there at two or three fathoms below the surface; and then, as he lay perfectly still, and our gig was also towing astern, we had the means of making a comparison of his length, and concluded that it was not much, if at all, under 18 feet; some even thought it exceeded 20 feet[*]. His presence naturally excited great interest amongst us, especially as he was attended, as usual, by seven or eight little

[*] Prince Canino relates that one Mediterranean species attains to 24 feet.

pilot-fish, which went actively and fearlessly round and round the great monster's head, and seemed to regard him quite as their protector and friend. I never witnessed anything that appeared more truly to indicate a perfect understanding between the shark and his little companions than on this occasion.

As some of the crew had seen him pass under the ship a little time previously upon some fowls' heads and offal being thrown overboard, and after the pilot-fish had previously been to it, he was supposed to have gone and eaten the refuse, as he certainly went to the spot. Now, therefore, there appeared a tempting chance of catching him with a bait. The shark-hook was consequently duly baited with a large piece of fat pork, and thrown from the quarter a few yards in front of his nose; the huge monster nevertheless remained all the while motionless, except his broad and thick fins, that alone appeared to move occasionally so as to steady his position. His little active and zebra-striped companions, however, seemed at first rather scared by the splash of the bait; but before it had sunk to the depth of a few feet, one or two advanced cautiously towards it, and then the whole seven or eight followed, and after carefully going round and round the bait as it slowly descended, and also reconnoitring and running up and down the rope attached, they darted off to the head of the shark, and then seemed to pass close over and under his nose, in the very precincts of his terrific jaws. We watched the motions of all with great interest, hoping to see him the next moment dart at the alluring bait; but the huge leviathan slowly turned his head and sailed away. It was, to all of us, exactly as if he had been informed by his little companions that there was danger in the tempting food; and so Mr. Shark and his little friends sailed away together, and were not again seen.

The frequent association of these little fish (which are about the size and form of the mackerel) with the shark is remarkable, as is also the place they take when swimming with him, just in front of or over his nose. When accompanying a ship, as they often do, the pilot-fish take up a position a few inches only in front of the cutwater, where they have been known to remain several days, with the exception of an occasional dive under the ship's bottom, whence they soon return to their station, where they so regulate their speed by that of the ship as to appear attached to it by an invisible wire. Instinct or experience has taught them, no doubt, that this is the safest place from their own special enemies, and a place of impunity, when in company with the shark; so they adopt it with the ship,—having also found that, when the shark feeds, crumbs fall for them from his terrible jaws.

CHAPTER XXI.

THE EAST COAST OF CRETE—GORGE OF KAROUBA—ZAKRO BAY—
CYCLOPEAN REMAINS—THE ANCIENT ITANUS—DESTRUCTION
OF IT AND PRÆSUS BY THE HIERAPYTNIANS—THE ANCIENT
NAME STILL APPLIED TO A NEIGHBOURING VILLAGE—THE
COINS OF ITANUS—THE APPROPRIATE EMBLEMS UPON THEM
—SITE OF THE SMALL TOWN OF AMPELUS—ROUTES TO RETURN
TO IERAPETRA.

To the south of Grandes Bay, the coast of Crete assumes a wild, forbidding aspect for several miles, indeed until opposite the white cliffy islands of Kouphonisi. Along all this part, including the barren headland of Cape Plaka, naked limestone steeps and cliffs frown upon the shore, but are here and there intersected by gorges and ravines.

The largest of these gorges and bays is at Zakro, six and a half miles south of Cape Plaka, where there is a small plain bordering the bay, about half a mile long and the same in breadth. There is anchorage also in the bay at convenient depths; but the locality has a wild, forbidding aspect from the sea, from the nakedness of the cliffs and mountains above.

This little plain of Zakro is enclosed by high steeps of grey limestone, and by cliffs which ascend from the plain in a series of natural terraces, like steps, each being the well-marked line and ledge of a former sealevel. The conical hill over the bluff on the north side of the bay most remarkably shows these several levels, presenting a somewhat pyramidal form, there being six or seven such evidences of the old sea-levels, which, as so many zones, almost encircle the hill.

The limestone is a hard, compact, bluish, stratified rock, dipping to the eastward at an angle of about 30° or 35°. In consequence of such an inclination, the upturned ends of the strata have been shorn off at each of these levels, by which the fact of their having been each the result of sea wear and encroachment is made too clear to be disputed, or to require vestiges of positive beaches upon them.

The north winds are less felt in this bay than at Grandes; but heavy squalls strike the sea two or three miles off the shore, which increase in violence and frequency off the bolder parts of the coast to the south of Zakro, and leave Zakro Bay less subject to them.

Behind Zakro there is a great sunken valley five or six miles long, and from one to two in breadth, which is not a plain, but filled up with a series of disturbed schists and slaty ridges like those of Grandes Bay; and the valley is of a similar geological age, and, like it, the result of a downcast, or the limit of a great displacement.

This sunken district or valley has several villages in it; but they are poor, although sometimes picturesquely situated. The karouba is the chief produce. There are two outlets to the valley, through narrow gorges. One, with a village called Karoub in it, which takes its name from the tree, lies to the north of Zakro Bay. At the mouth of the Karouba gorge there are some remains of an Hellenic ruin, which appears to have been a mere tower or coast-station defending the approach to the valley. The Karouba valley is reached by a road from the Topler Monastery, which passes through the hamlet of Angathe near Palaio Kastron, and crosses through a gap in the Samothe ridge.

The second and principal outlet of the sunken valley of Karouba is that at the Bay of Zakro, where a rivulet from it threads a serpentine course through an impracticable and tortuous gorge, a mere rent in the mountains, that originally opened under the great convulsions that raised them; and the stream flowing through it turns two or three mills at its entrance into the plain of Zakro.

From this description it must be evident to the reader (viz. from the combination of a rivulet, plain, bay, and high bounding ridge) that Zakro presents features highly favourable for the situation of a coast-city of the Cretans in early days. And in examining the crags and lower hills which enclose the little theatre-like plain, the Cyclopean remains of a very ancient and very considerable city were found, which, from their position on the coast, their character, and extent, can be no other than those of Itanus, since Scylax and some others, including Ptolemy, place this city in the most eastern part of Crete: but the name of Zakro, which the place now bears, has evidently no connexion with the ancient city.

The river flowing from the gorge divided the city into two parts, of which the remains are considerable and are of much interest, consisting entirely of Cyclopean walls and the foundations of rude and massively constructed buildings and terraces, ranged upon two steep ridges running into the plain on the north side of the river, with a sort of acropolis or fortified height over the gorge. On the south side of the river, similar remains occur on the lower spurs jutting from the surrounding precipices, which, however, are crowned on this side with some massive walls in addition, as it was there more approachable.

During a careful examination throughout the above site, I saw only a large stone trough, and three or four squared blocks, that showed evidences of a tool being used to trim the rude stones into a shape for buildingpurposes. The stratified character of the surrounding rocks, as at Olus, was favourable, however, for splitting the massive blocks into a form somewhat adapted for the Cyclopean style of construction; yet the massive character of the walls, terraces, and buildings shows that no mean power or skill was used in the construction of them. A Pelasgic character is thus stamped upon the entire remains of this city; for no Roman or middle-age ruin was visible anywhere, to show that it had had inhabitants in these later times; and if so, as at Olus, the rude habitations of its earlier people were used by them.

My chief reasons for believing the very early and once flourishing Cretan city of Itanus to have been at Zakro, in the absence of any name, at the site itself, similar to that of Itanus, are the following:—

The inscription at Topler Monastery records the fact of an alliance between Præsus and Itanus. Now, as the upland territories of Præsus and of this site are conterminous, an alliance was natural.

This alliance was doubtless for mutual defence against their rival neighbour, Hierapytna, as it is recorded that that town finally warred against and destroyed Præsus; and therefore it is reasonable to conclude that Hierapytna did not allow the allied flourishing coast-city to remain as its maritime rival after Præsus had fallen; and so Itanus probably shared the fate of Præsus. Then what would be the result to the inhabitants that escaped or were left? Why, they would naturally flee to another land, if able to do so; and if not, submit and retire to the furthest limits of their upland fastnesses, so as to lessen the recollection of their misfortune by locating at as great a distance from the scene of it as possible.

And it is precisely the latter of these two courses that they seem to have followed; for in the far-off highest of the upland plains above Zakro, where it is adjacent to the Præsian boundary, we now find a small village, apparently the representative of that remnant, having remarkably preserved the name of their desolated city in that now applied to this village, viz. Tsitano or Sitano, but with the usual prefix of the S, or Ts, that I have before noticed as frequent in the east of Crete. And not far from it, viz. on the opposite hills, we found a small square Hellenic fortress, which perhaps was the frontier outpost between the old city of Itanus and the territory of the Præsii.

By the coins of Itanus, which are not uncommon, we know it to have been an important trading-city in the early period of Cretan history; and as no coins of it, of the Roman period, I believe, exist, nor any remains of that date, its time of desertion is made clearly to be cotemporary with that of Præsus—about the time of Alexander probably, or not long after it.

The emblems upon the coins are also characteristic of the locality here assigned to Itanus:—the eagle, as inhabiting its overtowering cliffs and gorges; the triton, with trident in hand, in the field of the same coin or occupying the entire obverse of another very fine but earlier coin, as indicative of the early connexion of the inhabitants with the sea as traders and fishermen.

And Herodotus mentions one Corobinos, a purple-trader of Itanus, from whom the Theræans gained their knowledge of the Libyan coast, and under whose pilotage the first Greek colony went to Cyrene, under Battus, about 630 B.C., by order of the Delphian Oracle (Herod. iv. 153).

From the fact that Pliny notices Itanus only as a promontory around which were the islands of Onisia and Leuce, and the 'Stadiasmus' does not mention it at all, my view regarding its probable conquest and desertion receives further support. I have felt it the more necessary to give a full exposition of my reasons for placing the site of Itanus at Zakro, because Dr. Pococke places it at Palaio Kastron, in Grandes Bay; and, from his minute description of Kouphonisi, and the manner in which he mentions Zakro (although in a note only), he seems to have been in its neighbourhood. Nevertheless he does not appear to have landed at Zakro, but only to have passed near it in a boat; and therefore the opinion of the learned doctor cannot be founded upon a complete research.

Ampelus is mentioned by Pliny as being a town beyond Itanus, but by Ptolemy as a promontory only; and this town is apparently identified at some ruins, consisting mainly of the foundations of a small walled city, which exist upon the coast opposite the Cavallos Islets, at the end of a narrow, shelving, stony plain that borders the shore there, about three miles southward of Zakro.

The walls were built of quadrangular blocks of sandstone, from the rock which underlies this little coast-plain of Katocampo, as the place is called. The ruins of Ampelus are apparently not more than 300 yards long. Hence, from its size and the character of its walls, it seems to have succeeded Itanus on this part of the coast as a mere fishing-town.

Had Ampelus been of any size and of very ancient date, the hill over the adjacent point, westward of the present ruins, would doubtless have been chosen as a more inviting position, and more consistent with early Greek sites than its present. An open bay under it was doubtless its haven, under the partial shelter afforded by the two rocky Kavallos Islets that lie off it.

There is a mineral spring near, which is in repute for its medicinal properties; and Ampelus probably in part owed its existence to this cause. It is now without inhabitants, save the families of two or three shepherds.

A road ascends from Katocampo, or Ampelus, to the upland plains of Khadra and Zero, which is exceedingly rugged and steep; but there is no more practicable route along the coast to the westward. Therefore the traveller, if he ventures thus far by land, can retrace his steps by the way of the Topler Monastery to Sitia, or ascend the mountains leading from here to the plains of Zero and Khadra, or from

Zakro to that of Kataleone and Khadra, and thence take the southern route to Ierapetra along the south coast; and this route I recommend in preference to returning to Sitia Bay.

As my notice of this part of the island would be deficient without a reference to the White Islands of the Kouphonisi, which lie about two miles off its south-east headland, I shall describe them in the following chapter.

CHAPTER XXII.

THE KOUPHONISI ISLANDS—ROMAN RUINS—ANCIENT STATUE—
THE ISLAND OF OPHIUSA—CRETAN PIRATES IN EARLY TIMES—
ROMAN AND RHODIAN WAR AGAINST THEM—THE HAUNT OF
ALGERINE PIRATES—AN ENGLISH TRAVELLER TAKEN BY ONE
—CAPTAIN MANIAS—HIS PIRATICAL DEEDS AS A SFAKIOT
CHIEFTAIN—HIS DEATH IN MY SERVICE—A CHARACTER, BUT
NOT A TYPE OF THE RACE—A PATRIOT'S GRAVE.

THE largest of the Kouphonisi is a flattish and low island, about two miles in length, with three small islets close off it. There is a plain on its north side, nearly a mile in length, with the remains of a small town at its extremity and just over the north-west point of the island, which seems to have been of the Roman time, the wall which encloses it being built of small stones and mortar, with Roman bricks in horizontal layers between. The greater portion of the ruins, however, are buried beneath blown or drift sand, which has accumulated over them from the sandy shore near.

In the plain to the south of the small tower or fortress are three vaulted and solidly built cisterns, constructed in the same manner as the wall of the town. These cisterns communicated with each other

VOL. I.   R and with the town by an aqueduct, which remains in part visible, and can be traced also to the hills southward of the cisterns, whence there must have issued a spring in ancient days, and where in the winter season, I was told, there is still a small source. The largest of the cisterns was 650 feet long, divided into three longitudinal vaulted compartments, and was evidently built to hold for summer use the whole supply which the springs and rains would yield.

Near the south end of the town are some fragments of slender columns of grey and reddish-grey limestone, that may have belonged to a church, or more probably a temple, as a fragment of a draped figure in white marble, but much mutilated, was found on a sandhill near them.

On the peak forming the summit of the island, and situated over the steep white cliffs of the southern shore, there is a raised platform or pedestal of squared blocks of limestone, upon which was formerly placed a colossal figure in white marble, in a sitting position, like the one at Palaio Kastron. It now, however, lies on the side of the platform that supported it, and is split into two pieces, but was originally sculptured out of a fine block of Parian marble.

No ancient author seems to have mentioned this island as having been inhabited. Can it, then, have been the haunt of pirates originally, as it was during the middle ages, and even not many years since, as I

ISLAND OF OPHIUSA. 243

learned from my Sfakiot guide and interpreter, Captain Manias, so often mentioned in Pashley's 'Crete'? For Manias told me himself of his own early cruisings here; and I found the truth of his statements confirmed by his knowledge of every inlet or creek of this part of the coast, and, to my surprise, of the islands of Caso, Carpatho, and Castelorizzo also.

Pirates do not erect statues, however, to their heroes or chiefs; so that this town must have been originally a legitimate city, dependent upon Crete, and doubtless subject to Hierapytna. But what was its ancient name?

Pliny places the Onisia and the Leucæ or White Islands of Ophiusa, Butoa, and Aradus all opposite the Itanus promontory. The first-named (the Onisia), then, are most probably the Cavallos; for the Leucæ, or White Islands, are unmistakeably the Kouphonisi group, from their remarkably white aspect; and as the first-mentioned of the White Islands or Leucæ was probably the nearest to Itanus, as well as the largest, and was called by Pliny Ophiusa, its identity with Kouphonisi seems to be established, the modern appellation having been formed by corruption from Ophiusa.

Between the two islets lying off the point of the town there is a small natural harbour for coasting-craft, and where the wary corsair could be hid from view to all passers-by, and be ready to pounce sud-

R 2

denly upon any unfortunate trader that had been drifted too close by currents during the darkness and uncertainty of navigation by night.

That the corsair and pirate had long made the islands lying off the eastern extremity of Crete their haunt is well authenticated; and the several dangers which lie off Cape Sidero, and which were so little known previous to our surveys, were perhaps used as so many snares, into which a stranger was decoyed, and when surprised by them was embarrassed, so as to prevent escape. This appears to have been the case ever since the time of the Romans; for Diodorus the Sicilian, in a fragment touching upon the Cretan wars of the Romans, has given the following account of the piratical propensities of the Cretans:—

" The senate had often debates concerning the Cretans, alleging, and at length concluding, that they joined with the pirates and were sharers in the robberies; and therefore they decreed the Cretans should send in all their ships to Rome, even to a skiff of four oars, and resign the three hundred famous hostages, and send away Lasthenes and Paneres, and amongst them pay 4000 talents of silver. The Cretans, hearing what was decreed, went into a consultation about these commands imposed upon them. The more prudent amongst them advised them to be observant in all things to what was enjoined them. But those that were of Lasthenes's party and guilty of the same crimes, fearing that, being sent for to Rome, they should be there punished for their offences, stirred up the people to a sedition, advising them to maintain those liberties that they had ever, time out of mind, enjoyed."

Also, in his book xxvi. is the following account of war being declared by the Rhodians against them for piracy:—" The Cretans rigged out seven ships for piracy, and robbed many passengers at sea ; whereupon the merchants being altogether discouraged, the Rhodians, looking upon it to belong to them to redress this mischief, proclaimed war against the Cretans." And it was evidently off this part of Crete that one of our countrymen, a Dr. Veryard, was taken by pirates in the year 1668, when sailing from Candia to Alexandria in a Dutch merchant-vessel. For in his 'Book of Travels,' under the heading of " Voyage to the Levant," after a brief account of a journey to Mount Ida in Crete from Candia, he says, " I returned on board the Dutch vessel bound for Alexandria, and on the first day's sail (from Candia) we discovered a vessel at south south-east making towards us with all possible speed. Our captain, suspecting it an enemy, bore off, hoping the night would favour our escape; for though we had thirty guns mounted, yet we were not much above half manned, and consequently incapable of making any defence. What we did was to little purpose; for they came to us above an hour by sun, and two others came in sight, so that all three appeared under the colours of Algiers, and the first saluted us with a broadside. Three to one was a prodigious inequality; wherefore, after a small resistance, we suffered them to come on board; but I can hardly express the consternation we were in to see ourselves surprised by the enemies of the name of Christ, for indeed our spirits were so damped that we had hardly force enough to cry 'Quarter.'"

He then relates that they were shut up between decks, all but nine or ten men and boys, who were kept to work the ship, with the thirty Moors left on board by the corsair. "Of the passengers, there were besides myself Italians and Jews, who all equally deplored their hard fate: some blamed the stars, others quarrelled with fortune, others, more piously inclined, vowed vows to the saints on condition of escape. As for my own part, I never thought my curiosity dearbought till then. However, I endeavoured to make the best of a bad market, and encouraged my companions to an entire resignation to the divine will."

A terrible gale of wind overtook them on their voyage, which lasted two days, and separated them from their three companions; but on the third night, when it fell a calm, the Moors, being exhausted, fell asleep, which their deck-comrades perceiving, they found an opportunity for allowing those below to escape into the cook-room, when the arms were suddenly seized, and, the few Moors first aroused being shot down, the vessel was retaken; upon which they bore away for Malta and reached it in safety.

This story of our countryman's capture off here by Algerine pirates towards the end of the seventeenth century induces me to relate the capture of an ancestor of mine in the same century, a clergyman: but he was captured when in sight of Cork harbour, and was not so fortunate as the doctor; for he was carried to Algiers, and remained there some time in slavery: and when ransomed by the merchants of Genoa, he refused to take advantage of his freedom, prefering to remain, that he might contrive to administer the gospel in secret to his fellow-countrymen still in slavery there.

That Algerine pirates even resorted to our own coasts for the capture of Christian slaves does not appear to be generally known or believed as a fact in their history, or as recorded in our own; but this instance is too authentic to be doubted, as it is narrated in the sufferer's own handwriting, and the manuscript is in my possession as an heirloom, the author, my direct ancestor, being a Protestant clergyman, named Devereux Spratt, who was captured when on his passage to England, after the rebellion and the massacre of Protestants in the South of Ireland.

The narrative would be out of place here; so the reader who may feel an interest in it is referred to the Appendix.

The remarkable whiteness of the cliffs of the Kou phonisi renders them a conspicuous feature in this part of the coast of Crete, where otherwise all is dark and iron-bound by grey and almost sterile and inhospitable-looking mountains. The cliffs are not chalk, however, although so white; but their geology is of interest from their being composed of strata of two ages of the marine tertiary period, as well as containing a dyke of trap.

I refer for details to the Geological Appendix; for I am induced to linger on the thought of these old haunts of corsairs still; and I have spoken of Captain Manias, my pilot, as having been one in modern times. My learned predecessor in Cretan research, Mr. Pashley, has spoken highly of his patriotic deeds as a chief, or *capitaine*, of a band of Cretans during the revolution; for Manias was a true patriot, although at times also a pirate, but the latter, it is to be hoped, only from necessity. I will therefore speak only of his brighter deeds; for although we are on the scenes of some of his corsair life, we are also approaching his last resting-place, his grave, as poor Manias died in Her Majesty's service, as my interpreter and guide, a few days only after our first visit to these islands.

I will here relate, then, that on our first coming to the east end of Crete in H.M.S. 'Spitfire,' to commence its survey, and as we were running inside of the Yanisades Islands without any knowledge or even a previous hint of the existence of a danger near them, but were keeping simply a good look-out as usual, and proceeding very slowly, old Manias came aft on the quarter-deck, and quietly asked me if I did not think there might be some danger near. I had heard of none, I said, and hoped there was none. He, however, advised my keeping nearer the Yanisades Islands than the Cretan coast; and then told me of an anchorage in those islands, and a cave in which there was a little spring of water. I thought the advice good, on this display of his local knowledge of the islands, so I followed it, but was surprised at the information coming from him, as I could get it from no one else, nor even from him previously.

This fact, however, revealed to me that he knew perfectly all the dangers thereabouts, and, as I found afterwards by our surveys, that he had thus cautioned me when I was near a very treacherous one that lies about two miles from the land, and which I have named the "Spitfire rock" in consequence; but he evidently did not like to say too much then, lest he should excite a suspicion of his patriotic or piratical cruisings in these waters.

Now Manias was a Sfakiot chieftain; and they have the reputation of having been all more or less pirates as well as patriots in their time, as the older Casiot sailor and the older Castelorizziot resident also know. But their pirate deeds must die in their own breast:

I shall not record them here, nor many other of their deeds nearer home (and less excusable than what they did in concert with their countrymen against the common enemy), which I have heard from their own mouths; but the Cretan lowlanders, both Mahomedan and Christian, know them to their sorrow.

The patriot chieftain Manias shall sleep, therefore, with his piracies unwritten by me. Pashley has recorded his heroism during the revolution, has given his portrait, and thus raised a deep interest in the man as a type of a peculiar people in Crete. But he was a remarkable character, and displayed many noble traits, as does every true hero whom the love of freedom rouses in defence of his country or its cause; and there have been few like Manias among Sfakian worthies of modern times, even according to the account of the Cretans themselves. Manias's manners and character are therefore by no means to be taken as the type of all those hardy mountaineers, as Pashley's narrative rather leads his readers to infer. He was a specimen of lion-hearted patriotism, combined with lamb-like gentleness in all the common intercourse of life: his form and constitution were herculean; but his manner was fascinating, and his voice he could modulate to a tone as soft and persuasive as that of a maiden.

By these qualities and virtues, Manias had gained a high local repute amongst his countrymen, mainly in consequence of his heroism during the futile struggle for independence between 1820 and 1828—a long struggle between the two religions in Crete, that unhappily only ended in desolating the land, filling it with blood and misery, and throwing it back half a century or more. But his kindly speech and manner had so brightened and, indeed, gilded his fame, that he had many friends in every village, and an acquaintance in almost every man he met; for his manner was a true reflex of the bent of his mind and feelings. He was patient and gentle; and his heart was kindly, though stout: a lion or a lamb, he had no intermediate quality.

With feelings of respect, therefore, for his memory, and appreciating his good service to me, I approach his last resting-place, as he died of fever at Hierapytna, after piloting us round to it only a few days previously, and was buried by the side of the church of Agios Georgios (or St. George), which stands at the northern end of that dilapidated and fever-haunted town. He was buried as he had lived during the past five or six weeks with us, viz. in his clothes, and even in his boots—an article that is almost as inseparable from a Cretan peasant's limb as his skin, being seldom removed either for repose or for ablution.

Poor Manias left a widow and two or three children to mourn him, but with some property for their support, both in Sfakia and at Dramia, near Retimo. As I was myself prostrate at the time also with an attack of fever (that enemy to oriental travel and research), I could not follow his remains to their last rest, as I desired; neither would it have been consistent in me to have inscribed upon his tomb, " A Patriot's Grave;" I will therefore simply indite them upon these pages, in respect for his good name and his patriotism. But not a word regarding Grabusa or Grandes Bay shall blot the page of this memento of poor Manias. And do not desire it, good reader, or call it mistaken sympathy; for had you been a Greek, a Cretan Greek, at that same period, you, under the same circumstances (that is, if you had the heart), would not have been less, from the tyranny and misrule that then chafed the patriots' souls into flint and fire, and rubbed out the perception of moral right in its flashings of revenge, for domestic losses not to be repaid, and for mental and bodily sufferings not easily realizable to you.

CHAPTER XXIII.

RETURN TO IERAPETRA—ITS SITUATION AND NATURAL FACILITIES FOR FORMING A GOOD PORT—ITS IMPORTANCE IN EARLY CRETAN TIMES—ITS THREE THEATRES—ITS THREE HARBOURS—AN INSCRIPTION WITH THE NAME OF THE CITY—A LEPERS' VILLAGE—VISIT TO THE VILLAGE—THE NEGLECT OF THE LEPERS BY THE CRETANS—THE CHAPEL OF THE HOLY CROSS UPON A MOUNTAIN—MISDIRECTION OF MIND AND MEANS—CONSTANT RESORT OF THE SICK TO THE SHIPS FOR MEDICAL AID—THEIR WANTS AND WOUNDS ATTENDED TO BY THE DOCTOR—THE GOOD PHYSICIAN'S PLEASURES.

THE route to Ierapetra by the southern coast-road has nothing to attract attention, being tedious and long, as it occupies fully nine hours from Khadra, and lies near the shore during a great part of it—crossing, however, many narrow and uncultivated valleys and ridges, with a shepherd's farm or a water-mill here and there in some lonely but picturesque glen. Numerous ravines intersect the route, across which the road proceeds by a series of ascents and descents, sometimes more troublesome from their number than from their depth and steepness, until the last ridge is gained, which opens to view the low-walled and miserable town of Ierapetra, which I passed, on my entrance to the Sitia peninsula, without describing it.

Ierapetra, or Girapetra as it is also called, is the capital of the eastern peninsula of Crete, is the fourth city in the island, and is governed by a mudir, under the Pasha of Candia. It is situated upon a low part of the shore, near the extremity of a long undulating and slightly inclined plain which borders the south coast at the narrowest part of the island.

The plain thus extending behind the town is not alluvial, but somewhat rocky in parts; it is nevertheless for the most part very fertile, and is covered with a large grove of remarkably fine olive-trees. Just where Ierapetra stands, the plain is somewhat more undulating; and the roots of the lower hills, running through the centre of the isthmus lying behind it, approach so near the shore that a natural ledge of rocks originally jutted out from the undulating ground a little way into the sea, and thus afforded facilities for the construction of a harbour within them. Massive blocks were thrown by the ancients into the sea to form moles from the extremities of these reefs, and thus complete the harbour or harbours that were in part formed by nature.

Consequently, in ancient times, a town of considerable importance, named Hierapytna, arose upon this low part of the coast, although it is an unusual position for an early Greek city, and a weak one for defence, as was shown by its abandonment during the war with the Romans under Metellus, without any

IERAPETRA the anct HIERAPYTNA.

Agos Slavros

J. Schranz del. from a sketch by T.A.B.S.

M.& N. Hanhart imp.

resistance, the defenders having fled on his approach, although their chief had gathered all his strength there.

Hierapytna had apparently two harbours thus formed by nature and art, viz. an inner and outer one, both of which, however, have been destroyed, and are now for the most part filled with sand and débris subsequently thrown in by the sea and by man; and the modern town stands upon part of the outer of these ancient harbours. It is enclosed by a loopholed wall on the land side, which is a Turkish construction, leaving within it the inner port or naumachia thus cut off from the sea, and forming a malignant marsh that annually poisons the poor inhabitants with fever of a very malignant form.

Its inhabitants number about 2000, of whom rather more than half are Turks, and nearly every one of whom have had the fever during the past few years, and are, in consequence, a weakly, cadaverous-looking community, who depend more upon their olive-groves than hard labour.

Its chief trade is in oil, of which it exports 2000 tons in good seasons.

A square fort, that was erected by the Venetians, stands upon the southern basement of the old moles, and mounts a few old guns. It is garrisoned by a company of fifty Turkish troops and artillerymen.

The remains of the ancient city are deserving of a

brief description, as Hierapytna was evidently a fine city in its day, which seems to have been about the time of, or immediately prior to, the conquest of the island by the Roman Metellus; for it contained two theatres and an amphitheatre: one of the former and the latter are still distinguishable.

In the 'Museum of Classical Antiquities,' Mr. Falkener has published extracts from some manuscripts referring to the antiquities of Crete, which he found in the Venetian libraries.

The most important of these was that of Onorio Belli; but the original work, it appears, does not now exist, only some extracts of it, with some brief notices and some plans of the most perfect of the ancient theatres which existed in Crete when he was there. As an eminent classical architect, Mr. Falkener was therefore the more able to appreciate them. I acknowledge the value of this publication, although so fragmentary, and for some time thought it superseded any necessity for my now venturing to write upon Cretan antiquities; but I have been persuaded otherwise, and therefore venture to submit my pages to the public.

I give the following interesting extract from Onorio Belli, in reference to Hierapytna, because it shows the state of its ruins as he found them in 1590, and thus conveys an idea of the beauty and importance of this city when under the Romans. For the plan and

THE REMAINS OF HIERAPYTNA. 257

details of the theatres, made out by this able archæologist, I must refer to Mr. Falkener's work.

"About forty miles west of Cape Salmone, on the south coast, are the remains of the noble city of Hierapytna. The city was formerly called Cyrba, then Pydna, then Camiro, and lastly Hierapytna; the modern name is Girapetra. It appears to have been built in the manner of Alexandria, having opposite to it a small island connected to the city by a mole formed of a wall twenty feet in thickness, and serving as a gabion battery to a beautiful and commodious harbour.

"Hierapytna contained a naumachia, an amphitheatre, two theatres, temples, thermæ, and aqueducts. The modern city was ruined by a dreadful earthquake in 1508, which is described by Girolamo Donato, duke of Candia, the translation of whose letter I will give when I come to speak of the earthquakes which have happened to this island. Since that event the city has been reduced to a small castle, with a hamlet.

"The theatres of Hierapytna are highly remarkable from the peculiarity of their design. The smaller theatre, of which many of the seats remain, measuring two feet in width, was adorned with two orders of columns of the whitest marble, 5 quarters in diameter (17 inches English), of the Ionic order; the capitals and entablatures were of the most excellent workmanship, many of which have been sent to Venice by his Excellency the Proveditor General. The statues (of the scene) were of stucco: these I found entire on excavating a trench along the front; but on endeavouring to remove them, they fell to powder. Most of the columns have been destroyed by fire: those of the lower order were 10 feet high (11 feet 4 inches English). The columns of the upper order were 1 foot in diameter and 9 feet in height. The columns of the portico behind the scene correspond in size to those of the lower order; but they are of granite (pietra dura), like the two columns at Venice. These columns, which are so numerous here and at Gortyna, must have been brought from Egypt; for there is no stone of this description in the island of Candia; indeed the building-stone is very indifferent, being even softer than that of Creazzo and Sorzio. Many of the seats of the theatre remain in place; they measure two Vicentine feet in width.

"Among the ruins of the theatre are some inscriptions, of which, although much mutilated, I send you copies, hoping that you will be able to get them translated for me, and to forward them to me here; for, as you know, I am not sufficiently acquainted with the language to interpret them myself.

"The great theatre was partly excavated out of the mountain. The scene was of marble, relieved in parts with red-marked stone similar to that of Verona. It was most richly decorated with columns, cornices, and other ornaments, now, alas! a heap of ruins. The order was Ionic, which was the favourite order in these parts.

"The capitals are of most beautiful design and wonderful execution, and indeed all the architectural members are carved with the greatest care. Where the Corinthian order is employed, the capitals are far from possessing the beauty of those designed by Palladio, nor are the Doric columns to be compared with those at the Basilica at Vicenza.

"You will pay particular attention to the arrangement of the Scene in these two theatres of Hierapytna, which depart further from the directions of Vitruvius than any other theatres which I have seen, and probably from many that have been seen by others; but the parts behind the scene, including the hospitalia, are generally disposed according to the usual principle. The theatre had at least one row of bronze echeia, the cells for which are very visible, and indeed the best-preserved of any of these theatres. The ignorant inhabitants of the island, who do not know what a theatre was, call these cells ovens.

"The amphitheatre was dug between two little hills or rocks; and in order to complete the oval, six buttresses of solid masonry, without any decoration, were built at each extremity; between these were the stairs."

This amphitheatre I unexpectedly discovered when exploring the site previous to Mr. Falkener's publication of the above extract, no notice having been given of it in Tournefort, or Pashley, or any previous publication; for although Pashley also visited Ierapetra, he left the description of it for a future volume on Crete, of which he hints at the probable publication, or was satisfied with the notice of it by Tournefort, who, however, did not see this amphitheatre. And it is exactly as Belli has described it, viz. placed between two low hills, and, in order to complete the oval, six buttresses of masonry were built at each extremity of the opening separating the ridge, which is not more than fifty or sixty feet above the sea.

Mr. Falkener gives another extract, as a note to the manuscript of Maffei in which this author strongly expresses his difficulty of understanding what Belli meant by his description of the amphitheatre (see Falkener). But Belli's correctness is now verified in a very satisfactory manner by what actually remains.

The masonry of which it was chiefly built was small stones and mortar, but faced apparently in part with thin slabs of white and variegated marble, the fragments and chips of which are now found scattered near; but not a single squared block or stone seat is anywhere seen.

The rising ground in which it was made seems to be an old raised beach indurated into a sort of petrified conglomerate, through which there appears to have previously been an opening or quarry, that invited its selection for the site of an amphitheatre, as offering facilities for its construction.

The large theatre mentioned by Belli I found to be about 154 feet in diameter, as near as I could estimate it. Belli makes it five feet more. It is more conspicuous than the amphitheatre, and was likewise partially dug out of rising ground by the side of a neighbouring watercourse a little to the west of the amphitheatre; it faced the east. Nothing, however, of its ancient beauty can be made out from the mere semicircle of rubble masonry which now remains, or of the elegant portico with its many columns and statues shown by Belli to have existed in front of it, that part being now a corn-field. Thence no doubt came some of the marble statues that found their way to Venice, noticed in another manuscript, published by Mr. Falkener in his vol. ii. part 3; and thence, as we learn from this manuscript, was brought the statue now ornamenting the fountain of St. Salvadore in the town of Candia, figured by Pashley, and which, as I have also noticed above (see p. 44), is regarded with superstitious reverence by the lower classes of the Turkish community there. About midway between the theatre and amphitheatre, there were recently found two sculptured sarcophagi also, which have been removed to the British Museum. (See Chapter XXIV. for the description of them.)

The smaller theatre of Belli I had not originally made out when exploring the site; but when led to look for it by Mr. Falkener's publication of Belli's plan and description, I imagine I was enabled to identify it in a conspicuous mass of masonry standing on the top of a rising ground near the west extremity of the city, since it has some indications of having belonged to a building of a circular form. This ruin faces the north-west, and was not excavated into the rising ground, but entirely built above it. Near it, to the eastward, are some fragments of a handsome portico in white marble that had been recently dug up there,—which supports the idea.

But in none of the three theatres does a single seat now remain, nor are any of the niches that contained the harmonious vases for the transmission of sound, noticed by Belli, and of such interest in connexion with his account of the Cretan theatres, visible or traceable; so great has been the dilapidation of the ruins since the Venetian occupation. These vases were sometimes of earthenware and sometimes of metal, according to the wealth of the locality; and the former seem to have answered the purpose as well as the latter.

The chief part of the city occupied a level and low

THE HARBOURS. 263

plateau between a watercourse opening to the sea near the large theatre and amphitheatre, and another nearly a mile more to the west of it. This intermediate plateau is consequently scattered over with the foundations of several public buildings and habitations, with remains of aqueducts and cisterns; but these deserve no particular notice—except one large building, that lies prostrate with its foundations, but which, from its many compartments, seems to have been a palatial edifice of some importance: it stood near the south-west angle of the city.

The western watercourse is so steep that it was both a natural wall and fosse on that side; but no distinct line of walls or fortifications enclosing the entire city is now recognizable.

According to Belli, there were three harbours, inclusive of a naumachia: the other two, as distinct from the naumachia or inner port, cannot be clearly defined, although some massive foundations of moles or quays are traceable through the modern town, which, as I have before remarked, stands upon the very centre of the main harbour of the old Hierapytnians, and the Venetian castle upon the outer part of it.

In the western mole, which was built very solidly, although of stones and mortar, or rather pozzolana, there are still to be seen five or six perforated blocks, that projected from its sides to receive the ships' cables. These are visible near the south extreme of the modern town-wall, which is for a short distance built upon this mole. Within the town may be seen many fragments of columns both granite and marble (as well as other architectural fragments), that were brought from the old city, the styles and orders of which were chiefly Corinthian or composite, and thus indicate a Roman period.

From a recently repaired house in the town I copied the inscription (No. 21, Plate I., and noticed in the Appendix by the Rev. C. Babington) in which the name of Hierapytna occurs twice. I was informed that the stone upon which it was inscribed had been dug up only a few years since, and then built into the house of its proprietor, a Greek, to repair it after being injured by the recent earthquake of 1856. Earthquakes appear to have been of frequent occurrence in Crete from the earliest times; and in the very severe one of 1856, which was felt throughout the Levant, the inhabitants of Girapetra suffered much from its effects—every mosque, church, or house being more or less split and injured by it, and some destroyed entirely.

I will now dwell a little upon some features of interest in the neighbourhood of the town. The hills directly north of the town, the summits of which overlook both Ierapetra (or Girapetra) and the Mirabella Gulf, have their summit and northern face composed of the older limestone and shales, that form a sort of support for a group of soft brown marls and sands and sandstones, and also for a white tertiary marl and limestone, that repose against the south face of the ridge towards the Ierapetra plain.

These tertiary strata are apparently of two ages, and lie unconformably. They are also both of marine origin, as far as could be ascertained from the fossils present, which are here very scarce.

Upon one of the lower roots of these ridges, and about one mile north of Girapetra, is a little village, nothing striking in itself, but pleasantly situated upon a commanding and airy locality. An oleander-shaded rocky watercourse or torrent-bed passes beside it, in which runs a little rill during a part of the year; and a fine view is obtained from its rather neat-looking whitewashed habitations over the olive-grove extending from it to the town and the Libyan Sea beyond. "The peaceful retreat of the better class of the inhabitants of the fever-haunted and putrid town of Girapetra, no doubt," is probably the conclusion of the reader, or the traveller who chances to see its white buildings from a distance. But is it so? Alas! it is only another community of the polluted, the unclean! —a village of lepers, outcasts from every community. There are nearly one hundred poor wretches who are obliged to live apart from their families and homes while this loathsome disease creeps upon them, and to become dependent upon each other for the daily help they finally need, unaided and uncared for by their brethren of the towns. In this village I found a Cretan Turk located with his leper wife, and he was the only untainted inhabitant in it. He had resided with her for several years without becoming a leper likewise, and consequently had the privilege of free access to his mosque and to the neighbouring cafés. He was our guide through the village, and showed us all its miserable scenes.

Each Eparkhia in Crete has a separate locality for the lepers of its own district; and this is that of Ierapetra and Sitia.

The ignorant Cretans attribute the prevalence of this disease in their island in a great degree to impurity of habits; and hence their extreme disgust at it; but the educated, perhaps more rightly, attribute it to the great consumption of oil with their food: it being the principal produce, and cheap, is in consequence largely used by all, either pure or with the olives which with salt fish, often rancid or of the worst sort, and bad cheese, constitute the principal portion of their diet. They regard it as a very contagious disease; and the touch of a leper would paralyze them with fear. Yet the case of the Turk ought to remove their prejudice. But such prejudices are not easily removed unless the educated and better conditioned set an example to their less favoured brethren.

When I first visited this lepers' village, most of the stronger portion of the population were absent. As it was harvest-time, they were gleaning charity from their native or neighbouring villages and friends; and the remnant, that were left as being past such efforts, were objects that sickened the heart as well as the sight when we beheld their bloated countenances, covered with sores and blotches, and their otherwise disfigured limbs, as they held aloft, to implore for charity, their scaly and fingerless stumps for what were once hands. The unexpected sight of untainted strangers amongst them set all astir who could stir, as it was rare for them to see any but their own companions in affliction within their village, since no native comforter ever comes to them: few would enter it at any price. I was glad, however, that I had induced one intelligent Ierapetran to enter the village with me as an example to the rest; but his moral courage almost gave way when amongst them. For the voices of many failed them as they desired to greet us or implore our aid; and only a hoarse, unearthly sound proceeded from their throats — nay, apparently from their very stomachs. Some of them could not walk, but yet crawled forth from their hovels on the occasion; so grateful to them was the sight and sense of sympathy. What a sight of horror was that assemblage of lepers! it made the flesh to creep, although the heart desired to be strong in comfort and encouragement.

What is the natural conclusion from this sight, but that the Cretan community, exhibiting so little regard for the care and cure of their outcast leper brethren, have made extremely little advance in civilization? This state of social feeling is as much (if not more) a reproach to the whole community as to the local government, in not providing some hospital or some medical care for the purpose of dealing with the disease on its first appearance, nor providing a comfortable retreat for those who are beyond cure and individual care. For one of the first indications of healthy moral feeling in a community, together with the security of private rights and the advance of prosperity, is the provision made for the helpless poor; and whilst leprosy is thus so prevalent in Crete, and so neglected, one of the best signs of a hopeful social condition, and of fitness for self-government, is wanting.

The fine olive-grove growing on the undulating plain which borders the coast in the vicinity of Girapetra is confined on the west by a ridge of rather striking and picturesque appearance, from a number of rugged knolls and detached rocks that bristle on its otherwise smooth or gently swelling surface, and which, from a distance, look like huge blocks and fragments that a giant hand has hurled from the pinnacled summit crowning the ridge.

Upon this summit, at more than 3000 feet above the sea, there is a Greek chapel dedicated to the Holy Cross (Hagios Stavros), which having been recently restored and whitewashed, shines against the dark peaks of the Lasethe range bounding the view above and behind it, as a bright star resting upon the mount, and as if intentionally placed by the Cretan Christians as significant of the rising cross, thus elevated conspicuously over the recently fallen minarets of the towns.

But what an anomaly and inconsistency with the true spirit of their faith is found in close proximity to this elevated building erected to adore the symbol of Christianity! Upon this lofty hill the Holy Standard is set on high, and the prayer of the Cretan Christian thence ascends towards a loftier throne; but a smaller hill is near it—in sight in fact —crowned with a community of diseased, neglected outcasts of humanity, whose voice, too, must often be raised to the same throne, but in bitter suffering from the neglect experienced by them in their helpless condition. And does not that cry ascend also, good Cretans? and shall it not be heard against you? Your thoughts are turned hopefully to a coming struggle, and your purse devoted to the accumulation of arms and gunpowder, clandestinely bought under the disguised name of "black rice," in anticipation of a strife that, if begun, will again desolate your land with fire and sword, blood and misery. Let that "rice" damp and rot in its hiding-places, rather than be used for the purpose for which it was supplied by false friends, for their individual advantage, not yours. Rather, if you elevate the cross, carry out its principles towards your own co-religionists, who, through your neglect, are allowed to live in lingering misery of mind and body as outcasts, purely from the want of a lepers' hospital for their early cure or later relief.

The Turkish Government, I have been informed, do prevent them from starving, by allowing one oke of bread per day to each leper; and thus, in the eyes of most, a large part of its duty towards them is fulfilled—that is, if they really do receive it. But the want of care for their better tendance and cure, the want of sympathy for the 800 or 1000 suspected or confirmed lepers that are made outcasts from their villages and families the moment the plague-spot is declared to be upon them, is a reproach to the whole community of Cretans.

When employed upon the surveys of the eastern parts of Crete, previous to the Crimean war, several who suspected themselves lepers came to the ship for medical advice, amongst many others afflicted with divers diseases who daily journeyed to her from all districts, all of whom were most patiently and charitably attended to by Dr. Smart, the surgeon, in the first instance, and afterwards by his successor, Dr. Willcox, at the cost of much labour and time on their part, extra to their duties; and it was gratifying to all of us who could only sympathize, and not administer, to see the wants of the halt and sick so humanely attended to—often after long journeys from distant parts of the island to us in the hope of some relief, and often after long suffering from neglect or the injudicious treatment of ignorant itinerant empirics.

Thus they came to us at all times and hours, and we received them, Dr. Smart even establishing a sort of hospital in an adjacent hut whilst we were anchored in Grandes Bay for the shelter and convenience the bay afforded us during the progress of the survey of the eastern coast; and there he successfully performed the amputation of an arm for an adult female peasant living within the Sitia province—an event that caused considerable sensation in the island. I here, therefore, thankfully and with most pleasurable satisfaction record this devotion of time and skill to so good, so charitable a cause on the part of Dr. Smart and Dr. Willcox, the latter of whom, having continued to serve under me during the subsequent years, has enlarged my obligations by continuing to give his skill and time in some other places, where relief could not otherwise have been obtained.

There is, perhaps, no act of charity so comforting as that of giving relief to the sick in the way of medical or surgical treatment; and the gratification that must arise from every act of such devotion of talent and skill is therefore to be envied. There can be no higher pleasure than the recollection of such acts; and in few places was there so large a field for them as in Crete when we began our survey of it; and as it can be enjoyed only by those who possess that skill, their privilege is therefore great who possess and in philanthropy and charity use it. The professional pride, too, which attaches to the possession of a diploma will, no doubt, stimulate many to its exercise whenever opportunity offers or helpless importunity solicits, and they know that they alone can do what is required.

Dr. Smart's attention to the lepers that came to him led to a closer study of their disease; and many there were who, suspecting themselves possessing the foul spot, with fear and trembling came and exhibited the blotch or sore in secret, but returned to their homes new creatures in mental feelings on receiving the assurance that their fears were groundless, that they were clean. And it led to his writing an able and interesting paper, which appeared in the 'Medical Times,' upon this disease.

In 1853 my late friend Dr. Hjorth, a son of a Dane, and the head of the Health Department in Crete, was induced also to write a small pamphlet on the sanitary condition of Crete. He there points out the hopeful prospect of greatly reducing, if not entirely eradicating as in other civilized countries, the malady which is so prevalent in that country as to render outcast nearly 1000 of its inhabitants.

And he feelingly remarks, " Whoever walks out of the gate of one of the large towns, especially if it be on a Saturday, is distressed by the hideous sight of many of these unhappy beings sitting by the roadside imploring charity. It is impossible to behold with indifference the condition of these unfortunate people, or to meditate that as soon as they are branded with the name of leper they are driven away from parents, children, relatives, and friends, like criminals, deprived of the power of earning their livelihood in an honest manner by labour, and reduced to the degrading state of begging."

Dr. Hjorth suggests a hospital exclusively for the lepers, and appeals to the Turkish government. But if the inhabitants themselves do not feel and move for their suffering brethren, what can be expected in this way from the very authorities they themselves oppose in other acts of improvement.

CHAPTER XXIV.

DISCOVERY OF TWO SARCOPHAGI—THEIR PURCHASE AND REMOVAL TO THE BRITISH MUSEUM—A GHOST STORY—DESCRIPTION OF THE LARGER SARCOPHAGUS—THE SITUATION IN WHICH THE SARCOPHAGI WERE FOUND, NOT IN SITU—CONJECTURES UPON THEIR ORIGIN AND ORIGINAL SITES.

IT having come to my knowledge that two sculptured sarcophagi had been recently found near the Theatre at Ierapetra, the trustees of the British Museum, on being informed of it by me, were induced to become the purchasers of them from the Greek family in whose property they were found. The purchase having been effected, their removal was effected also by the officers and crew of H.M.S. 'Medina,' during the latter part of December 1860 and the beginning of January 1861, but with considerable labour and difficulty, in consequence of the exposed position of the anchorage of Ierapetra at that season, and the great weight and the situation of the tombs.

As the largest of these tombs weighed nearly seven tons, a very substantial pier had to be made upon this open sandy coast before it could be embarked; and as it had to be removed some distance, over heavy ground or sand, to the most sheltered part of the bay, the operation was both slow and tedious. This duty, however, was performed with great zeal by the shore party under the direction of Messrs. Wilkinson and Drew, and its shipment by Mr. Stokes, master, aided by our chief boatswain's mate and perfect seaman John Douglas: and as the larger tomb was an interesting as well as a fine specimen of art, although much mutilated and cracked, great care was taken to preserve it, as far as possible, from further injury during its removal; and to prevent it being injured wantonly or by local enemies (there being a party there who were opposed to our removal of the relic), Mr. Wilkinson thought it advisable to sleep inside the tomb until it had arrived within the walls of the town: yet it did not wholly escape mischief; for some wanton hand destroyed what remained of the face of Hector.

The sarcophagus having thus been brought to within a few yards of the land gate of Ierapetra, upon the top of which a Turkish sentry nightly walked his solitary watches, when from time to time he called the hours, with his face towards his post and therefore turned away from the town, his eyes looked directly down upon these tombs of the dead, which, after many centuries of repose, were now being transported from their hallowed resting-place by the rude hand of strangers.

It was a subject for reflection to a meditative mind,

even though he were but a Turkish sentinel. The midnight hour, too, favoured the mind's play in phantom spectres and ghosts, more especially on that night, as the moon's light was dimmed by heavy clouds that hung over the adjacent mountains, and there was lightning and thunder, and a storm of wind now and then swept over the town. Whether our sentinel was meditative, or whether he had previously any apprehension of the ghosts of the men whose tombs were being so ruthlessly removed by the hands of infidels, I cannot tell; but I can aver that as he thus had his eyes upon the two marble sarcophagi, and had commenced his occasional call of "All's well," to quiet the fears and alarms of the slumbering natives within, those eyes were suddenly fixed, as they beheld a tall figure, enshrined in a windingsheet, and white as a spectre, suddenly rise out of one of the tombs. The words of the affrighted Turk stuck in his throat before they were half uttered, as if grasped by a vice; and then, as if struck by an unseen hand, he as suddenly dropped down from his post behind the thick screen of walls and gates of the city; and neither he nor any other sentry of that guard ever ventured to mount to the summit of that gateway again whilst the tombs were there, nor was the gate opened by the serjeant of the guard until broad daylight had appeared to ensure them from another vision of the spectre, the ghost of the tomb.

SCULPTURE ON THE SARCOPHAGUS. 277

The account of that sight has no doubt since been often repeated in the barrack by the serjeant and his party on guard during that eventful night. Many a tale of terror and legend, regarding ghosts and spectres, has arisen from a circumstance or circumstances as explicable and simple, if explanation had been sought for at the time; and that the ghost of the hero who was buried in the tomb some twenty centuries before had not appeared to the sentry on that night it would probably be as hard to convince them, or their many subsequent hearers at their distant homes, as to disabuse people of their belief in the stories told of ghosts in some benighted parts of our own land.

The larger tomb is very interesting, as containing a representation of some of the more striking events connected with the life of Achilles, the hero of the siege of Troy. It was sculptured on all four sides; but three only seem to have been finished. Hence it appears to have been originally intended to stand close to some temple or sacred way.

The style of art is undoubtedly very good; and as we know so little of the early Cretan sculpture, beyond its having been in high repute, and having had an early school, whence came several good masters, without going back to the father of Cretan and of Greek sculpture, Dædalus himself, we may be justified in supposing this to have been the work of one of its best masters,—leaving it to the modern masters of the art to determine the exact date, and to point out its beauties and defects, when hereafter exposed to public view at the British Museum. The fine grouping of the figures of the front piece, as well as the figures on the end faces, cannot fail to strike even an ordinary eye, as also the exquisite finish of the deeply chiselled eggwork above, and chaste interlaced or plaited moulding which ornamented the lower part of this fine relic (that resembles the carving upon the beautiful Ionic temple of Minerva Polias, in the Acropolis at Athens), and therefore to awaken deeper regret that the features of all the figures upon it were irreparably mutilated previously to its discovery.

The back field represents the triumph of Achilles over the body of Hector, which he is dragging by the heels behind his chariot before Troy. This, however, is only a rough, unfinished representation, but gave the key to the recognition of the other sculptured faces in all their details.

The front of the sarcophagus has a representation of the discovery of Achilles at the court of Lycomedes of Scyros, the two prominent figures in the group being Achilles and Deidamia, who are seated in chairs. It is a finely executed group, containing, with heralds and attendants, some dozen figures, as will be seen by the view here given.

The two ends have more exclusive reference to

ACHILLES AT THE COURT OF LYCOMEDES.

Achilles. One depicts him in his youth, under the instruction of the wise centaur Chiron, who taught him the gymnastic exercises and music, with his other accomplishments; here, therefore, he is in the act of going through some of his athletic attitudes; the other represents him when in the zenith of his manhood and power, but when under humiliation and grief at the death of his friend Patroclus, to whom also he had lent his armour,—a fit subject and circumstance to herald his final triumph. Thetis, or Iris, then appears to console him in his grief, and promises to provide him with new armour to avenge the death of his friend, some parts of which she seems to be here actually presenting to him; whilst Hephæstus or Vulcan himself is behind her, in intent labour upon a new shield for his future use and glory. Of this, from its better state of preservation and its interesting character, I give a sketch also.

The interest naturally attaching to this fine relic awakens a desire to know whence it originally came, and for whom it was intended, since it was evidently not *in situ* where found at Ierapetra; and therefore a record here of its exact position when found is perhaps desirable, to prevent the rise and spread of false conjectures upon it.

During some excavations made by one Kluveraki, an independent Greek of Ierapetra, between the theatre and amphitheatre at the east end of the city,

ACHILLES, THETIS, AND VULCAN.

a sunken chamber was struck upon, about 11 feet square, and from 6 to 8 feet below the soil. The chamber was without vaulting or covering of masonry, and was entirely filled with rubbish and earth, on clearing away which the two marble sarcophagi were found, as represented below, with their lids removed and broken. But as poor Kluveraki soon after was taken ill and died, and local superstition attributed it to the supernatural spirit he had disturbed, the sarcophagi were neglected by the family, and would have become in a few years worthless from mischief and exposure.

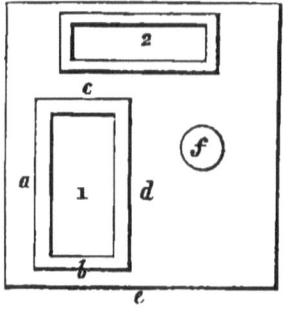

a. Triumph of Achilles over Hector.
b. Lamentation of Achilles at the death of Patrocles.
c. Instruction of Achilles by Chiron.
d. Achilles at the court of Lycomedes.
e. Old wall.
f. Composite capital.

Although both sarcophagi are in white Parian marble, the smaller sarcophagus, No. 2, found with it, is less ancient, and of very inferior art, representing festoons and heads only: it was no doubt intended for the wife of the individual who had then appropriated the large sarcophagus for his own body, and had evidently removed it into this sunken chamber from some other, perhaps distant locality.

The walls of the chamber were of small stones and mortar, or pozzolana, from their solidity; and the front wall (e) seemed, from its depth and durability, to have been a part of the old town-wall that faced the bay on this side.

The larger tomb also showed that it had been broken into before its removal here, by a hole existing in its north face (c), which, from the position of the small sarcophagus so close against it as we found it to be (in fact, touching in some parts), could not have been made after the two were placed in this chamber. The flooring of the chamber was found to be formed of thin, flat stones, indiscriminately mixed with Roman tiles, showing likewise the late time at which they were placed in this vault.

Moreover the tomb itself, from the better preservation of the lower part of it, and the worn condition of the upper, shows that it originally stood for a long time in some exposed position, and that this lower part must have been preserved by the accumulation of the soil around it to that height previously to its removal to the chamber in which it was recently found.

Whence did it originally come? is probably the question of the inquisitive student as he views this fine tomb, or of the reader as he peruses these crude remarks upon the interesting relic and beautiful work of art.

Heroes and monarchs alone were worthy of such a tomb and monument, wherever it stood originally, whether Hierapytna or elsewhere. But Hierapytna was never a city of such celebrity as to possess either, so far as we know of Cretan history.

To whom, of all the Cretans, was such a monument so appropriate as to the hero king Idomeneus himself, one of the suitors of Helen, and the companion of Achilles in the great war, having led the eighty Cretan ships which this then flourishing island sent to that war? and he is said, too, to have returned in safety to Crete, with his followers, and to have had his tomb or monument at Gnossus, and also to have been afterwards worshipped there as a god. Hero-worship is still practised at the same locality, as I have before shown in the Pasha's Tomb outside the fortifications of Candia; and the Roman statue at the Venetian fountain of St. Salvador, within the town of Candia, is another instance of such worship, even in the present time: it is curious that this statue actually came from Ierapetra, as we learn from the manuscript of Belli, to embellish the Venetian fountain in which it is built. May we not, then, suppose the converse to have taken place with respect to the sarcophagus in question? namely that it came from the old capital, Gnossus, at some very late period of its decline, to become the tomb of a Hierapytnian of the late Roman time (which it evidently was, from the position in which it was found, and from the character of the sunken chamber or walled sepulchre it was buried in)? And as a small composite capital was likewise found with it in this chamber, all the facts show that it was deposited here at some late period.

I believe, moreover, that the smaller sarcophagus had a previous owner and occupant elsewhere. May it not, then, have been the very tomb or monument to Idomeneus which some late authors have alluded to as having existed at Gnossus, but which must have been a restoration after the original had fallen to ruin, and at a time when art and taste in Greece and Crete were such as to render an illustration of the prominent features of the siege of Troy the natural and appropriate embellishment upon it?

Now, the popular admiration of the Homeric poem was perhaps at no time greater than in the century subsequent to the great sculptor Phidias, when Alexander gave popularity to the incidents recorded in it, by his well-known admiration of the Homeric record, and his own heroic deeds in the same land; and the style of art, the finish of the detail of the sculpture, and its ornament of egg-work and plaited moulding seem to correspond best with the works of that time rather than a later.

Although Crete was a school of the art from the earliest period, and sent many masters of renown into Greece, and although its sculpture has been highly spoken of by ancient authors, no actual monument has been mentioned as of especial note for its merit as a specimen of art,—this tomb of Idomeneus being merely noticed, by late authors only (Diodorus Siculus and others), as having existed and been worshipped at Gnossus; yet, having been so noticed, and as it was dedicated to Crete's great Trojan hero, it must have been a monument worthy of the man and of the art that flourished within the island.

Some of the early coins of Crete undoubtedly show very high art in design and taste, but fail in completeness of form as medals, from this having been evidently there considered secondary to the former; and although illustrations of the 'Iliad' upon sarcophagi became common in the later period of the Roman empire, yet the style of art of this sarcophagus must fix its date at a much earlier period, probably about that of Alexander or not long after; and thus it seems probable that this may have been the very monument or tomb noticed by Diodorus at Gnossus to its Trojan hero Idomeneus, since no other Cretan was so worthy of so fine a work.

Although there were some in the town of Ierapetra who were covertly opposing my efforts to secure these relics for our national Museum, probably from having been influenced in favour of some other nation, yet the greater portion of the population, Greek as well as Turk, were entirely in my favour, and took much interest in the mode of removal of them from their sunken chambers to the ship; and I was particularly indebted to the father of our respected Vice-Consul at Candia, Signor Colocherino, for his influence on the occasion—a loyal Ionian who highly appreciated the British protectorate, and took every opportunity of showing that he did so; and even the old Cadi of Ierapetra joined in the general anxiety for our success; and as, from the season of the year, the operation was attended with many difficulties, he came to help, and encourage the natives to assist us, during the embarkation.

I must also relate a circumstance indicative of the good feeling of the chief members of the Greek community of Ierapetra on another occasion, when the ship was seen to be in some difficulty and danger. A gale of wind having set in from the south-east before I could embark men enough from the shore party to weigh my anchor, having only a badly constructed windlass, I was obliged to hastily slip my cable; but in turning ahead, the floats of the starboard paddle-wheel drew the bight of the buoy-rope into the wheel, and rolled up a turn or two of the cable round it before we were made aware of the fact; and whilst we were thus helplessly lying in the trough of the sea with head paying off towards the shore during the long minutes required to clear it, the good people of Ierapetra happened to be coming out of church from their morning's service (for it was a Sunday), and saw that we were in some difficulty, apparently drifting towards the surf. All instantly ran back to the church to desire the priest to join with them in a prayer for the safety of the captain and crew; but before the prayer was concluded we had happily freed ourselves from the chain-cable without any damage, although the position was for a few minutes very awkward, and the risk of losing one of our paddle wheels seemed imminent, involving the danger of having to ride out the gale too near the shore, with only one paddle wheel to help us in case of need. I relate this display of good feeling by our Ierapetra friends with much gratification and grateful recollection.

289

CHAPTER XXV.

THE VILLAGE OF ANATOLI—VALLEY OF MYRTO—VILLAGE OF MALIA WITHIN IT—TOURNEFORT'S "SIMPLING" JOURNEY TO IT— ROUTE FROM GIRAPETRA TO ARVI—A GIANT'S TOMB—PASHLEY'S LEARNED DESCRIPTION OF THE CONFLICT OF OTOS AND EPHIALTES, SONS OF A GIANT, AGAINST THE GOD ARES— PROTRUSION OF PORPHYRITIC TRAP—SITE OF THE TEMPLE OF JUPITER ARBIUS—CLEFT MOUNTAIN OVER IT—THE PROBABLE ORIGIN OF THE TEMPLE AT ITS BASE—GEOLOGICAL NOTICE OF THE ADJACENT COAST DEPOSITS—KERATON ROCK AND BAY— VAST NUMBER OF OLIVE-TREES—ROUTE TO VIANO—VIANO THE ANCIENT BIENNUS—ROUTE TOWARDS THE MESSARA—ROMAN AQUEDUCT—A FIGHTING TURK—TCHIFOOT KASTELLI.

I RETURN now to the Chapel of the Holy Cross, noticed in the last chapter, and proceed with my description to the westward.

Below it, upon the south slope of the mountain, is the village of Anatoli, nestled between two of the knolls I have spoken of upon its surface, and surrounded by well-wooded and fertile terraces and fields. It was thought, from the information of some natives, that here were some Hellenic ruins, and so, probably, the site of an ancient city; but when examined by Lieut. Mansell, they proved to be simply those of a Genoese or Venetian tower, or pyrgo, made strong as

VOL. I.   U

a secure residence for the proprietor of the village or governor of the district. Nor did the coins found there by the villagers indicate anything earlier than these times; but a small bronze figure of an athlete was purchased from the priest of the village, and probably came originally from Hierapytna. It is no doubt a representation of some good work in marble, and is not unlike a torso that I presented to the British Museum, that came from that city.

The western face of the Anatoli ridge descends to the deep valley of Myrto, which penetrates into the heart of the Lasethe Mountains. The river Myrto, flowing down it, is the boundary between the Eparkhia of Sitia and Rhizo; and its waters turn two or three mills, near the sea, where the Vasiliko Dromo or main coast-road from Girapetra to Candia crosses it.

The Myrto valley has two or three villages in its upper part, the largest of which is Malia, containing upwards of two hundred families, and situated on the slopes of a well-wooded and wild basin of abrupt hills. A mountain-source, of some size and beauty, issues from an aperture near the village of Kalomafka.

Tournefort spent three days in exploring this valley on a botanical excursion from Girapetra, and, passing Kalomafki and Anatoli, he came to Malia, and thence on to the upper regions of the Lasethe. Thus " simpling " along the border of the first snows, that then rested (June 7th, 1700) upon the summit and sides of this mountain—a margin of snow which, according to my observations, is at that time of the year about 6500 feet above the sea—he says that he there " met with the ilex, oaks, maples (*Acer Cretica*) with leaves slashed in three points." He says also, "Nothing is more surprising than a sort of plane-tree (*Prunus Creticus*) with which all these rocks are embellished, and which flourishes in proportion to the melting of the snow: its stems are not more than half a foot in height; the branches are very bushy, and loaded with flowers of a flesh-colour; it grows hardly bigger than a white gooseberry."

The celebrated botanist and traveller also makes it appear that the wild olive-tree, which is found with the above shrubs, is indigenous to these mountains, by the following remark:—" If Hercules the Cretan had been informed that these trees grew in Crete, he would not have given himself the trouble of going amongst the hyperboreans to bring them into Greece," quoting Pausanias for the statement.

The road from Girapetra to Arbi or Arvi has been already described by Pashley, whose ground I am now again beginning to tread upon; so that in my brief description of the island as a sequel to his learned work, I shall not prevent my reader from fully appreciating the interest of the story with which his description of this route is garnished in a learned dissertation upon the traditional grave of a twice-forty-feet giant (!) that was shown him near Sikologo, a village situate four or five miles from the mouth of the Myrto valley, and the classical learning connected with the marvellous mythological tale of the contest between the sons of the giant (Otos and Ephialtes) and the god Ares; for the learned traveller supposes this story to have had its origin at this locality, from the present tradition regarding this giant's tomb—this *saranda pikes*, or forty pikes of man; and he shows that it was near the Cretan town of Biennus, whose position he also determined by finding that the principal village or town situated over this part of the coast still bears the name of Biano or Viano. I refer, therefore, to his erudite work, vol. i. pp. 279–283.

Pashley, however, has only partially touched upon the features he met with in the way; so from the mouth of the Myrto, and along the sea-coast, I will take up the physical features there developed as an additional subject of meditation for the reader whilst he is wandering towards Arvi in imagination, or the traveller as he passes along the road leading over the rocky steeps and myrtled vales that intervene; for here especially this beautiful shrub flourishes in profuse luxuriance wherever there is water to counteract the drought of the sunny southern aspect, mingled with the oleander, arbute, mastic, and juniper, affording sometimes a refreshing shade, and at others sending forth a delicious fragrance, as the traveller brushes through them and startles at the same time a homely blackbird from the thicket, to recall, by its well-known *twit-twit-tweet* when so disturbed, the land of his home more vividly to his memory.

This part of the topography of the interior was completed by my late coadjutor Lieut. (now Commander) Mansell, during the progress of the examination of and soundings off the coast; but he was not more fortunate than Mr. Pashley in the discovery of any ancient city of importance between Girapetra and Arvi.

The coast, after passing the valley of Myrto, is marked by high white cliffs of tertiary marls and gypsum, the strata of which are much displaced by a mass of porphyritic trap that has risen through them, and which has also much shattered or split the masses of grey hippurite limestone that were also uplifted by it, and upon the flanks of which the tertiary strata reposed.

To the west of this disturbance is a small narrow valley, and a plain that extends to the sea from the foot of a steep and bare rock, that is singularly rent from summit to base by a yawning fissure, nearly 1000 feet high, and from the bottom of which issues a gurgling stream that cascades from an upland plain close above it; but its waters are absorbed by the thirsty little plain through which it then descends to the coast at Arvi, long before it reaches the sea.

Near the mouth of this valley is a small modern chapel, which seems to stand upon the site of an ancient temple, from some relics that have been found there; and there is some appearance of a small town having also occupied the site. By the name it now bears of Arvi, Pashley identified it as the site of the temple of Jupiter Arbius, which name, according to Cramer, was also applied to a mountain of Crete ("Arbius, a mountain where Jupiter was worshipped under that name," Cramer, vol. iii. p. 392). It was here, as Pashley has shown, that the elaborately sculptured sarcophagus presented by Admiral Sir P. Malcolm to the Cambridge Museum, and figured in the first volume of Pashley's work, was found; it represents the triumph of Dionysius: but as a work of art it is greatly inferior to that from Hierapytna, now in the British Museum, and descends, moreover, from a much later period.

The annexed view of the valley of Arvi and the cleft mountain above it, from near the site of the temple, is striking as a picture, and the phenomenon interesting, so proximate to the comparatively recent volcanic outpouring before noticed, to which doubtless the remarkable rent in the mountain here shown in part owes its origin, as well as two or three smaller rents in its vicinity, each of which also gives outlet to two or three streams from small upland basins above, that, without these rents for the es-

CLEFT MOUNTAIN. 295

cape of their waters, would be lakes instead of fertile plains.

CLEFT MOUNTAIN OF ARVI, THE ANCIENT ARBIUS.

In this remarkable feature, we probably see the reason for the erection of a temple to the God of Thunder at this locality, under the name of Jupiter Arbius. To whom but the God of Thunder could a temple be so appropriately dedicated when associated with such an apparent fracture from some great volcanic movement, and so proximate also to a protrusion of igneous matter, that showed its comparatively recent origin by the disturbance of the strata it burst through, and thus naturally connected it in the minds of its early people with earthquakes, and the terrors of the thunderings and of the lightning's flash, occasionally sent forth by Jupiter himself to indicate his anger or his power.

I have frequently observed in the Levant that many of the Greek mythological traditions which are associated with Vulcan or Jupiter are remarkable for their connexion with apparent volcanic phenomena, or with rocks of volcanic origin, and thus display an early knowledge of the localities which have been in bygone times the foci of great or small igneous movements or eruptions, as submarine or suboreal uprisings or outpourings. I need only refer to Lemnos (fabled to be the forge of Vulcan) and its entirely volcanic origin; and here at Arvi is another instance. It follows then, either that the early Greeks, whether Pelasgians or others, were eye-witnesses of some of those eruptions, so as to hand down the traditions, or that, in a limited sense, they were geologists.

Pashley notices the great abundance of fossil shells in the cliffs near Arvi. These I found to be chiefly those of living Pectunculi, and to be in a remnant of a very modern tertiary deposit—most probably post-pliocene, as it is only about forty feet above the present sea—which must have been about the depth in fathoms it was deposited in.

At two miles west of Arvi there rises a remarkable rock, called Keraton, which is surrounded by a middle-age or Venetian fortress; but there is a tradition of its having been an Hellenic site also, vestiges of which are said to be found under the west side of the horn-shaped rock when cultivating its terraced side there, the ruins being now covered by the soil.

Dr. Cramer, in his most valuable work, suggests that " Castel Keraton possibly represents the town of the Ceraitæ, mentioned by Polybius as being allied with Lyctus;" and although Pashley treats this with contempt, I am strongly of the same opinion as the learned Doctor. The singular horn-like form of this peak, which is just 2000 feet above the sea, and only about a mile from it, perhaps suggested the appellation.

A fine open bay lies under the Keraton to the west, and a plain covered with young olives, through which flows a stream that descends from a small cliff or gorge like that of Arvi, being the outlet of the waters issuing from the enchanted little mountain retreat of Viano, the most secluded and charming upland basin in Crete, the name of which suggested its identity with the ancient Biennos, both to Dr. Cramer and to Pashley; and this seems confirmed by the position given to it in the 'Stadiasmus,' in which it is placed midway between Hierapytna and Lebena the southern port of Gortyna, although not lying upon the coast.

I anchored in Keraton Bay in the 'Medina,' not far from the mouth of the Anapodhari, the largest river in Crete, but which in the summer season is reduced to a mere rivulet, that meanders through a wide pebbly bed and is finally lost in the sandy beach at its outlet to the sea, very much like what the famed Scamander of the Troad is at this same season; but in winter, when the rains fall heavily upon the mountains, it is swollen to a wide and impassable torrent, and would then likewise justify all the apparently exaggerated description given of the whirling currents and deep pools of the Scamander by Homer. The main road from Ierapetra to Candia crosses it, by a bridge of three arches, at about five miles from the sea; and from its mouth to the bridge there is no road by the side of its course, as it traverses a narrow impassable rent or gorge for some distance, whence it issues at about two miles from the sea.

Two miles west of the Anapothari (or Anapodhari), is another mountain rivulet issuing through a rocky gorge; but it has its rise in the mountains adjacent, not more than five miles from its outlet: it is called the Sudsuro, and has been confounded with the Anapothari by Pashley and previous travellers through being a stronger stream at its mouth than the latter, and more spoken of by the natives in consequence. I shall refer to it more fully after a trip to Viano and to the valley of the Messara.

To get to Viano I was obliged to send there for mules; for not an inhabitant but shepherds dwells within two or three miles of the sea along the whole coast between the valley of Myrto and Kaloi Limenes (vulgarly called Kalos Limiones), and not a boat is to be found upon it either. The heat of the climate of the south coast, and the greater insalubrity of its valleys in consequence, has driven its scanty population to the upland districts, one or two hours' distance from the shore and its malarious plains.

Being provided with horses sent to me from Viano, I started for it on a July day. The road began to ascend, through a thicket of wild shrubs, from the western point of Keraton Bay. These trees were chiefly a species of stunted, bushy cypresses, mingled with the karoub and wild olive. I ask my guide why the latter are not cultivated; he answers, " We have enough to attend to already," and states that in Keraton Bay alone there are between 50,000 and 60,000 olive-trees.

Halfway up the hill we pass by a ruined metoki, with a water-mill turned by a rapid rill which rushes down the steep; here the olive-trees have been carefully cleared of their companions, and brought into bearing by pruning, grafting, and cultivation. The shade of the grove was a grateful shelter from a July sun; the myrtle, too, gave both freshness and fragrance to the scene. In an hour we reach a cleft in the mountain, like that of Arvi, by which the rivulet from the Viano plain escapes. As we near it, rock-pigeons dart upwards from the gorge in flocks. The same occurred at the gorge of Arvi when we were there, where they are so numerous that the natives, who are keen connoisseurs of pure water, refused to drink it near the gorge, on account of the impurity their droppings are supposed to impart to the rivulet, although the water rushes so copiously and is as clear as crystal. What would a Cretan say to a drop of the Thames?

We are accompanied in our ascent by a Greek peasant of Khadra driving his three donkeys, each of which is laden with sacks of chopped straw from his *halone* (threshing-floor) near the mouth of the Anapothari, to which he makes three trips a day in this broiling sun; but as it is his winter provender for his cattle, he cheerfully toils backwards and forwards with his poor load, enlivening the journey with a nasal song in the intervals between smoking his pipe.

The little upland plain of Khadra suddenly comes into view upon reaching the col by which it is entered; but no clear ground appears there, it being entirely covered with olives. The village, too, is close on our left, with others before us. At the col the road crosses the stream, just above the gorge, which now is under us; for its summit is just at the outlet of the Khadra valley, from the edge of which the lively streamlet leaps into the abyss-like cleft in the rock below, and murmurs at its fall, sending up a misty spray from the bottom.

Skirting the village of Apostoliano, at the junction of the two plains, we next enter the plain of Biano, or Viano, nestled in an almost complete circle of mountains. This plain is only in part covered with olive-trees. Deep ditches drain its centre of the water that would otherwise lodge there, and thus there are some fields of corn where otherwise it would be a swamp. Viano itself rises in part above the plain, on either side of a rocky ravine and pointed ridge, under which descends a labyrinth of little enclosures as gardens, each of which is thickly overgrown with fruit-trees, and they are rendered thus fertile by a considerable rill that passes through the village.

I pitch my tent in one of them. The aga being absent, his secretary presses me to enter the Strangers' House. (The reader already knows my reason for avoiding all such hospitable overtures when it can be done without offence, and when the weather will admit of tenting in the open air.) The Demarkh also assists to render my location agreeable, and I am promised by him better mules on the morrow for my trip into the Messara.

Viano is the capital of the Eparkhia of Rhizo (or Arkadia, as it was formerly called), a district that extends between the Myrto and Anapothari rivers to the edge of the hills which confine the Pediada. It was the association of the name of Arkadia with this part which no doubt induced Pashley to place Arkadia on the eastern flank of the Lasethe; and hence he tries to make the ruins near Kritza, the undoubted Olus, to agree with the distance of thirty miles, given in the Peutinger Table, between Biennos and Arkadia, by supposing it to have been measured as a crow's flight across the lofty mountains which intervene—a mode of measurement, I need hardly add, that cannot be at all consistent when the only practicable route is by a great circuit round the base of the mountains, and far exceeds that distance, as he is obliged to admit.

But as Pashley had not proved that Biennos was really at Viano by any existing ancient vestiges, I was very diligent to inquire for such, as I had heard from Mansell that some existed upon the spur over the Apano Viano; and soon after daylight I ascended to the top of the hill, and, in the ascent, I passed by the ruin of a goodly habitation of some wealthy Venetian, with its four or five front windows of the upper floor still remaining.

The top of the hill over the village, although small, I found to contain some vestiges of ancient terraces, as well as foundations of walls of an early date, between Cyclopean and Hellenic, which, with some tombs and cisterns also seen upon it, left no doubt of the existence of the acropolis of a small town earlier than the middle-age or Venetian period, and that this must have been the Biennos (or Bienna) of the olden times; otherwise there might be a doubt as to whether this ancient town was not more properly identified at Castel Keraton, so proximate to it.

Viano contains about three hundred houses, nearly equally divided between Mahomedans and Christians, the latter having the majority; and it is a most delightful mountain retreat for one desirous of escaping from the busy scenes of the lower world or the insalubrity of the lower plains, above which it is elevated some 1800 feet, being nearly on a level with the crest of Keraton castle and peak. At this elevation the olive nevertheless flourishes here, although, in the upland of the Sitia, at the same elevation it is not seen. The reason evidently is, that, in addition to a south aspect, the high peaks directly over it on the north shelter it from the cold blasts from that quarter.

The Demarkh of the village fulfils his promise: three fine mules are ready for my further journey by the time I return from the examination of the ruins above the village; and he sends his son also to be my guide, to the great disappointment of a young Turk whom the Muduri's representative and secretary wished to send with me instead.

Pashley descended to the Messara by the western road from Viano, and crossed the Anapothari by the three-arched bridge over it. I took one to the northwest, leading over a gap in the mountains there; but the shortest road to Candia is by another and higher pass due north of Viano, which is more direct, and leads through the villages of Empero and Nepedeto, and from the latter across the Pediada plain. My route descended direct into the deep valley of Martha, on the other side of the mountains over Viano, by a zigzag slippery road, which cuts into beds of loose brown shales and schists, from which I could procure no fossil to identify their age or origin.

From Martha, a poor village of ten houses, I cross over gravel hills to Kasame, and thence descend into an open valley, that leads down from the great Pediada Plain, and has a few fruit-gardens by the side of a stream flowing from it, belonging to the inhabitants of Kasame.

As I approach Ene, a hamlet on the west side of the river, I come in sight of some masses of ruins in a hollow or small plain behind two or three eminences on its east side.

These ruins I soon perceived to be the remains of an aqueduct of the Roman time, having been arched and built with horizontal courses of Roman brick or tile. The aqueduct is also traceable on the hills approaching, but on a level with the ground. The foundations of some buildings of the same age, as well as those of two or three churches, are seen near the aqueduct, and upon the top of the hill close over the river, to which the aqueduct led. Much pottery in the soil, with fragments of building-materials scattered here and there on the hills and plains behind, show that here was situated a town of some importance in the time of the Romans, if not earlier; but no circuit of enclosing walls is anywhere indicated.

The name Ene Kephale, and the tradition that it was the chief city of the district, identify it as Inatus.

The river passing under the Ene Kephale must therefore be the Inatus, a river which is mentioned in connexion with this city (and thus assists to confirm its identity) as being a distinct river from the Pothereus (the modern Anapothari), having its source in the Lasethe mountains, and thus in the territory of the Lyctians; whilst the latter river (the Pothereus) was said to flow between the territory of the Gortynians and Gnossians.

The peasantry at Ene showed me only Roman coins of the lower empire that are found in its soil; and as it is not known to have struck coins of its own either in late or in more ancient times as an independent republic, Inatus seems therefore to have arisen in importance upon the decline of the earlier and neighbouring cities Biennus and Priansus, which latter I identify at the mouth of the Sudsuro, as I shall by-and-by show.

From Ene I proceed over low ridges of very fertile but poorly cultivated land, through Makera, Badia, and Pirate, to Aposoleme, where I arrive at sunset, and pitch my tent, from the absence of a better spot, upon the uneven surface of a corn-field near it. These are all Turkish villages, as are nearly all that are situated amongst the lesser hills which border the great plain of Messara on the north,—Kalyvia, the nearest to the Anapothari, being the only entirely Greek village; and consequently my Greek guide, the son of the Demarkh of Viano, much wished me to encamp there, as he had never been to any of the Turkish villages before, and they are seldom visited by Greeks of other districts.

As I entered Badia a burly Turk, with a Cretan cast of features, came out of a mean-looking cottage to welcome me; and when I asked for water, and drank it, he in return asked me for rum, from the vulgar impression generally prevalent in the East that this spirit is the Englishman's nectar! and he looked, too, as if the stronger beverages were more grateful to his palate than pure water.

When I left the village, which my young Greek guide seemed very glad of, he remarked that our friend was one of the fighting Turks, and was always ready for an affray with any Christian—a sort of Mahomedan Manias, no doubt, although his appearance rather indicated him to be of Cretan extraction and therefore Christian descent: but some of this description are represented as more bigoted and ill-affected towards the present Christians than the pure Turk; while many others now in Crete are still Christians in private, although Mahomedans in public through fear of declaring themselves whilst located so exclusively amongst the followers of the false Prophet.

The hills or ridges descending towards the Messara from the north side vary from 200 to 600 feet in height, and are intersected by steep-sided valleys in most parts. Yet all are capable of great fertility, if more populous; but a few olive-trees near each village, a detached vegetable-garden, and some open patches of corn-land are the amount of cultivation they present at present.

The hills are chiefly composed of soft white and grey tertiary marls, marly sands, and gravels, the strata all inclining at a small angle to the south, and thus towards the Messara, from the central backbone; near to Pirate and Aposoleme I procured several fossils. But here and there a mass of the secondary limestone raises its head above the tertiary strata, as an islet or rock in the sea.

The Turkish peasantry we met working in the fields showed us the greatest civility everywhere. Twice we had presents of cucumbers; others gave us honey in the comb; and some, hard pears; so that my old interpreter, Spero, and even the son of the Demarkh of Viano remarked that they were not such bad people, *for Turks*, after all: for the natural prejudice could not be overcome entirely.

I passed through the half-dilapidated village of Kephali, then towards Tchifoot Kastelli, across a wide, desolate valley without any appearance of cultivation or habitation within it, in which flows the most western branch of the Anapothari; but although the stream has a wide, gravelly bed, that indicates the size to which it sometimes attains, it at this season dwindles to the dimensions of a shallow meandering brook hardly ankle-deep.

Crossing this, and ascending the western side of the valley, we pass near a picturesque mass of rock upon the top of the ridges, which, when seen near, proved to be merely a weather-worn mass of conglomerate, but which at a distance had the appearance of a ruined castle, insomuch that I for some time mistook it for that of Tchifoot Kastelli, which I was in search of: but that old fortress did not appear until we had crossed another ridge, and were close upon it. Then the square-headed and almost insular rock upon which its walls and towers bristle, suddenly rose before us from the opposite side of a peaceful and fertile glade, in which were a few fine valoneas and fruit-trees growing near a spring that bubbled up through the soil and irrigated in its course a few vegetable-gardens.

A Turkish hamlet also stands near the bottom of the ridge on this side of it; and as we are passing, one of the Turkish inhabitants immediately comes forward and offers to accompany us as our guide to the fortress, presuming that to be the object of our visit. The way winds round by its south face, ascending there from the neck of a narrow ridge that connects it with the higher summits to the southward; and we soon enter this old castle, whose dilapidated walls and towers bristle round the margin of an inclined plateau of nearly a quarter of a mile in diameter, which crowns the top of the rock, and enclose numerous ruined habitations, both Turkish and of earlier times. Two or three Turkish lepers were entering the castle at the same time, in quest of charity. They had a mule in common for the conveyance of the corn, olives, cheese, or other articles that the benevolent gave them; and in this way the poorest and least afflicted make long journeys during the harvest season.

CHAPTER XXVI.

TCHIFOOT KASTELLI—THE SUPPOSED SITE OF ARKADIA—PASHLEY'S ERRONEOUS VIEWS REGARDING ITS POSITION—PLINY'S DESCRIPTION OF ITS FOUNTAINS—TCHIFOOT KASTELLI PROVES TO BE ONLY A MIDDLE-AGE FORTRESS—PROBABLE ORIGIN OF THE NAME—RETURN TO THE TENT—INFORMATION OF OTHER RUINS—PROCEED TO THEM—IDENTIFY THEM AS ARKADIA—THEIR DESCRIPTION.

THE ruins at Tchifoot Kastelli having been described to me as very ancient, and reputed by the natives to be Hellenic, I approached this old castle with considerable anxiety and interest, from the supposition that it might be the hitherto undetermined site of Arkadia, which, in opposition to the opinion of Pashley, I felt must be in this neighbourhood, and not on the east side of the Lasethe Mountains as he presumed and believed it to be. He was no doubt led to form this opinion partly by the fact that the name of Arkadia was formerly and is often even now applied to the eparkhia of Rhizo, extending to the south-east roots of the Lasethe. Yet this eparkhia of Arkadia, or Rhizo, also extends to near Tchifoot Kastelli, the river Anapothari close under it being the boundary between it and Monofatsi; so that the argument, after all, is just as much in favour of the view that it was at or near Tchifoot Kastelli as at the foot of the Lasethe, at the other extreme of the eparkhia.

Arkadia was an early bishop's see of some note, Cramer showing that, in the Acts of the Second Council of Nicæa, mention is made of a Bishop of Arkadia; and a rich monastery of this name existing on the west side of Mount Ida, in the eparkhia of Amari, had tended to confuse all writers on Crete before Pashley, by leading them to suppose that the monastery must represent the ancient Arkadia—since its coins show the latter to have been a city of some importance in ancient times, and its subsequent repute as the see of an early Christian bishop might naturally suggest its having a monastic association still.

Pashley, however, showed the error of this view when, having arrived at the modern village of Arkadia, four or five miles to the north of Tchifoot Kastelli, near the Monastery of Saint George, he was led by the name to refer to it as follows:—" Tournefort, wandering still more incautiously than Dr. Cramer from the positive topographic indications of the old authors, no sooner arrives at the richest and most beautiful convent in the island, at least fifty miles west of Gnossus, than he takes it for all that remains of the ancient city, of which, as it appears to him, it had preserved the name. Sieber, too, thinks that, without all doubt, the monastery occupies the site of the ancient city. This supposition is too absurd to need any refutation, and nothing but the far superior scholarship of the learned author of the 'Description of Ancient Greece' (Cramer) would induce me to detain my reader with an examination of a point on which his views are almost as untenable and ungrounded as those of Tournefort and Sieber.

"It will be very easy to show that Arkadia must have been somewhere in the modern eparkhia of Mirabella, or on its confines in the direction of Rhizo Kastro or Hierapetra. I have already mentioned the evidence of the Peutinger Table. We know moreover from Pliny that Arcadia was in a district abounding in rivers and fountains—a description which cannot be applied to the country near Arkadia, but is applicable to many parts of the mountains about Lasethe, and to the whole of Rhizo Kastro. Lastly, the diocese of the Greek Bishop of Arkadia does not approach this village of Arkadia, but contains the district of Rhizo Kastro, and borders on the mountains of Lasethe and Mirabello. More might be said about Arkadia; but while in this village we are on ground so far distant from the probable site of that ancient city, that it seems undesirable now to dwell any longer on the question." (See Pashley's 'Crete,' vol. i. p. 231.)

The district had only been partially examined by me when the Russian war interrupted the completion of our surveys in Crete; and feeling sure that Pashley was as much in error as the authors he has censured, and that the Arkadia of Pliny and the seat of the early bishopric must be in this neighbourhood, the name of Arkadia being still applied to one of the villages of the locality seemed so much to confirm this idea, that, as no other ruins had been discovered during the progress of the survey, excepting the doubtful Tchifoot Kastelli, I was induced to suppose that the ancient city might have stood at Agio Thoma, in the same neighbourhood, where there are some few remains and rock inscriptions that indicate an Hellenic site of some kind or another, although apparently not a large one. But the notice of Arkadia by Pliny (xxxi. 4) records a special characteristic of this city, related of it by Theophrastus. He shows that it must have stood in a strong position, that its neighbourhood abounded with rivulets, and that within the city were springs which are said to have dried up (ceased to flow) when it fell into the hands of the enemy, but recovered their supply when the city was retaken.

Hence the springs I observed under the Tchifoot Kastelli, of which there are several, one flowing into an old reservoir on the side of the rock much above the others, seemed at first to favour the placing of Arkadia here; but my examination of the ruins that crowned this rocky summit proved to me that not a vestige that was Hellenic could be traced in any of them—not a vestige that might be attributed even to the Roman period; all was evidently of the middle ages. Towers, walls, and ruins were all built of small stones and mortar, some still two, some three stories high, and others extensively vaulted beneath. Over the dark apertures of the latter my guide (a Turk of the district) delighted to pause and tell wonderful tales of deeply hidden treasures that were guarded by spirits, and of dungeons where the old kings of the castle kept their faithless wives, &c.

I was forced to listen to them for a time, but was at last obliged to tell him that it was nothing but an old castle of the Franks, and not the Hellenic city I supposed; for it was soon clear to my mind, from the character of the fortress, that it was not even Venetian. I therefore concluded that it must be the very fortress that was said to have been built somewhere in the centre of the island by Boniface during his short possession of Crete; and this idea was confirmed by my recollecting that Tchifoot Kastelli is just within the eparkhia of Monophatsi, and just without the confines of Arkadia, and that the name of Monophatsi was manifestly the modern Greek corruption of Boniface, and that therefore the adjacent district had received, and still retained, the former name of this evidence of the Franco-Genoese possession of Crete.

Disappointed, however, in the more interesting

hope regarding its having been Arkadia, I could not help sitting down on the higher crest of the rock to admire the commanding view it gives over the several ravines and valleys that surround it. The view, although a pleasing one, was not very extensive, as north, west, and south higher ridges rose above it, at no greater distance than from three to four miles, while Ida overtopped them in the distance.

The day was hot, so I was glad to rest upon so airy on eminence; for it was a July sun that shone upon the scene, and had turned all vegetation brown, except some patches of heather and shrub upon the higher hills, and some flowering oleanders which meandered down every ravine that channelled them, indicating that there was moisture beneath.

The name of Tchifoot Kastelli, or Jew Castle, is one which I have found here and there scattered over the East, applied to some isolated and strongly fortified fortress of the middle ages; but the origin of this name always puzzled me, since the fortresses evidently could not have belonged to any of this outcast and persecuted community as a possession at any time; yet the Jew's Castle is a name which several middle-age fortresses have received, in the Greek as well as in the Turkish parts in the East, under the names of Ovreo Kastro, or Tchifoot Kastelli, the probable origin of which (possibly the real one) struck me whilst contemplating the castle from the top of the rock,—viz. the finding amongst the ruins at some time a hoarded stock of gold or ancient coins, the gathering of some old miser who resided within it; for the association of a Jew with hoarded money was natural in times when they were persecuted more for their possession of it than their persuasion or religion. The traditional tales of the Turkish guide regarding buried moneys, and guarding spirits, suggested this idea to me here; and I am induced to offer it as a clue to a better.

As none of the Turks who were with me at the top of Tchifoot Kastelli could, or rather would, inform me of any other ancient site in the neighbourhood, I gladly returned to the shade of the large trees in the glade beneath the castellated rock. I was hungry, too, after my early journey and labour, and wanted some dinner; but neither bread, eggs, nor fowls could I buy: sour milk and boiled new wheat they said we could have in plenty, but nothing more. I wondered at this apparent incivility, but was at length told that, amongst the fifteen families that lived there, only four or five had any poultry left, "as they were all eaten by the Greeks" who assembled in the neighbourhood in the previous year, when the Turks were obliged to retire to their fortresses. An old cock was at last obtained at a war price; and it was soon in the pot, with some rice, for a stew, under the skilful cooking of Spero, a trusty old servant from

Smyrna, and interpreter to this survey for nearly twenty years.

The cooking was an attraction to some of the Turks of the village, who were now resting during the midday sun from their labours at the threshing-floors; or they may have come only for the love of a gossip with the stranger. The subject of old ruins was naturally referred to by me again; and at length one of the Turks pointed to the high mountain visible on the opposite side of the wide valley separating Tchifoot Kastelli from the northern ranges, and said that there was another palaio kastron at the top of two high crags there. Glad thus to have a hope revived, I immediately looked with my glass, but could see nothing to verify it. The face of the mountain under the two crags, however, showed indications of being apparently more than naturally terraced; and upon each of the terraces had evidently been some patches of corn. A ruin of some building was likewise visible halfway down, which he said was that of an old monastery. Others present, however, denied its being the site of an old city, stating that the top was only a mandri, or place with walls for keeping sheep; and the evident desire of the most influential of the party was now to divert me from giving attention to it and going there; so that I could gain no more information from them then. One of the party, however, an older man than the rest, and both sick and poor, lingered about the shade of the tree after the rest had left, and after a while he voluntarily told Spero that there really was an old city there, and a very large one, which was also built with large stones, and added that it was the kephale (or chief city) of the district, where a king once lived, who married the daughter of the prince of Tchifoot Kastelli after he had conquered it. Such was the statement of the old Turk as to the local traditions connected with the spot, who, being now alone, did not fear to tell me of it; for he was poor, and evidently wanted a nourishing meal. I looked again in consequence of this information, but still saw no walls of a palaio kastron of any kind such as he insisted did exist there, the name of which he said was Axe Kephala.

But, thinking the information reliable, I resolved to proceed there, to settle the point, as it was desirable to discover the true site of Arkadia, which was still doubtful through my failing to identify it here as I had expected. As the poor old man still remained, he gladly shared with Spero a portion of the savoury stew in return for the information. Unfortunately a small piece of salt pork had been put into the stew to flavour it; but, as the poor man was not cognizant of it, I hope it neither troubled his conscience nor the digestion of a comforting meal. Perhaps, too, he had some lingering sentiments of Christianity from his ancestors, and therefore his sense of

HALT AT MELIDOKHORI. 319

guilt, if he had any subsequently, about Spero's suspicious stew, would be extenuated, we must hope, by the greatness of the temptation of an empty stomach and craving appetite.

We descended by the ravine from the village down to the bed of the Anapothari, and crossed it above the Turkish village of Sore, situated on a small eminence on the other side. Some Turks were busy around a threshing-floor on its outskirts, and we went to them to inquire respecting the truth of the existence of an old city on the high crags over them; and I was pleased to find they unhesitatingly confirmed it, advising us to go to Melidokhori, a village on the north-east face of the hill, and ascend to it thence. I took their advice, and reached Melidokhori in a little more than two hours after leaving Tchifoot Kastelli; for I halted on the way, to take a hasty sketch of the picturesque appearance of the latter as it rose like a pillar behind us when descending under its north face.

At Melidokhori, a miserable Turkish village of about ten families, near the foot of the hill, I accordingly halted to pitch my tent, and then accosted an old man, who was idly leaning on his staff near the ruins of an early Greek chapel, to ask for some one to accompany me as my guide to the old castle above. To my surprise, he willingly undertook it himself for the sum I offered, and immediately took a firm grasp of his staff and tramped off before me. His wife, however, had overheard the conversation, and called aloud to prevent him, insisting that it was too far for him; so I pressed him to take Spero's mule, which he consented to do, but reluctantly, appearing slightly offended at being thought to require it; for he was still active, although bowed and wrinkled by the sorrows of a long life in troubled times.

We proceeded together up the north face of the mountain, without following any path, as it was neither too steep nor very rough, nor embarrassed by cultivation; some wild pear-trees, oaks, and valoneas, however, which showed the influence of the northern breezes upon the vegetation by their stunted character, grew here and there on this bleaker aspect of the mountain. Some masses of rock also peeped out occasionally above the surface soil, under one of which, not far from the top, was a small spring. One of the Arkadian fountains noticed by Pliny! was my natural exclamation and exciting hope, on seeing it.

In half an hour we had reached the saddle between the two high crags of limestone that stand upon the mountain-brow, and at once the fact was clear that it was indeed, in all probability, an Arkadian fountain we had passed; for there were portions of the old walls of a city before us, that could be no other than Arkadia— a fine piece of Hellenic wall, flanked with square towers, but facing the north, although extending

THE ANCIENT ARKADIA FOUND 321

from one crag to the other on the crest of the col or gap between them. It was evident, then, that we were still outside the city, and that the south face of the mountain, where I had seen the many terraces, was its true position; yet here were some few vestiges of scattered terraces and buildings, and pottery also, fully establishing that so fine a Greek city and site must be the long-missed Arkadia—which was actually in view of Pashley when he halted at the village that still retains its name, not three miles from the ruins of which he was in search. It is therefore strange that the Greeks of the neighbouring Monastery of St. George had no tradition respecting the true position of a city that was the seat of a very early bishopric, and is still a bishopric at the present time. Revolutions, however, such as have from time to time occurred in Crete among people of diverse religious sentiments are destructive of traditions as well as records; for if retained for a time, they can only be whispered, and so become lost or so perverted as finally not to be recognized—like the story told by the old Turk, regarding its being the castle of the king who married the daughter of the prince whom he conquered. Whether this had any connexion with the conquests and loves of old Boniface, I must leave the reader to settle as he pleases.

This Cretan city of Arkadia was evidently of note in very early times, and even disputed with Mount

VOL. I. Y

Ida the honour of being the birthplace of Zeus, as shown by the poet Callimachus, quoted by Dapper. Hence the reason of its early and only known coin having the head of Jupiter upon it; and as Arkadia was also an episcopal see of the third rank at an early Christian period, it combines an early mythological with a Christian interest.

This Arkadia, then, without doubt, was the kephale polis or chief city of the district, as my old guide also called it. He now first took me round to the west side of the western crag that overlooks it, and where it can be best ascended, whence I soon entered within a small acropolis that enclosed its limited summit, the walls of which are of an irregular but somewhat quadrangular shape, following that of the hill, and of a rude style, although not very massive; but at the south-east angle there was a fine specimen of a massive Cyclopean tower or angle of the fortress, to indicate its early date. Within the acropolis is a fallen ruin of later time, probably a church or monastery, with a large cistern connected with it; but the old Turk, pointing to it, said it was the mint or treasury of the king.

Leaving him to search over it and to follow with the mules, I scrambled down over the east face of the hill, and reached the wall extending across the gap between the crags; but I did not ascend to the eastern crag, as it appeared to have nothing on its summit but the wall itself, and was smaller than the western crag. This wall, connecting the two crags, is built of quadrangular blocks in regular courses, and with square towers at intervals, but projecting to defend the approach to it from the north, the two peaks or crags also outflanking the whole.

I then descended over the southern face of the hill, from the col between the crags, and immediately came upon innumerable artificial terraces and fallen buildings of the early style, like those of Olus in the Mirabella—some large, with their compartments traceable, but all nearly level with the ground, and the chief portion lying in a natural theatre-like hollow between two swelling slopes that descend southwards from the two crags; but a spur of rock, or cliff, from the western crag juts out considerably on that side of the hollow, so as to overhang much of the upper part of the city, and also to overlook a deep ravine to the westward of it. The face of this swell or ridge, descending from the western rock, is so steep that few vestiges of buildings have remained upon it. But the swell seems to have been the western boundary of the city, although no traces of walls exist there; for the city must have been enclosed by walls that descended upon the crest of this ridge, as it was upon the ridge from the eastern crag, where the wall is in several parts to be traced. There must also have been a southern boundary-wall low down the hill, as well as the northern one on the col between the crags; but, having been built upon softer ground, it must have fallen down, and either been swept into the valley below, from the steepness of the hill there, or buried in the soil and fragments accumulated from above, for the hill-face and lower terraces are covered with the débris of the city walls and habitations.

In passing under the cliffy spur projecting from the western acropolis or crag, I came to a cleft in the rock, on its west side, with a small spring issuing from it, and with artificial basins and conduits in front of it, that are evidently as old as the city.

Here, then, was a spring that, although not within the city, was so completely under the command of the acropolis and its overhanging cliffs, that a few stones hurled from their summit could easily defend its approach. Thus the Arkadian damsels could resort to it for their necessary supply of water until the city itself fell into the hands of the enemy; and whenever this calamity befell them, the early authors relate that the springs dried up, and only returned when the city was retaken from the enemy.

Lower down the mount, also, but within the bounds of the city, there is another spring more copious than the former, which, although forming a small marshy puddle before it, trickles for a small distance, and is then altogether absorbed by the soil; but its track can yet be traced in its descent by the grass and

THE MONASTERY. 325

rushes that grow over it. These two springs, therefore, render the evidence of the identity of the city more complete; for doubtless they were the magic fountains referred to by Pliny and others.

The ruins of the monastery I had not time to visit, or, indeed, to examine the entire city in so minute a manner as would alone satify an archæologist of keener research; for the evening shades overtook me whilst still on the mountain, and I had therefore to hasten my return to my tent. In doing so, my old guide showed me some tombs on the eastern side of the city, that had not long since been found. They were merely simple graves, formed of rough slabs of stone in some cases, and of large tiles in others, judging from the fragments seen on the surface near.

The site of Arkadia was truly a fine one in every respect; for it was a strong position, had a southern aspect, and overlooked a great portion of its territory, and moreover was sufficiently supplied with water. The foregoing sketch of its ground-plan will best convey an idea of its situation and extent, and perhaps render my long and rather detailed account more intelligible.

CHAPTER XXVII.

THE MESSARA PLAIN—ITS TWO RIVERS—PROCEED TO PANAGIA—
MUSSULMAN HOSPITALITY—THE EFFECTS OF THE GREEK
MOVEMENT AGAINST THE TURKS DURING THE PAST YEAR—
DISAPPOINTING VISIT TO REPORTED RUINS OVER PANAGIA—
SEARCH FOR THE HOMERIC RHYTION—DISCOVER RUINS AT
ROTAS—IDENTIFY THE SITE AS RHYTION—KASTELLI THE AN-
CIENT STELÆ—SUDSURO THE ANCIENT PRIANSUS—ITS SITUA-
TION—SUDSURO BAY—ROCK CHAPEL.

HAVING thus satisfactorily determined the site of Arkadia, I now return by the southern margin of the valley of the Messara to the mouth of the Anapothari in search of the Homeric cities of Rhytion, Stelæ, and Priansus, which were cities in this neighbourhood that remained as yet undetermined. The Messara valley is confined on the south by a long range of mountains rising abruptly from the coast, over which, at about the centre of the range, is its highest summit, at 5700 feet above the sea, and called Kophino. The Kophino Peak is a remarkable feature from all sides, more particularly from the sea, rearing itself like a square hump, and consequently makes a good landmark for knowing this part of the coast when approaching from the southward.

The Messara plain is but thinly cultivated at present, as, although numerous villages are scattered along its margin, they are but half populated and in partial ruin. The plain is not a dead level, and therefore not alluvial, but rises gradually from the two extremes to its centre, between the two opposite villages of Sternes and Asimi, where it is about 600 or 700 feet above the sea; but the rise is so gradual on either side, that the height is not perceptible even when looking along or across the plain. In this respect its incline is like the deceptive steppes of Russia, often considerable, although appearing flat.

The waters from the mountains and ravines on either side, therefore, flow east and west from this point, and, uniting, form two considerable main torrents, which cut deeply into the substrata of gravel and sands of the plain, and form small rivulets within them.

The western is called the Metropoli Potamos, and is by some supposed to be the ancient Lethæus that flowed past Gortyna, although that rivulet seems to have been only the tributary that divided the city of Gortyna. That running to the east is the Anapothari (or ancient Pothereus), and swells to a considerable river during winter, being capable, it is said, of then bearing large trees to the sea. These two rivers insulate the Kophino range. Desiring to get a commanding view over this fine open valley, I proceeded to the village of Panagia, on the south side of it, and near the most elevated part. This village, although named after the Holy Virgin, I found to be entirely Mahomedan, consisting of about fifteen families. At the pressing invitation of an old Turk, who found me pitching my tent near the entrance to it, I removed to his house, which was new, with an upper room made purposely for the use of strangers,—being induced to do so by the promise which its cleanly appearance gave me of probable freedom from my usual night enemies, the B's and F's.

Every Turkish village in Crete, as elsewhere, is supposed to possess a strangers' room; and as it is a mark of distinction to have the privilege of lodging a stranger, in addition to the act being considered by every good Mussulman a duty, the owner of the strangers' house is generally the most wealthy or most charitable Mussulman of the village. My tent was therefore dispensed with for this clean and newly floored house, rather than offend the good-natured proprietor who pressed my acceptance of it. The old man and his wife occupied a sort of dungeon below; whilst his son stretched himself at full length upon the roof, in the enjoyment of the cool and pure atmosphere of the locality.

The family supper being got ready at dusk, it was given for our use first, viz. a bowl of boiled vegetables and oil. Not a fowl or an egg could be got;

for all the former, as at Tchifoot Kastcli, had been eaten up by the Greeks from Sfakia and the adjacent villages during the demonstration of the last year, when the Turkish peasants of the district were everywhere driven into the fortresses. I was thus obliged to be content with this simple fare, improved by my own good tea. One poor Turk of the village deeply lamented the loss of his seventeen turkeys, and our host the loss of all his copper kettles and household utensils, in addition to his poultry and crop. Yet there was no expression of revenge against the depredators who had so impoverished them; for the Cretan Mussulman peasant is generally a humiliated being at the present day, as he feels the weakness of his government, and lives in constant fear of a revolution and of an exterminating religious war in connexion with it. That their day of domination and oppression is gone they know; and the Greeks do not now fear openly to tell them so, and with impunity, as I have heard. But the lowland Cretans generally, both Mahommedans and Christians, desire now to live in peace and harmony, having too often experienced that it is they who have first to bear the brunt of any struggle, and suffer most, as both patriot and foe fall at once upon *their* defenceless lands and villages, until exhausted. Therefore, under such apprehensions and alarms as have occurred recently, very few are disposed to extend their cultivation and improve their

EFFECTS OF THE GREEK REVOLUTION. 231

lands beyond what is absolutely necessary for subsistence.

In no part of Crete have the effects of the last revolution (although now nearly forty years ago) been less recovered from than in the Messara valley. Every village is in partial ruin still; some, indeed, have half their houses in the condition in which that revolution left them. The blackened walls and roofless hovels show still the brand of war; and ruined churches tell, too, of a religious as well as a domestic strife, with its horrors of violence and revengeful barbarity. Those who remember the oppressed condition of the Greeks of past times, however, cannot but in some degree excuse their present hatred against their old Ottoman oppressors; for every family has traditions of wrong and suffering, if the members now living have not actually experienced it.

Early the next morning I ascended to some ruins reported to be ancient, half an hour up the mountains adjacent; but they proved to be only those of a mountain-farm and a church; and immediately upon my return to the village, I proceeded to the eastward, along the skirt of the plain.

The next village of Sternes is Greek, and here my hopes were somewhat raised both by the name (meaning cisterns) and by reports; but it seems to have derived the name merely from the remains of an old cistern within a vineyard. As Pashley and both

Lieuts. Mansell and Wilkinson had passed along this side of the plain without finding any ancient site, I now almost despaired of doing so, as I could hear of none except that of Korakas (or Khorakas), which they had both determined to be only that of a monastery; it is, however, a picturesque and complicated old ruin, crowning the top and sides of an isolated conical rock that rises on the edge of the plain, near the modern village of the same name, which I reached about an hour from Panagia.

The neighbourhood is fertile, and the spot more striking and pleasing than any other on this border of the plain; nothing, however, indicated its being the site of any such old Homeric city as Rhytion, for which I was in diligent search, as I felt that this end of the great valley must have had its city, as well as the western part its Gortyna and Phæstus, besides some minor places, and that Rhytion was undoubtedly somewhere near this part, if not actually within it.

I had expected much from Agia Photia, near Sternes, from the description given of it at the latter place by a communicative Greek I met on the road, that it was full of old ruins; its position, too—at the centre of the great valley, and at the head of the two rivers that flowed east and west through it—was promising. I certainly found ruins there, but only those of an old Venetian house and of modern Greek houses; for, of these, six or eight only, out of nearly forty that originally belonged to it, were now inhabited. It was, indeed, full of ruins, which were still black by fire, and the people apparently the poorest of the poor; the brand of the last great social war was its characteristic still.

After passing round the foot of the hills under Korakas, which here make a sort of bend, we descried another bay, at the opposite point of which I immediately observed a small hill, with a ruined church or tower upon it, just over the village of Rotas, which was also visible. My eye was immediately directed to this ruin and to the rocky eminence upon which it was; and as we neared, there appeared terraces on the side of it facing the plain. The hill was naturally rugged and bare, and no walls appeared to rise upon the slope in connexion with the terraces; but on coming still nearer, by the aid of my telescope I saw that the terraces were artificial, and apparently Cyclopean. Leaving my mules to proceed towards, and wait for me near, the village situated at the other end of the hill, I ascended its western base on reaching it, and immediately came upon the remains of massive walls that had extended up its narrow brow, and which, it was apparent, originally enclosed a rather large and very ancient Hellenic city. The hill proved to be almost insulated, being only joined to the main ridges by a very narrow and low neck at its south-east end.

It is nearly a mile long, and about 400 feet high above the plain, being also very steep on its south side, but less so on its north face, yet still so steep as to have required massive terraces for the support of the streets or houses of the old city; and some of these are evidently of the earliest time, although not in the most massive Cyclopean style, and they are still from three to eight feet high. Over the village are three churches of the middle-age period. One of them has been enlarged, and seems, from the foundations extending from it, to have been a monastery also.

The smallest of the three churches stands near the summit. It has a Gothic entrance, and may be (as the natives said) of the Genoese period; for, as no Roman remains were seen—not a single vestige anywhere,—the place seems to have been deserted from before the Roman period until the time of the middle ages, or that of Boniface, when the churches were probably erected, and a town again rose upon the site.

This, then, must have been the Homeric Rhytion which is named as proximate to Gortyna, and which I was in search of. Pashley conjectured that it was in this neighbourhood, and must have passed close under its wall when he crossed the valley. And some may imagine the name of Rotas, now preserved in the village, to be a relic of its more ancient name Rhytion, and to be a confirmation of the identity.

MOSQUITOS AND FEVER. 335

But there are other evidences, besides the character of the ruins and the name, to support it. For Rhytion is said to have been once deserted by its inhabitants on account of a species of fly that infested it; and I find that a part of the plain in front of Rotas is now rank and marshy—in fact, the only part of the Messara that is so; and the few Turks who inhabit the village say that they cannot sleep outside of their houses as at other villages, in consequence of the swarms of mosquitos that rise from the plain, which probably were the fly that anciently infested it; they are also much subject to fever, and many of the inhabitants have left in consequence: it is therefore apparent that both the fever and the fly have always been the local pests. One house, however, was being repaired for a newly married couple when I arrived in the village; and as I descended the hill alone, and had explored it alone, the natives working upon its roof were taken by surprise to see me thus suddenly appear amongst them from the ruins above; for I was the first Frank that had been to them, they said, evidently jealous and annoyed at my having done so; and under the influence of a half-blind and infirm old Turk, who came out of his hovel on hearing that a stranger had explored the ruins, they were induced to be positively uncivil, and would give me no information. It was a display of the old feeling; and this accounts in some degree for Arkadia and Rhytion having so long remained concealed from the Christian traveller. But the Venetians were equally unacquainted with both sites.

Not an individual that I inquired of previously gave me the least indication of finding an ancient site at Rotas. Pashley, although unsuccessful himself, was also so satisfied that Rhytion was somewhere in this part of the Messara, from the authors who mention it, besides Homer and Strabo (the latter of whom says it belonged to the Gortynians), that he was, singularly enough, induced to make the following remark regarding the village of Rotas—" But I can hardly suppose that this modern village of Rotas affords an indication of the situation of the ancient Rhytion,"— thus misleading himself from its actual situation.

The most remarkable feature in this part of the Messara is the high insulated hill of Kastelli (or Kastellianah) at its eastern extremity, round the base of which the Anapothari winds on its way to the south coast. It is a very commanding table-topped hill, rising to the height of 700 or 800 feet above the plain, and steep all round, except on the south, where it is easily ascended by the narrow neck or col that connects it with the Kophino range ; but it is not a mass of limestone, like the long-backed hill of Rotas, but composed of soft tertiary sands and gravels, excepting its cap, which is a hard calcareous layer of the same period, and forms an inclined crust or plateau upon its summit. The remains now upon it are those only of a middle-age town or fortress commanding this extreme of the Messara, of which it appears to have been the main stronghold at that time as well as under the Venetians, who called it the Castel Belvedere.

It has the remains of five churches, some cisterns, and a spring upon the plateau crowning it, but nothing approaching Hellenic, although it doubtless must have been an ancient site, from the advantages of its position and strength, whence Pashley, without examination, considered it to have been Inatos; but that city, particularly in respect to its distance from Gortyna and Lebena given in the Peutinger Table, is better identified at Ene, a village and ruins a few miles north, and which I have before described.

Pashley also quotes Stephanus of Byzantium for a town called Stelæ, which he shows is near to or intermediate with the two towns of Paræsos and Rhythimna (no doubt confounded by Stephanus for Priansos and Rhytion). I therefore think that Stelæ stood upon this remarkable hill of Kastelli, or Belvedere; and the name of the adjacent village of Kastellianah seems to favour this conclusion by the probability of the corruption in later times of Stelæ into Kastelli, whence, finally, its proximate village took the name Kastellianah, with the final syllable *nah*, according to a Cretan peculiarity in this part, exemplified in the names of some adjacent villages, as Thavrianah and Babalianah.

The only road from the eastern part of the Messara to the coast is through Kastellianah over the schistose and shaly ridge intervening between it and the Bay of Sudsuro, which I follow from here to reach my ship at the mouth of the Anapothari. An ascent of half an hour brings us in sight of the Libyan Sea again; and in two hours more we descend to the coast, near the mouth of the little river Sudsuro, which river, however, or the valley in which it flows, we come in sight of directly the top of the ridge over Kastellianah is reached: the mountain descends very precipitously to it in most parts; and the road is a mere mountain-track, seldom used except by shepherds and now and then a pedlar merchant, generally a Sfakian, who passes from village to village, and hamlet to hamlet, buying stock or crop, and selling small wares and taking in exchange honey, wax, and cheese.

However, little of the produce of the eastern part of the Messara now finds its way to the south coast, its natural place of export, partly from the difficulty of the present mountain-track to it. But in ancient times its port was no doubt Sudsuro Bay, at the mouth of the Sudsuro, where there are some remains, hereafter to be described, which I conclude must be those of Priansus: and although Priansus seems, from its coins and the early notices of it, to have been an important city in the earlier times, yet it must have been deserted or dwindled into insignificance in later periods of Cretan history; for neither Pliny, Ptolemy, nor the 'Stadiasmus' mention it, or rather it seems then to have been confounded with Bienna or Biennus and Inatus, perhaps from being then merely their place of export, and having few inhabitants.

The coast about Sudsuro Bay is wild and picturesque. A deep-blue sea laves its cliffs and shingle shore, and bold crags and hills rise from it. The ruins of Priansos lie on either side of the steep rocky peaks and banks confining the narrow gorge through which the mountain-river of Sudsuro issues to the sea. A small flexure of this unusually straight coast renders Sudsuro Bay the most sheltered along the whole of the south coast to the eastward of Fair Havens, and it affords a good summer anchorage for all classes of vessels. This sheltered position was doubtless the main inducement for the raising of a town here in ancient times, as the nearest trading-point of the eastern part of the Messara; for, although so difficult to reach now, a good road communicated between the plain and town in ancient times; but it is now not practicable, vestiges only of the road remaining visible within the gorge and valley of Sudsuro.

The produce of the Messara is also now carried overland to the town of Candia, owing partially to the difficulty of the road to Sudsuro, and to the risks of the sea-voyage all the way round to Candia in coasting-craft; for foreign vessels are not allowed to take cargoes, except in one of the fortified ports on the north coast.

We found a convenient anchorage for the ship on a shelving bank of sand that extends nearly half a mile from the mouth of the Sudsuro; but the bank then descends almost precipitously, resembling in its steepness the sides of the bay and the mountain over it.

In ancient times it must have been used as a beach-harbour only, if used at all in winter, just as Lebena, a seaport of Gortyna, more to the west, where vessels could only be hauled ashore; for there is a strip of shingle shore and narrow plain along the Bay of Sudsuro, on either side of the gorge, and this plain is now partially cultivated by some inhabitants of Viano.

There are foundations of ancient buildings, and other vestiges, scattered over this low ground, besides some ruined walls upon the rocky crags on either side of the gorge, one of which seems to have been crowned by a small middle-age fortress. There is a small relic of a Cyclopean platform or wall also near the modern chapel which stands on the east side of the Sudsuro, near its mouth, indicating probably that the chapel was on the site occupied by a temple at some early period.

Within the gorge, just above its first bend, there are the remains of a wide and well-built causeway or terraced road, which, I have before mentioned, led up the valley and across the hills into the Messara, to Rhytion; and vestiges of a ruined bridge are seen at the entrance of the gorge. A fragment of an Ionic pilaster and a diagonally fluted column in grey marble, with some few squared blocks, were, however, the only evidences of a temple or other building that possessed any architectural design; but these are sufficient to show that an ancient city existed here, which must have been the Priansus of earlier authors, and the Præsus of Strabo, who mentions it as adjoining the territory of Lebena, although he evidently confounded the eastern Præsus with it when referring to the Dictæan Jupiter, as I have before shown.

The coins of Priansus have Poseidon upon the reverse, to indicate its situation on the shore; and the palm tree by his side apparently denotes it as being in a part of Crete where this tree, perhaps, flourished and bore fruit in early times. It may also be taken as an indication of alliance with Hierapytna, which has the same tree upon its coins; and Dr. Cramer notices an inscription, now in the Oxford Museum, which mentions an alliance between Hierapytna and Priansus.

As no palms appeared to exist now at Sudsuro, I inquired if they were ever known to grow there, and was immediately informed that there are ten or twelve growing near the chapel of Agios Niketas, over the rocky coast about a mile to the westward of Cape Sudsuro, and was thus induced to visit them and the rock chapel.

This chapel is within a cavern or grotto there, regarding which a marvellous story, illustrative of Cretan superstition and credulity, was told me, which I shall relate in the following chapter.

CHAPTER XXVIII.

ROCK GROTTO AND CHAPEL OF NIKETAS—BARBARY CORSAIR—
MIRACULOUS ESCAPE OF SOME CRETANS FROM THE PIRATES—
THE FLIGHT OF A CRETAN VIRGIN—THE RIVER SUDSURO—A
WATERFALL—THE CITY OF LEBENA—TEMPLE OF ÆSCULAPIUS
—THE RUINS OF THE CITY.

FROM Cape Sudsuro, towards the west, the mountains rise abruptly from the shore for a distance of about fifteen miles; bare crags form their crests, and steep ravines channel their sides. The chapel of Agios Niketas is situated just beyond the first of these ravines after passing Cape Sudsuro, upon a small cultivated slope, which in ancient times was terraced to support the soil. It was the only spot, for that distance, along the steep part of the coast, that showed any capabilities of cultivation; but it is neglected now, the church being the only inducement for the natives ever to visit it. A small rill trickles down the ravine near the chapel, giving nourishment to the few beforementioned palm trees growing over it, as well as to a few luxuriant oleanders, which always spring up where there is any moisture in a mountain-ravine and refresh the oriental landscape, in the hottest days of summer, with their tufts of gay flowers and evergreen clothing.

The chapel is at present merely a smoky-looking cave beneath a large detached mass of rock lying on the slope, the entrance to which is walled in by a barrier of loose stones, only about breast-high; for even this outlying spot did not escape the brand of the destroyer during the late civil and religious revolution. But there are still the remains of a building which once extended far beyond the present limits.

The roof of the cavern, although very uneven, is also elaborately painted, representing, as far as could now be made out, the remarkable events in the life of the Saviour and of Niketas, and showed that considerable cost and artistic care had been bestowed upon it; for the recent scaling-off of parts of the painted surface revealed that there was a previous painting beneath, of quite a different subject or differently treated.

This rock chapel may have been a retreat of some hermit, in times when such locations were numerous in the East. I found within it a small mutilated Testament, a wooden spoon, some incense, matches, and a lamp without oil, as evidences of its sanctity and occasional use.

That which gives it special interest with the natives at present is the story of an event that is said to have occurred about four or five centuries ago. It is as follows:—The church was crowded with Christians from the adjacent villages, on the eve of the festival of their patron saint Agios Niketas, so as to be ready (as is usual with the Greeks) for the matin service at day-break. But the fires which the assembled party had lighted near it, having been observed at sea by a Barbary corsair then cruising off the island, guided his approach to the spot, and under the darkness of the night he landed his crew in a neighbouring cove. Thus unobserved, they stole up to the church, and, finding it full of the natives, closed the door and windows upon them, and waited for day, the better to secure for embarkation their captives within.

These, therefore, discovering the reality of their condition when the door was closed and secured, uplifted their voices in a general prayer to St. Niketas. The lamentation and prayer were heard; for the priest soon after informed them that the saint had shown him a way of escape—through the back part of the cavern, by opening a small aperture there, communicating with another cavern, that led finally out upon the mountain-slope over the rock. Through this aperture, then, they all silently crept, unseen and unheard by their captors, excepting one little girl that had fallen asleep in a corner of the chapel.

When daylight came, therefore, and the church was opened, she alone was left as a prize for the Barbary corsair; and in consequence of her remarkable beauty she was made the domestic slave of the chief of the crew.

Some part of the story is probably founded on fact; but priestcraft founded two miracles upon it: first, the miraculous opening through the back of the cave by the saint, which no doubt was always known to the priest and was only closed up by a thin partition; the second was the miraculous return of the girl on some subsequent anniversary of the saint's day, in the following manner:—

It happened that on that anniversary, whilst the poor girl was in attendance on the corsair with his early cup of coffee, she suddenly remembered that it was the anniversary of her captivity, and burst into tears. Being pressed to state the cause, she did so, but received an angry reproof from the barbarian for her folly in not having long ere this forgotten her home and family. But before the harsh pirate had finished his anger the damsel disappeared from his sight; for St. Niketas (who in the Greek calendar is reverenced as a sort of Bellerophon, having the power of aërial flight on a white-winged steed) had taken her up; and the girl was restored by the saint then and there, whence she had been taken, to the arms and joy of her family. Some marks upon a rock are shown, too, which, it is affirmed, indicate where the horse's foot touched the ground when the saint alighted with the girl. Hence it is natural that St. Niketas, and the church too, should have their due share of respect on every returning anniversary of his worship, from so credulous and benighted a Christian community as the Greeks of southern Crete.

The river Sudsuro is a beautifully crystal stream, that runs all the year round, and cascades over large boulders that partially choke its bed in the bottom of the gorge. This river is a very convenient one for a ship, on her passage to Alexandria, to water at, as it flows to the sea as a strong stream.

The water is clear and pure, having only a short course from its source in the adjacent mountains; and the present name seems to be compounded of the Turkish words for milk and water; but it bore the same name, I believe, in the time of the Venetians, in which case we must trace it to an earlier race than the Turkish, or to a different derivation. Ptolemy notices a river Catarrhactes somewhere here.

In the early season of the year, when the mountain-springs run freely and every ravine has its rill, the union of several of these on the southern crest of Mount Kophino forms two streamlets, which descend from its summit at about seven miles west of the Sudsuro and two miles east of the remarkable hump of Kophino, and then fall over a high cliff under the outlet of one of these upland valleys or ravines, forming there two picturesque waterfalls, which have a descent of from 200 to 300 feet or more, and are about 1500 feet above the sea.

We saw them first in the spring (after visiting Sudsuro), at which season they are strong, and we at once decided that they must be the Catarrhactes mentioned by Ptolemy as being " between Inatus and Lebena;" but when we passed the spot again in the middle of the summer there was no fall of water, all had dried up, leaving only the white streak down the face of the cliff, which a deposit of calcareous incrustation from its action had left upon the surface. Which, then, was the Catarrhactes of Ptolemy? was it the modern Sudsuro, or the upland winter waterfalls near Kophino?

When the north wind blows strong, and its force is checked by the walls of mountains presented by the Lasethe range on one side and Mount Ida on the other, it rushes over these crests of the Kophino Mountains with terrible force, falling in white squalls that plough up the sea into columns of spray—wind-falls truly, but which would almost rival the waterfalls in their force and effect upon a sailing-vessel that happened to be so near the coast as to be under their stroke at such a time; for they are as much cataracts of wind as the falls are of water.

But to be able to observe to advantage a remarkable headland which Ptolemy has handed down to us as Cape Leon (from its resemblance to a lion), a vessel must sail or steam along it within a distance of two or three miles; and then a shaggy-shouldered, bluff-faced couching lion is really a form which the modern Cape Leda may be said to resemble.

Cape Leda is nearly twenty miles from Sudsuro Bay; and the shelter formed by this small but conspicuous headland against the prevailing westerly winds, together with the possibility of forcing by cultivation some produce out of the hills behind it, and the fact of its being directly opposite to Gortyna, with an easy communication through a gap in the mountains, led no doubt to the establishment there of a small coasting-town. For when the sickly citizen of Gortyna, or the befevered natives of the adjacent parts of Crete, found no relief from the medicines and hygienic empiricisms of the early times, it was natural that the invalid should be tempted to try the air of the proximate sea-coast or its Libyan-sea bathing.

Thus Lebena was early celebrated for its salubrity, and for a temple dedicated to Æsculapius, as noticed by several authors. It was natural that the inhabitants should raise there a temple to the god of health, for it was the Brighton of the central part of Crete; and it finally became the emporium of Gortyna.

When we first visited the ruins of Lebena, the priests of a neighbouring monastery called the site "the Lasea" (of the Acts) "that was nigh unto Fair Havens;" but that city I discovered afterwards to be much nearer Fair Havens, as I shall show.

That the remains now existing at Leda are those of Lebena was established by several facts. First, it is the only spot where the inhabitants of Gortyna could establish a port so conveniently. Secondly, the ruins and inscriptions found there more particularly confirm it. I found many fragments of a beautiful temple, lying near a Greek chapel called Agios Ioannes, which no doubt are relics of the very temple of Æsculapius of which mention is made; and it was near the probable site of this temple that I dug up the pedestal, containing a votive inscription, which is now in the Fitzwilliam Museum of Cambridge. (See Appendix.)

The following sketch will give an idea of the situation of this interesting city, rising gently from the little shingly bay upon the flank of the lion-shaped headland of Cape Leon, under which it was sheltered from the prevailing westerly winds and sea.

Several ravines intersected the site; but the intermediate slopes are not very abrupt, yet sufficiently so to have required in some places artificial terraces for the support of the buildings. No walls appear to have enclosed it, neither was there an acropolis. although the summit over Cape Leda, the back of the Lion, was just such a position as the early Greeks would have chosen for such an upper city or fortress, had it been in early times anything more than a temporary location for the restoration of health.

The ruins now existing are chiefly remains of several

vaulted buildings and cisterns, the foundations of early Christian churches and habitations, and of the facings of the terraces that supported them; all, however, that remain are built with mortar and unhewn fragments of stone, together with the materials of earlier buildings, amongst which are found many marble columns.

About the centre of the city, and near the chapel of Agios Joannes, two columns are still erect, that seemed to be *in situ*, as belonging to the interior of an early Christian church, by the foundations in connexion with them; but immediately below these columns, to the east, is an ancient platform or terrace that must have been the site of a temple—no doubt that of Æsculapius; for among the fragments near are several other columns, with blocks of Parian marble, and a fragment of a well-finished and peculiarly ornamented capital, and a base of a column, of the same marble. Upon this platform also lay the inscribed pedestal before referred to; but it was more than half buried in the soil, and, until dug out by us, the inscription was not discovered: it was also inverted.

Lower down there was found, lying in a watercourse, another pedestal, that had two almost illegible inscriptions, one being with the inscription reversed, and thus showing that the pedestal had been subsequently used for some other purpose, and overturned for the second inscription. Both these pedestals appear to have supported statues; and a fragment of a foot of a colossal statue in white marble was found near the shore. The natives informed me also that some years ago an entire statue was found here, by persons who were digging for stone to make lime, and was broken into pieces more convenient to remove to the kiln, the marble, from its whiteness, being considered more desirable as making a better lime. Consequently the foot was the only fragment that had remained; and, from the quality of the marble, it was very probably that of Æsculapius.

There were no other ruins worthy of notice, except those of a vaulted building by the side of the rocky hill lying to the east of the city, which may have been granaries, and the remains of a larger and well-built Christian church on the south face of the same hill, near which are several columns and other fragments that were used in its construction, but which no doubt came from the temple of Æsculapius or some other early building.

According to Strabo, Lebena was the scene of the Treatise on Love, by Theophrastus; but by the same authority it was said to be 70 stadia inland—a statement incompatible with these ruins being those of Lebena. But the error of placing Præsus near Lebena, which I have shown in a former chapter, leads to the inference that it is due to some transcriber, and not to the geographer, who, having lived at Gnossus, must have been better informed.

That this was Lebena the seaport of the Gortynians, and that it contained a temple of some beauty to correspond with the temple of Æsculapius, which was said to have been built upon the model of that of Cyrene, and was resorted to by strangers, is fully shown by its situation and remains. Yet there may have been an inland town of Lebena, besides this on the coast, if Strabo is correctly transcribed. Onorio Belli seems to have identified it with some inland site, where he says a large spring and aqueducts exist, as well as a bridge and other remains (Class. Ant. No. viii.), but which I did not hear of when in that part of Crete.

AN unavoidable delay in the publication of the volumes, after the printing of the Cretan Vocabulary, has fortunately enabled Viscount Strangford, late Oriental Secretary to the British Embassy at Constantinople (to whom I am indebted for the translation of the Vocabulary), to add also the following brief but learned dissertation on the Cretan and other Modern Greek dialects, a subject as yet little investigated.

# APPENDIX.

1.—ON CRETAN AND MODERN GREEK.

By VISCOUNT STRANGFORD.

COLLOQUIAL modern Greek (its slight and loose-fitting Turkish and Italian elements apart) is spoken with tolerable uniformity in nearly all the districts where it is the vernacular language. It is thereby strongly contrasted with the countless dialectic variations, falling into four main types, ultimately reducible to two, which characterized the ancient Greek of the early and the classical period. This uniformity arose from the diffusion of Attic as the basis of a common dialect after the Macedonian conquests. It continued its progress during the Roman dominion, and was at length fully established under and by means of the centralization of the Byzantine Empire*. A quasi-classical dialect, retaining the ancient grammar and vocabulary to the best of the speaker's ability and knowledge, was spoken in formal life at Constantinople by the Court, the Patriarchate, and the upper classes until the Turkish conquest; but the popular language of everyday life had gradually assumed a form essentially identical with the speech of the present day in grammar, and only differing in vocabulary by the absence of Turkish, the comparative absence of Italian, and the retention of some Latin words. The forms and idiom

* The fancy of calling modern Greek the "Æolo-Doric," which originated with the poet Christopulo, and has since been taken up by dilettante students of modern Greek among ourselves, is but a fancy. It would be easy to show two Ionisms for one Æolism or Dorism in it. Such seeming cases of either peculiarity as occur here and there probably arise from the natural growth of phonetic change, rather than from any retention of the ancient form.

of the modern language are at least as old as the tenth century. Its pronunciation, certainly not classical, is much older than that date; and though its various peculiarities are by no means all of the same uniform degree of antiquity, some of them probably belong to the later classical epoch*. The long period during which Byzantine centralization exercised its influence was sufficient to establish this popular speech, so formed, with a minimum of variation in all parts of the Empire; so that true provincial dialects, analogous in any degree to those of Italy or England, are only found in remote and outlying islands, or in districts early detached from the rest by Mahometan or Frank conquest. Provincial dialects, in fact, are only found in a form more or less marked in the ratio of the greater or less historical independence of the provinces during the Lower Empire.

Putting aside the interesting dialect of the Greek peasantry at the back of Trebizond, and the Tzakonic dialect, still spoken in a few villages on the east coast of Laconia (which, indeed, is not a dialect of modern Greek at all, but the repre-

* We in England cannot teach scholastically a foreign and a dead language like the Hellenic with the simultaneous retention of both accent and quantity, nor can we conceive without effort how any language can have been so pronounced. Yet they did undoubtedly coexist in pronunciation for a long period, without either interfering with the other, when ancient Greek was a living language. To comparative philologists such a coexistence is not only intelligible, but seems a matter of course. Our classical scholars, being generally unacquainted with the existence or nature of other Aryan languages akin to Greek, do not bear in mind the fact that to this day the Lithuanian of East Prussia fully retains the simultaneous use of tone-accent and quantity; and the same is the case in Illyrian or Servian—to say nothing of the accentual system of Vedic Sanskrit, strongly allied to that of the Greek. Nor can the modern Greek, for his part, conceive how, for example, his ancestors' words εἰμὶ, πλατὺς, could be pronounced by accent, yet without the accent changing the time of the vowel from short to long as in his own pronunciation. Recent Lithuanian grammars will teach him how this is done in the corresponding words *esmì*, *platùs*, of that remarkable language. Controversy on the subject of Hellenic

sentative of the ancient speech of the Kaukones*, being a sub-dialect of the ancient Doric come down to us in a state of extreme corruption, yet not without traces of even pre-Hellenic antiquity), the main body of modern Greek speech may be considered as tending to diverge into two types, which it is convenient to call the continental and the insular. This, of course, has reference only to the speech of the uneducated, the sole refuge of true dialects in our time : the educated (and they are more numerous in proportion to the population in Greek countries than anywhere else in Europe, as regards the elements of education and something more) speak the same language everywhere. The most marked test of the two divisions, among many others of idiom and vocabulary and some of forms, is to be found in the 3rd person plural of verbs, ending on the continent and in the standard speech in -ν, but in the islands in -σι. Thus λέγουσι or λέσι, εἴπασι, 'κτυπήσασι are said in the latter for λέγουν or λένε, εἶπαν or εἴπανε, 'κτυπήσανε. The speech of the islands shades off into its extremest variation in the south-eastern group, in Chios, in Rhodes, in Cyprus, and in Crete. In the last two islands it may be said most nearly to amount to true dialect; but the deviation even there is very far short of the absolute mutual unintelligibility which we see in, for instance, the 'Exmoor Scolding,' when contrasted with the Lancashire of 'Tim Bobbin,' or even in the difference between two adjacent Italian dialects, such as Turinese and Milanese, or Neapolitan and the polished Sicilian of the Abbate Meli. Cretan has even a literature of its own, formed in direct imitation of that of Italy during the Venetian domination. The 'Erotókritos,'

pronunciation is simply worthless and a waste of time, unless based on the principles established by the comparative study of the Aryan tongues.

* The common derivation of Tzakonia from Laconia involves a letter-change which is quite untenable. The change of κα into τζα has several analogies, as τζακίζω, τζακόνω, &c., " I break, work mischief, quarrel," &c., from κακός.

a long half-heroic half-chivalrous poem by Vincenzo Cornaro, is the earliest of these. It was written in the 16th century (at the end of the 16th or beginning of the 17th, according to Leake; but shortly before 1737, according to Mr. E. A. Sophocles); its Cretan character is well-marked; and parts of it are said even now to be remembered and recited by the Cretan peasantry, much as parts of Tasso by the Venetian gondoliers. The 'Voskopúla' or Shepherdess, a pastoral poem by one Nikóla of Apokórona, and the 'Erophile,' a tragedy, of which the story and title, as well as the method and style, were taken from the Italian, have also come down to us. The latter has many Cretan peculiarities: it also contains perhaps the earliest instance of Italian metre applied to Greek, such as has since become a favourite form of versification in the Ionian Islands, and is so delightful to read in the humorous political flings of Lascarato.

The dialect now spoken is described by Pashley as differing from that of the above books to some extent, principally by the admixture of Turkish words which have crept in since the conquest of the island by the Porte: but these, after all, are but few, and it must be borne in mind that the authors of these works, though they did not go out of their way to avoid provincialism, yet certainly did not seek to represent its peculiarities in full. A few songs taken down by Pashley, a specimen or two in M. Khurmúzi's work on Crete, a long vampire-story given by Mr. Pashley in the words of his Sfakiot guide, and the talk of the Cretan in a play by M. Khurmúzi, the author of the present vocabulary, constitute all the written specimens of modern Cretan known to me. This last production, called 'Babel' (ἡ Βαβυλωνία, ἡ κατὰ τόπους διαφθορὰ τῆς Ἑλληνικῆς γλώσσης), is what we should term a "screaming farce," and is exceedingly entertaining. It will remind classical scholars, and those who look at everything modern Greek through ancient-Greek magnifying-glasses, of the plays of Aristophanes : in reality it and similar modern comedies, like so much else that is modern Greek, are partly Italian, partly Turkish in their origin and character. A number of Greeks are celebrating the victory of Navarino in a wine-shop; an Albanian becomes quarrelsome in his cups and fires his pistol at a Cretan, who has taxed the Albanian with having come to Crete and eaten up all the κουράδια in the island. The Cretan uses the word as meaning "sheep"; but the Albanian takes it in the sense it bears everywhere else, that of σκατά, being, in fact, the ordinary gross oriental idiom with which readers of Morier's novels are familiar under the veiled translation of "eating dirt." A row ensues, and an Ionian Dogberry comes in and marches everybody off to prison. The fun of the play, which is exceedingly rich and well kept up, lies in the attempts made by the Ionian to get at a coherent story from the different witnesses when cross-examined : he talks something which is as much Italian as Greek, and he has to do with an Asiatic Greek whose idioms are mere Turkish, with a schoolmaster who will talk ancient Greek, with a rough Moreote merchant, and so on. The confusion which arises is, of course, much exaggerated, and is impossible in real life, but it is very amusing. The Cretan, unfortunately, being wounded, has little share in the dialogue; but enough is given to show the nature of the dialect.

Differences of accent prevail among the Cretan provinces—probably slight, and as imperceptible to foreigners as those which exist between different provinces or counties in Ireland, and are to be detected by natives alone. This is generally the case in Greece; and it requires experience to enable a stranger to distinguish even an Ionian islander's accent from that of a continental : nothing at all is met with corresponding to the difference between our West-countrymen and North-countrymen. In Crete the leading distinction is between the mountaineers, or 'Λορεῖται, and lowlanders, or Κατωμερῖται.

Concurrently with this, the provinces group themselves into districts—the Western, the Sfakian, that of Retimo and the neighbourhood of Mount Ida, that of Megalokastron, the Eastern, and the South Central (comprising the two provinces of Pyrghiótissa and Kenúrion). The differences are to be defined as germs of dialect rather than actual dialect: a few special words and a local accent seem to constitute the whole amount: thus Σταμόνα (i.e. στάσου μόνος), *Hold hard, be quiet*, is peculiar to Lasíthi, and ἔρωτας, for the Cretan dittany, to Mylopótamo.

The speech of the Sfakiots is distinguished from that of the rest of the island by the persistent substitution of ρ for λ, by some difference in their vocabulary, and by general retention of the extreme Cretan type. Owing to their secluded position and little intercouse with the rest of the island, they have been sheltered from the influence of the modern Greek educational system, elsewhere so strong and all-pervading. But this system, bearing for its firstfruits an ardent surface-desire for national union and centralization, which, so long as foreign domination endures, and until he attains his wishes, is sufficient to stifle the original municipal instinct and naturally centrifugal tendency of the true Greek in all ages, has taken firm root in the island. This must end by obliterating all but the faintest traces of a popular dialect, there as elsewhere— displacing a real form of speech which might have been made to bear the same relation to classical Greek that Italian bears to Latin, and substituting in its stead a strange language, now, perhaps, unavoidable and past remedy, in which a revived or factitious ancient vocabulary is galvanized, rather than animated, by the idiom of modern French newspaper-writing.

It is in words rather than forms that Cretan is best distinguished from the dialect of other islands. Many of these are classical words lost elsewhere, or are otherwise of interest to the philologist. Of the first class are κατέχω ("I know") for the common ηξεύρω, πέμπω (θὰ πέψω) for στέλνω, θὰ θέσω for θὰ βάλω, ἄγομαι or πορίζω for πηγαίνω, derivatives of νέμω and ψέγω in ἐγγαλονόμος, ξερονόμι, ψεγάδι; ἀρίδι (ἄρις), "a gimlet"; ἀροδαμὸς for ὀρόδαμνος, "a twig"; χαλέπα (from χαλεπὸς), "a difficult hill"; φθαρμὸς, "the evil eye," from ὀθφαλμὸς; the ploughman's cries of ἄνω, ἔσω, &c.; σκλώπα for σκώπα from σκώψ, an owl; ἔδιωξε, "it has occurred to me," very probably for ἔδοξε—an excellent preservation, δοκῶ being utterly lost,—with many others. The Italian words differ from those in use elsewhere, as βετέμα, "a crop," It. vendemmia; ροζονάρω, "I speak," It. ragionare; μαρτὶ, "a fatted sheep" (i. e. fatted for the festival of San Martino); βιτσάτο, "thin," i. e. poor or vitiated; πούρι, the It. pure, used as a mere expletive or weight-giver to the phrase, like γιαμὰ (from the It. giammai) in the southern Ionian islands, or μαθὲς at Smyrna; ματινάδα, "a popular song," and many others. There are a few points indicating some special connexion or intercourse with the southern Morea. Besides the local name of Tzákonas (distinctly indicating a colony from the mainland), in Leake's vocabulary of the Tzakonic dialect we find κέφαλ' ἀρία, written in two words, interpreted τὸ κεφάλι μου πονεῖ, "my head aches." But it is manifestly the Cretan κεφαλαρία, i. e. κεφαλαλγία, for the ordinary πονοκέφαλο, a headache, with the Cretan change of λ into ρ: νομεῖς or νομείαι, again, for shepherds, are only found elsewhere in the Cretan words given above. Some local names, chiefly in the western promontory of Crete, contain the patronymic termination usual among the Mainotes, but nowhere else (-άκος, as in Leotzákos, Dimitrákos, Dimitrakarákos) — Spaniákos, Priniákos, Mustákos, Trakiniákos, &c. To these may be added the name Kalamatianà in proof of Moreote affinity. The natural bridge is the island of

Cerigo. But half a century's routine occupation of this island, a most primitive and secluded district, has now ended without a scrap of information on its dialectic or indeed any other peculiarities having once been contributed to the public knowledge by the apathetic ruling race. It may here be said that the local name Sklavokhóri, occurring more than once in Crete, shows that the island was not without its share of Slavonian settlements; and the name Katzivelianà (from κατσίβελος, fem. κατσιβέλα, like γύφτος or τσιγγενές, "a gipsy") must indicate a gipsy colony. Of dialect, properly speaking, contemporary with, or even prior to classical Greek, it is, perhaps, just possible to detect a trace here and there. Ἄρκαλος, "a badger," seems to be connected somehow with ἄρκτος, ἄρκος, whence the modern ἀρκοῦδι. Apokórona, the modern name of the ancient Hippokoronion, may possibly preserve, as in Cyprus, a Cretan vernacular pronunciation of the word ἵππος (ἴκϝος, originally akvas), retaining the original initial vowel as perfectly as we see it in the East-Aryan or Indo-Persian and the Lithuanian corresponding words, well known to comparative philologists (açva, aspa, aszwà), slightly modified in the Gothic and Celtic words and the Latin *equus*, further modified in the classical Greek, but wonderfully maintained to this day in Cyprus: ἄππαρος or ἄππαρον is there used for the Cretan κτῆμα and the ordinary ἄλογον. It must be remembered, with regard to this word, that in Cyprus a doubled consonant is still really a doubled consonant, pronounced as clearly as in Italian or Arabic: thus ἄλλο is not pronounced as a modern Greek pronounces it, but like the Italian *allo*—an invaluable relic of Hellenic pronunciation, which is alone enough to make the Cyprian dialect outweigh all the others in philological importance.

I subjoin a Cyprian view of the Cretan dialect, taken from the '*Vavilonía*.' Οἱ Κρητιτζοὶ μιλοῦσιν τὰ λωὰ τὰ λόγια τους, καὶ τὴν ἀχελομαλοῦσα λέσιν τη νύφη, τὸ λαμπρὸν λέσιν το φωτιά, τὸν ἄπαρο λέσιν το χτῆμα, καὶ ταῖς κουδέλαις λέσιν ταῖς κουράδια.

In this it is the Cretan whose words, except the last one, are the same as the ordinary Greek, and the Cyprian that deviates. Ἀχελομαλοῦσα, "eel-ringleted one," for the common νύφη or νύμφη, "bride," is worth noting in this last dialect. Ἄπαρο is here spelt with only one π; but this must be mere carelessness: I have twice heard the word pronounced with a π doubled, and by Cyprians in each instance—one a gardener, the other a professor. Before proceeding to give M. Khurmúzi's vocabulary, I cannot refrain from quoting from the body of his little work the following form of disenchantment used for the relief of eye-stricken or bewitched persons, not only as a long specimen of Cretan dialect, but also for its curiosity as a bit of "folk-lore."

Πιστεύουσι τὰς νεραΐδας, τὰ φαντάσματα, τὰ στοιχειά, τὴν βασκανιάν, τὰς μαγείας, τρέμουν τὰς κατάρας, κ. τ. λ., καὶ εἰς μὲν τὸν τόπον ὅπου ὑποπτευθῶσιν ἢ ἀκούσουν ὅτι κατοικοῦν νεραΐδες ἢ στοιχειά, παντελῶς δὲν πλησιάζουν· ἂν δὲ κατὰ δυστυχιὰν περάσῃ τις ἀπ' ἐκεῖ ἢ κοιμηθῇ πλησίον, καὶ ἀσθενήσῃ, ἢ εὐθὺς ἢ μετὰ καιρόν, τότε λέγουν ὅτι ἔχει βυστιριά, τῆς ὁποίας τὸ ἀντιφάρμακον εἶναι τὸ διάβασμα. Τὴν δὲ βασκανιάν, τὴν ὁποῖαν ὀνομάζουν φθαρμόν, ἐξορκίζουν οὕτω τὰ γραΐδια· δένει (τὸ γραΐδιον) τρεῖς κόκκους ἅλατος εἰς τὴν ἄκραν ἑνὸς μανδηλιοῦ, καὶ ἀφ' οὗ τὸ μετρήσῃ μὲ τὸν πῆχυν του, πλησιάζει εἰς τὸν ἀσθενῆ, ἐγγίζει τὸν κόμπον (μὲ τὸ ἅλας) εἰς τὸ μέτωπόν του, ἔπειτα εἰς τὴν γῆν τρεῖς φοραῖς λέγον " εἰς τὸ ὄνομα τοῦ Πατρὸς κ. τ. λ." ἔπειτα ἀρχίζει "Ποῦ πᾶς φθαρμέ, ποῦ πᾶς κακέ, ποῦ πᾶς κακαποδομένε; φύγε ἀπὸ τὰς 72 φλέβας τοῦ παιδιοῦ μου (δεῖνα) καὶ ἄμε στὰ ὄρη στὰ βουνά, ποῦ πετεινὸς δὲ κράζει καὶ σκύλος δὲ γαυγίζει, νἄυρης τ' ἄγριο θεριὸ νὰ πιῆς ἀπ' τὸ αἷμα του νὰ φᾶς ἀπ' τὸ κρέας του (χασμιριέται)·

ελούσθηκ' ή κιουρά μας ή Παναγία, κτενίσθηκε και στο θρονί της κάθισε και περάσασιν οι αγγέλοι οι αρχαγγέλοι και φθαρμίσασί την (χασμιριέται), και πάγει αφέντης ο χριστός και της λέγει· 'ηντά 'χεις μάνα ηντά 'χεις μητέρα;' 'ελούσθηκα παιδί μου χτενίσθηκα και στο θρονί μου κάθισα και περάσασ' οι αγγέλοι οι αρχαγγέλοι και φθαρμίσασί με ' (χασμιριέται)· 'καλέ μάνα καλέ μητέρα δεν ευρέθηκε χριστιανός αγιασμένος και την αγιά Πέφτη λουτουργημένος, να παρ' αλάτσι απ' την αλική, ή τρία φύλλ' απ' την ελιά, και να 'πή μια φορά το Πάτερ ημών δύο φοραίς το Πάτερ ημών (έως τας εννέα).'" Τον εξορκισμόν τούτον τον λέγει τρις χασμουριούμενον συγχρόνως, έπειτα ξαναμετρά με τον πήχυν του το μανδήλι, και το βγάζει κοντώτερον 6 δάκτυλα από τον πρώτον μέτρον.

"They believe in the Neraïdes[*], in apparitions, ghosts, the evil eye, and witchcraft; they dread curses, &c.; and they never by any chance go near any place which they suspect or hear to be haunted by the water-nymphs or ghosts. If, by ill-luck, any one should pass by or sleep in such a neighbourhood, and should then happen to fall ill, either at once or after some time, they say of him that he has the Vistirià, the proper antidote to which is reading Scripture over him. As for the evil eye, by them called Phtharmòs, it is exorcised by old women in this way. The old woman ties up three grains of salt in the end of a handkerchief, measures it along her arm, and then touches the sick man's forehead with the knot, and afterwards touches the ground three times with it, saying, 'In the name of the Father,' &c. After which she begins, 'Whither goest, evil eye? whither goest, wretch? whither goest, miserable one? Fly out of the

[*] These modern nymphs are called by the name of the ancient Nereids, but their attributes are those of the Naiads. As the ancient word νηρὸς, whence their name was derived (as also the common modern word for water), is not limited to salt water, it is possible that this usage may be of high antiquity in the vernacular.

seventy-two veins of my son So-and-so, and be off to the mountains and hills, where no cocks crow and no dogs bark, to find the wild beast, that you may drink his blood and eat his flesh (she yawns). Our Lady * the Virgin has bathed and combed herself, and sat on her throne, and the angels and archangels have passed by, and have bewitched her (yawns) ; and the Lord Christ goes by and says to her, " what is it, my mother †, what is the matter? " " I have bathed, my son, and combed myself, and sat on my throne, and the angels and archangels have passed by me and bewitched me " (yawns). " Well, mother, no Christian has been found [query, can no Christian be found ?] made holy by the Eucharist and by church service on Holy Thursday, to take salt from the salt-cellar, or three leaves from the olive tree, and say, Our Father, &c., once, Our Father, &c., twice (up to nine times)." ' The old woman utters this exorcism three times, yawning at the same time, and then measures the handkerchief over again along her arm, bringing it out shorter than the first measurement by six fingers."

In concluding these brief remarks, I cannot do better than refer such of my readers as may be desirous of obtaining clear and correct views upon the very interesting subject of

* κιουρὰ, for κυρὰ, being like our conventional English pronunciation of υ. This is found in ancient dialects, as τὰν τιούχαν for τὴν τύχην in a Bœotian inscription, and is a marked characteristic of the Tzakonic dialect. Υ, probably pronounced like the French u in the later classical, the Roman, and the early Byzantine periods, has retained or reverted to its earlier sound in a very large number of words belonging to the colloquial language, now written with ου. Similarly, words like θεριὸ, ξερὸ, σίδερο must have arisen out of the earlier sound of η as a long ε.

† ἤντα is generally used for τὶ in Chios and the south-eastern islands. Koraës explains it as a contraction of τὶ εἶναι τὰ (for ἅ); as τὶ εἶναι τὰ λέγεις for τὶ λέγεις, " what is it you are saying ? " for " what are you saying ? " the intermediate τῆντα being found in the earliest modern Greek poetry of the Turkish period.

the true origin and growth of modern Greek, a subject hitherto always treated confusedly, with party spirit, and with insufficient knowledge, to the admirable summary which forms the preface of Mr. E. A. Sophocles's (of Cambridge, Mass., U.S.A.) 'Dictionary of Later and Byzantine Greek.'

VOCABULARY OF CRETAN GREEK.

A.

Cretan Greek.	Modern Greek.	
ἀγκοῦσα	στενοχωρία	Oppression, uneasiness.
ἄγομαι	πηγαίνω	I go.
ἀθιβολή	ὑπόθεσις, ὁμιλία	Business, affair.
ἄθος	στάκτη	Ashes.
αἰγούγια	ἀλοίμονον	Alas!
ἀκάτεχος	ἀνίδιος, ἄπρακτος	A man without experience
ἀναβόλεμα	ἀνήφορος	An ascent, a hill (going or looking upwards).
ἀναγκεμένοι	φρενοβλαβεῖς, πάσχοντες	Madmen, those afflicted in mind.
ἀνάδια	ἄντικρυ	Opposite.
ἀναλαμπή	φλόγα	Flame.
ἀναλώματα	ἀκαταστασίαι πολιτικαί.	Political disturbances.
ἀναντρανίζω	βλέπω ἀσκαρδαμυκτί	To look fixedly.
ἀναστοροῦμαι	ἐνθυμοῦμαι	I remember.
ἄνω	λέγουν τοὺς βόας ὅταν γεωργοῦν νὰ κλίνουν πρὸς τὸ ἀγεώργητον.	The word ἄνω is used to the oxen when they are tilling the ground, to direct them to the part unploughed.
ἀπαρθινά	ἀληθινά	True.

Cretan Greek.	Modern Greek.	
ἀποβολή	ἀντὶ τοῦ ἴχνους, διότι ζητοῦντες τι ζῷον καὶ εὑρόντες τὴν κόπρον τοῦ λέγουν· ἰδοῦ ἡ ἀποβολή του.	This term is used when they come upon the trace of a lost animal; and when they find its manure they say, literally, " droppings."
ἀπόγι	ἀγιάζι	Hoar frost, dew.
ἀπομονάροι	ἐναπολειφθέντες, ζῶντες.	Survivors.
ἀπορόχια	βρουβοβλάσταρα.	Lichen, or seaweed.
ἀποταχυάς	πρίν	Before.
ἀπύρι	θειάφι	Brimstone.
ἀραγός	ἀσκὶ μικρόν, ἀσκόπουλο	A small water-skin.
ἀργατινή	ἑσπέρα	Evening.
ἀρίδι	τρυπάνι	Gimlet.
ἄρκαλος	ἄσβος	Badger.
ἀροδαμός	βλαστὸς νέος τῶν ἐλαιῶν	A young olive-shoot.
ἄρτικας	ἀγριοσέλινον, μαγκοῦτα.	Wild parsley.
ἀφόρισι	ὑποψία	Suspicion.
ἀφορμάρης	φρενήρης	Mad, hot-headed.
ἀφόρμησι	φρενοβλαβία	Madness.
ἀφοροῦμαι	ὑποπτεύομαι	I suspect.
ἀτσέλεγος	σποργίτης	Sparrow.
ἄχνα	σιωπή, τζιμουδιά	Silence, quiet.

B.

βαβούρα	βοή	A shout or cry.
βαρεμένη	ἔγκυος	A woman in the family-way.
βαστάγι	σχοινάκι	A small rope.
βετέμα	εὐφορία ἐλαιῶν	Good olive-crop.
βίσαλα	κεράμια, τοῦβλα	Tiles, bricks.

Cretan Greek.	Modern Greek.	
βιτσάτο*	λιγνόν	Lean.
βλάβος	ἔχει βλάβος, ὁ τόπος εἶναι νοσώδης.	Sickness, unhealthiness (said of places).
βλεπάτωρας	δραγάτης	A vine-dresser.
βλέπησι	προσοχή	Attention.
βλέπομαι	προφυλάττομαι, προσέχω ἐμαυτόν.	I take care of myself, I look out.
βοσκήθηκα	ἐχόρτασα	I am satisfied, or have eaten enough.
βούργια	σακούλι	A bag.
βουργίδι	σακουλάκι	A small bag.
βυστιριά	ἀσθένεια προερχομένη ἀπὸ στοιχεῖα, ἀερικό.	Sickness which comes from malevolence of ghosts.

Γ.

γέρα	γηρατεῖα	Old age.
γαργερό	λερομένο	Dirty.
'γγαλονόμος ('γγαλο- for ἐγγαλο-).	ποιμὴν τῶν προβάτων ἀλμεγομένων.	The shepherd in charge of milch ewes.
γιαγέρνω	ἐπιστρέφω	I return.
γιοργά	ὀγρήγορα, καὶ ἰδιαιτέρως τὸ ταχὺ βῆμα τῶν ζώων.	Quickly (properly said of the brisk pace of animals).
γιότσα	ἀποπληξία	Apoplexy.
γκαύτω	ἀναχωρῶ	I start, quit, go.
γλακηχτής	ταχύπους	One who walks fast.
γλακῶ	τρέχω	I run.
γουλέ	κομάτι	A morsel.
γυολίδι	κομάτι, κεφαλοτύρι	A piece of, the top of a cheese.

* Literally "vitiated."

Δ.

Cretan Greek.	Modern Greek.	
δακτυλίδωμα	ἀρραβῶνα	Betrothal.
δάμακας	ξηρότειχος	A bare wall, without mortar.
δαμάκι	ὀλίγο	A little.
δαμινή	σιαγανή	Slow.
δέτης	βράχος μικρὸς εἰς εἶδος τοίχου.	A small rock in the shape of a wall.
δευτερογούλης	ἰούλιος	July.
διαρμίζω	βάζω εἰς τάξιν, συγυρίζω	I arrange.
διμηνήτης	εἶδος σίτου μελανοῦ διαμένοντος δύω μῆνας εἰς τὴν γῆν.	A kind of brown wheat which remains for two months in the ground.
δόμοι	λωρίον εἰς πολλὰς δίπλας ῥαμένον, καὶ τιθέμενον ὑπὸ τὰ ὑποδήματα (κόθορνοι).	A piece of leather thong which is closely folded and used by shepherds for the soles of their shoes against the slipperiness and wear of their mountains.
δροσιά	τίποτε	Nothing.
δῶρον	τίποτε	Nothing. But used by the Cretan sometimes when asking for a present or gift (using the true Greek word instead of the Oriental μπαχτίσι commonly used elsewhere).

E.

ἔγγαλα	τὰ ἀλμεγόμενα	Milch cows, ewes, &c.
ἐδά	τώρα	Now.

370   APPENDIX.

Cretan Greek.	Modern Greek.	
ἔδιωξε	μοῦ ἦλθε κατανοῦν, μὲ ἐφάνη νὰ τὸ κάμω οὕτω.	I remembered, it has come into my head, &c.
ἐπά	ἐδώ	Here.
ἐργῶ	κρυόνω	I feel cold.
ἔρωτας	δίκταμος	The Cretan dittany, concerning which there is much in Tournefort and Pashley.
ἔσω	νὰ κλίνουν οἱ βύες, ὅταν γεωργοῦν πρὸς τὸ γεωργημένον.	Is used in directing the oxen to approach the ploughed part when they are tilling the ground, as ἄνω, to send them to the unploughed.
ἔχνος	ζῶον οἰκιακόν, σκύλος, γάτα, ὄρνιθα κ.τ.λ.	A domestic animal, as dog, cat, fowl, &c.

Z.

ζάλο	βῆμα	A pace or step.
ζημιό	λοιπόν	Therefore, however, then.
ζουγλός	ἀνάπηρος (σακάτης)	Lame or disabled.
ζυγόνω	κυνηγῶ	I sport, or hunt.
ζουρίδα	κουνάδι	Polecat or stoat.

Θ.

θές (common everywhere as well as Crete).	θέλεις	Do you wish?
θέσε	πλάγιασε	Lie down, or repose.
θέττω	πλαγιάζω	I lie down to sleep.

ON CRETAN AND MODERN GREEK. 371

K.

Cretan Greek.	Modern Greek.	
κεφαλαριά	κεφαλόπονος	A headache.
κακαποδομένος	ἄθλιος	A miserable man.
κακαποδώνω	δυστυχῶ	I am unfortunate.
κακαφόρεσι	ὑποψία	Suspicion.
κακόσορτος	κακότυχος, ταλαίπωρος	An unfortunate man. (common all over the islands).
κακασύβαστος	δύστροπος	A perverse man.
καλουργιά	τὸ πρῶτον γεώργημα	The first cultivation or break-up of land.
καμνίζω	χαμηλύνω, κλειω τὰ βλέφαρα	I look downwards, shut the eyelids.
καμπανίζω	ζυγιάζω	I weigh.
καμπανός	στατέρι	Scales, steelyard.
κανάκια	χάδια	Caressing.
κανακεμένος	χαδεμένος	One who is caressed.
κανακεύω	χαδεύω	I caress, soothe, flatter.
καρφίχτης	καθρέπτης	A looking-glass.
κάσα	λέρα	Dirt.
καταλῶ	φθείρω	To destroy.
καταχανάς	βρουκόλακας	A vampire (see an entire chapter in Pashley).
κατεχάρης	εἰδήμων	A man with his wits about him.
κατέχω	γινώσκω, ἠξεύρω	I know.
κατηγορημένη	ἀδύνατος	A feeble woman.
κατίνα	ράχη	Back.
κεντιά	σφάχτης	Acute pain, twinge.
κεντῶ	ἀνάπτω	I light.
κιαουλιάς	καθόλου	At all (ordinary modern Greek, κιόλας).

Cretan Greek.	Modern Greek.	
κοιλιοδρόμι	διάρροια	Diarrhœa.
κοιτάζει	κουρμιάζει	(The hen) is sitting.
κοίτη	ὀρνιθόσπητον	Hen-coop.
κοκοσάλι	χαλάζι	Hail.
κομπόνουμαι	ἀπατῶμαι	I am deceived.
κοπέλι	παιδίον	A boy.
κοπελιάρης	ἔφηβος	A young man.
κορμιάζω	μουδιάζω	To have a limb asleep, to jar upon the nerves.
κορμός	νεοσσὸς περιστερᾶς, πιπίνι.	A young pigeon.
κοῦβος	φραγκόκοτα, γάλλος	A turkey.
κουζουλός (common elsewhere).	ἀνόητος, βλάξ	A silly fellow.
κουνενός	ὑδροδοχεῖον πήλινον	An earthen jug.
κουράδι	κοπάδι	A flock, or herd.
κούρταλα	χειροκτυπήματα, παλαμάκια.	The clapping of hands.
κουτσουνάρα	βρύσις αὐτόματος	A fountain, or natural spring.
κρεμαστά	κάτωθεν τοῦ σημείου, ὑπὸ τὸν σκοπόν.	Under the mark or object indicated. (Opposed to σκεπαστά).
κτῆμα	κτῆνος	A beast of burden or labour
κτηματσερός	ὄνος	An ass.

Λ.

λαλῶ	ἐλαύνω	I drive.
λέρια	προβατοκούδουνα	Sheep-bells.

ON CRETAN AND MODERN GREEK. 373

Cretan Greek.	Modern Greek.	
λήξης	. . . λαίμαργος	. . . . . A greedy fellow.
λιγοψυχιά	. . στενοχωρία	. . . . Oppressed, fatigued.
λιγόψυχος	. . στενόκαρδος	. . . . Uneasiness.
λιγοψυχῶ	. . στενοχωροῦμαι	. . . I am fatigued, or bored.
λοβιά	. . . ἡ θήκη τῶν ὀσπρίων	. . A granary.
λογάρι	. . . θησαυρός	. . . . . A treasure.

M.

μαδάρα	. . . ὄρος πετρώδης	. . . A stony mountain.
μαλάκα	. . . μυζιθρώτυρον	. . . . The μυζῆθρα of Greece: fresh cheese made from buttermilk.
μάλαμα	. . . ὁ ἀλωνισμένος πλὴν ἀλίχνιστος σῖτος.	Wheat thrashed, but not winnowed.
μαγλινό	. . . λεῖον	. . . . . . Smooth.
μαλιά	. . . λογομαχία	. . . . . A dispute.
μάλτα	. . . πορτοκάλι	. . . . . An orange.
μονάρι	. . . πέλεκυς	. . . . . An axe.
μαργόνω (common everywhere).	κρυόνω	. . . . . . I feel cold, shiver.
μάροπον	. . ἀρνὶ χρονιάρικον	. . . A yearling lamb.
μαρουβάς	. . τὸ κρασὶ ἀφοῦ σαραντήσῃ, παλαιὸς οἶνος.	Old wine.
μαρούβισε	. . ἐπάλιωσε τὸ κρασί, πίνεται.	The wine is old, it is drinkable.
μαρτί	. . . ἀρνὶ σιτευτόν	. . . . A fatted sheep.
μαρτή	. . . εἶδος κριθῆς σπειρομένης τὸν Μάρτιον, καὶ τῆς ὁποίας ὁ στάχυς εἶναι δίγωνος.	A kind of barley which is sown in the month of March, and the ear of which is two-cornered.
μασέλα	. . . σιαγών .	. . . Jaw.

374   APPENDIX.

Cretan Greek.	Modern Greek.	
μαστόρισσα	. μαμή	A midwife.
ματινάδα	. . τραγούδι	A song, ballad. Apparently a "mattinata" from Italian, like a "serenata."
μελίτακας	. . μύρμιγξ	An ant.
μιγόμι	. . . φορτεῖον	A burden, cargo.
μίστατο	. . . μέτρος ῥευστῶν δέκα ὀκάδων.	A liquid measure of ten Okes.
μιτάτο (properly μητάτα).	μανδρί, στάνη (common in Byzantine writers for a lodging or enclosure, from the Latin *metata*, castra *metata*).	A sheepfold.
μονοτάρου	. . διὰ μιᾶς	At once.
μουζούρι	. . . κοιλόν	A bushel.
μποτόνια	. . . περιδείριον	A necklace.
μπράτη	. . . εἰδήσματα	Information.

N.

νάκαρα	. . . δύναμις	Strength.
'ντήρησις	. . συστολή	Reserve, shame.
'ντηριοῦμαι	. . συστέλλομαι	I am ashamed.
νύχι	. . . . τουφεκόπετρα	A gun-flint, *lit.* a fingernail.

Ξ.

ξαμόνω	. . . σημαδεύω	I aim at.
ξάμου	. . . φροντίς μου*	It concerns me, or is my affair.

* φροντίς μου, if Greek at all, is written Greek, not idiomatic. Probably ξάμου, ξάσου are equivalent to the ordinary Greek ἔννοια μου, ἔννοια σου, meaning, in practice, "never mind," "don't trouble yourself," also "take care," "I'll take care" (*lit.* "it is my business," "your business"), for which φροντίς μου would be *fine* Greek.

Cretan Greek.	Modern Greek.	
ξάσου	. . . φροντίς σου	It concerns you, or is your affair.
ξεμύγηση	. . φυγὴ ἔντρομος καὶ βιαία	Hurried flight.
ξεμύστευση	. σωτηρία, ἀπαλλαγὴ δεινῶν.	Escape or safety from dangers.
ξεμυστεύω	. . ἀπαλλάττω, ἐλευθερόνω	To deliver or set free.
ξεπαραλῶ	. . ξυλόνω	To undo, cut the seam.
ξερά	. . . . τὰ καλάμια τῶν ποδῶν .	The shin-bones.
ξερονόμι	. . . χόρτον ξηρόν	Dry fodder.
ξέσυρε	. . . παραμέρησε	Get out of the way.
ξετρέχω	. . . ἀκολουθῶ, τρέχω κατόπιν τινός.	I follow, I run after some one.

Ο.

ὄμπανε	. . . ἀπόψε	To-night.
ὀργιά (ὀργυιά, a yard measure).	σπάγκος	Twine.
οὔγια	. . . ἀλοίμονον	Alas!!

Π.

παῖδα	. . . βάσανον	Trouble.
πεδουκλόνουμαι	ἐμπερδεύονται οἱ πόδες μου.	My feet are hampered. (It is usual Greek.)
παιδομή	. . . βάσανον	Trouble, grief.
παντέρμος	. . πάντι ἔρημος	Entirely barren.
παπούρα	. . γήλοφος	A ridge of earth.
παραβολή	. . ὅταν γεωργοῦν οἱ βόες καὶ φθάσουν εἰς τὴν ἄκραν, νὰ ἐπιστρέψουν.	Word used when the oxen are ploughing the ground, and reach the end of the furrow.

Cretan Greek.	Modern Greek.	
παρασύρα	σάρωμα	Sweepings.
παρασύρω	σαρώνω	I sweep.
πάσπαλα	κόνις	Dust.
πασπατεύω	ψάχνω, ψηλαφῶ	I touch, search by feeling.
πεδούλι	κομμάτι πετζίου	A piece of leather.
πηλά	λάσπη	Mud.
πηλώθω	στιβάζω	I pile up.
ποθές	πουθενά, εἰς κανὲν μέρος	Somewhere (anywhere, nowhere).
πορίζω	ἐξέρχομαι	I come out.
πόρος	δίοδος	Passage, transit.
ποταμίδα	ἀηδόνι	Nightingale.
ποῦλο	φάσκελο	The middle finger stretched out in cursing an adversary, as if imprecating blindness.
πρᾶμα	τίποτε	Nothing.
πράσσω	μανθάνω	I learn.
πρίκα (common everywhere.)	πίκρα, λύπη	Sorrow or grief.
πρόδωκα	παρεδόθην εἰς τὸν ἐχθρόν	I surrender or have been betrayed to the enemy.
προσκάδα	ἔνεδρα	An ambuscade.
πρωτογόνατος	πρωτότοκος	Firstborn.
πρωτογούλης	ἰούνιος	June.

P.

ράσσω	δράττω	To reap, bind in sheaves.
ρέμπεται	ἐπαίρεται	Is taken, seized.
ροζονάρω	ὁμιλῶ	I speak (*It.* ragionare).
ρούκουνας	ἀγκονή, γωνία	A corner.

Σ.

Cretan Greek.	Modern Greek.	
σακάζω	ἀποκόπτω τοῦ γάλακτος	To wean the child.
σάρακας	πριόνι	A saw.
σίβια	ὅλως, διόλου	Altogether, entirely.
σιμοσάτωρας	σύντροφος κατὰ τὸ ἥμισυ	A partner of halves, an equal sharer.
σκεπαστά	ἄνωθεν τοῦ σημείου, τοῦ σκοποῦ.	Above the mark or object pointed out. See κρεμαστά.
σκευρώνω	κάμπτω, στραβόνω	To bend.
σκιάς	κἄν	Even, if even.
σκλόπα	γλαῦκα	An owl.
σκολινός	χοῖρος	A pig.
σκοράρω	διαβαίνω	I go, pass through.
σωμίλιγκα	λοιμική	Plague.
σώπατο	ἐπίπεδον	A plain, on a level.
σοῦρο (It. súghero).	φελλός	Cork.
σταμόνα	(στάσου μόνος) ἡσύχασε	Be quiet, stay still.
στοῦπα	χιόνι	Snow.
στειρονόμος	ὁ ποιμὴν τῶν στειρῶν προβάτων.	The shepherd of the barren ewes.
συβάζω *	συμφωνῶ	I make an agreement.
σύβασι *	συμφωνία	An agreement.
σύγκλησι	χείμαρρος	A ravine, torrent.
συγκόκαλη	ἡ ἀποκρέω	The carnival.
συργουλιστά	κολακευτικά	Flatteringly.
σφάκα	ἡ πικροδάφνη	The bitter laurel.
σώχωρο	τὸ περιφραγμένον ἐκλεκτὸν χωράφι.	The well-fenced inner field or enclosure.

* Common everywhere.

T.

Cretan Greek.	Modern Greek.	
ταγή	βρώμη	Oats.
τάξε	ὑπόθεσε	Suppose.
ταρός	ἄνεμος σφοδρότατος	A very strong wind.
τάρταλα	λάφυρα	Spoil, plunder.
ταῦτέρου	αὔριον	To-morrow.
τσινιά	κλοτσιά	A kick.
τσινῶ	κλοτσῶ	I kick.
τσίτα	σουβλὶ ξύλινον	A wooden spit.
τσιπραγά	δίδυμα	Twins.
τουρί	κατήφορος	A steep descent.
τουρλῶ	γλυστρῶ	I slip, or slide.
τουπjὰ	τυροδοχεῖα	Skins for cheeses.
τριτάρης	σύντροφος κατὰ τὸ $\frac{1}{3}$	A sharer of thirds.

Υ.

ὑστεροβύζης	ὑστερότοκος	The lastborn.

Φ.

φαμέγιος	ὑπηρέτης	A servant.
φθαρμίζω	βασκάνω	To bewitch.
φθαρμός	βασκανία	Sorcery, evil eye.
φιοῦ	ὅταν βρωμᾷ τι, ὕβρις	Exclamation of disgust at a bad smell.
φουντούλης	ὑπερήφανος	A conceited man, coxcomb (*Turkish* fodol).
φρασκιά	μελισσοδοχεῖα, κυψέλια	Beehives.
φρύον	κράμβη	Cabbage.

X.

Cretan Greek.	Modern Greek.	
χαλέπα	πετρόλοφος	A stony hill.
χαμήλωσε	κάθισε	Sit down.
χαντῶ	νομίζω	I suppose.
χαράκι	λίθος	A stone, marble.
χαροκόπος *	ξεφαντωτής	Pleasure-seeker.
χαστουκιά	σβερκιά	A blow on the nape of the neck.
χαυτοῦμαι	τρώγω	I eat.
χουρχούδα	ρόπαλον	A club.
χρειασίδι	πήλινον ἀγγεῖον, γαβάθα	An earthen vessel.
χῦμα	κατήφορος	A hill (looking down, as ἀνήφορος is a hill looking or going up).
χυτά	κατηφορικά	Downhill.

Ψ.

ψακί	φαρμάκι	Poison.
ψακόνω	φαρμακόνω	I poison.
ψεγάδι	ἐλάττωμα	A defect or fault.

NOTES.

ἀγκοῦσα, *i.e.* "the strangler."
ἄγομαι. In the original the words stand ἄγωμε, πήγενε, which seems impossible, as a present ἀγώμω cannot be conceived. Perhaps it should be ἄγωμεν, ἆς πάμεν, *i.e.* "let us go," "come along," "*allons.*" The root is extinct everywhere, just as the Latin *ago* in modern Romanic tongues.
ἄθος. For ἄνθος.
ἀνάδια. Probably a corruption of ἐνάντια.
ἀπόγι. Lit. "earth-radiation."

* Common everywhere.

ἀποpόχια. I do not know the Greek explanatory word, and cannot find it in any of the dictionaries. It must be remembered that these last have hitherto made it a point of honour to suppress or ignore the so-called " vulgar " Greek. βρουβο- is doubtless from βρύον.

ἀποταχυάς. *Lege* ἀποταχειᾶς: interesting as preserving the Hellenic use of ἀπὸ with a genitive.

ἀργατινή, *i.e.* " the late," like τὸ βράδυ, or the Spanish *tarde*.

βούργια, βουργίδι. The Latin *bulga*, of Gaulish origin, as we are told; *Bulgas Galli sacculos scorteos vocant*. The Irish affinities are well known. It is our word *bellows*.

γιότσα. From the Italian *ghiozzo*, " drop." Compare the Turkish *damla*, " drop," and " apoplexy."

δόμοι. *Bands*; from δέω, doubtless, though the accentuation δομοὶ might be expected in that case.

ἐπά. 'Εδεπὰ *i.e.* ἐδὰ + ἐπὰ, is common in most of the islands instead of ἐδὼ (an inversion of ὦδε rather than from ἔνδον).

ἐργῶ. Perhaps from ῥιγῶ.

ἔσω. A word which is retained nowhere else, being supplanted by μέσα.

ἔχνος. Apparently formed from ἔχω, on the analogy of κτῆνος, a " possession," " chattel," " cattle."

ζουρίδα. *Zorrilla*, properly " a little fox," is used in colonial Spanish for a variety of skunk or polecat, Buffon's " zorille."

θέσε, θέττω. Here given as neuter, but in the Greek play used as actives—" μὰ τὰ πάσπαλα που θὰ θέσω στὸν "Αιδη," " by the ashes I shall lay in the grave."

καλουργιά. The vernacular form of the now common word καλλιέργεια, which, however, is a revived word, brought in from books, or rather constructed on ancient principles. The good Cretan family name of Kalerges, in the sense of " a farmer," is more likely to be from this indigenous source than from any vague meaning of " doer of good deeds."

κάσα. Found elsewhere in the sense of " scurf," " head-grease."

κοπέλι. Perfectly common everywhere; also in the Wallachian, *copil*. The derivation from κόπτομαι can hardly be admitted. Κόπελος is used in Byzantine writings for a bastard. On the whole, the word is more probably of Greek than of Romanic or barbaric origin.

κούρταλα. From κρόταλον. Κουρτηλίζω is common everywhere, and as old as the 12th century.

ληξης. Probably λείξης or λείξιος, from λείχω.

λιγοψυχῶ, &c. These words are used elsewhere, like the more usual λιγοθυμῶ, λειποθυμῶ, in the sense of fainting rather than mere oppression.

λοβιά. From Hellenic λοβὸς, "peascod."

μαλάκα. The word μυζήθρα is probably expressive of the straining or squeezing process, calling to mind Virgil's "*pressi copia lactis.*" Μαλάκα seems to be a form of the old word for *milk*, common to most of the Indo-European languages, which has run together or formed an etymological confluence with the word μαλακὸς, itself ultimately from the same root, much as *mulcere* and *mulgere* in Latin. The Cretan word reappears at the other end of Europe, among our own islands: "*mulcán* (gloss glassia, *i. e.* γαλαξία? a kind of milk frumity) is O'Reilly's *mulachán*, 'a kind of soft cheese.'" (Whitley Stokes, 'Irish Glosses,' No. 243.)

μασέλα. From the Italian rather than the Latin stage of *maxilla*. The Latin stage is preserved in μαξιλλάρι, "a pillow." Compare Chaucer's *Wanger* and the Arabic *mukhadda* (whence Spanish *almohada*), both meaning "cheek" or "jawpiece."

ματινάδα. Pashley spells the word μαδινάδα. The oldest work in the Brescian dialect (1554) consists in part of a " canzone villereccia," entitled "*Matinada, id est Stramboggio che fa il Gian alla Togna.*" (Biondelli, 'Saggio sui dialetti gallo-italici,' 163.)

μίστατο. Perhaps from an assumed ἡμίστατον in Hellenic. Compare the Latin *dimidiana*, whence our *demi-john, dame-jaune*, &c.

μουζούρι is not from *modius*, nor even the It. *misura*, but rather from the Byzantine μινσούριν, a confluence of the Latin *mensura, mensa*, and *missus*. It is a dry measure containing 15 okes (the oke = 2¾ pounds) of wheat, or 12 of barley. Its half is a πινάκι, its quarter a πρατικὸ, and its sixteenth an ἀξάγι.

μονάρι. Query μανάρι, It. *mannaja*.

μποτόνια. A neuter plural. Properly pendants, or *button*-shaped ornaments. It. *bottone*.

μπράτη. Compare below πράσσω (μανθάνω), *i. e.* "to work for information,' "strive to learn." The formation seems irregular, unless the word is for ἐμπράκτη. Πράσσω and ποιῶ are generally extinct, the latter, however, being retained in common use in the Trebizond country.

ξεμυστεύω. But in the 'Vavilonía' it means "to set free soul from body," "to kill," "smash," "*écraser.*" "Τὸν ἐξεμύστευγα δεδιμ, τὸν ἔπεμπα στὸν Ἅδη," "I say that I'd have smashed that man, and sent him down to Hell, Sir."

ξεπαραλῶ. In this word -λῶ is from λύω : in καταλῶ (φθείρω), given above, it is probably from ὅλλυμι. The present λῶ for λύω is a natural consequence or suggestion arising from the aorist ἔλυσα. As a general rule in vernacular Greek, all verbs whose aorist is -ησα, -ισα, -υσα, alike pronounced -isa, can form a present in -ῶ upon the model of the contract verbs, whatever it may have been in the ancient, or may also be in the "revived" written language. Thus, as ἐφίλησα is from φιλῶ, and ἠγάπησα from ἀγαπῶ, so ἔσβυσα has suggested a colloquial present σβῶ by the side of σβύω or σβύνω: ἔπτυσα has φτῶ as well as πτύω: ἐκόστισα, κοστῶ (constare, costare) as well as κοστίζω. It may be seen by this how the grammatical modifications of the ancient language which constitute modern Greek have arisen naturally out of changes in pronunciation. Ἐμεῖς and ἐμᾶς, and ἐσεῖς and ἐσᾶς, must have arisen from the impossibility of working the language in daily life, as soon as ἡμεῖς and ὑμεῖς came to be pronounced in exactly the same way; and so with many other instances.

προσκάδα. It. imboscata.

πρωτογούλης, i.e. "the fore July," as δευτερογούλης is "the latter July." The other variant names for months in Greek are *the Reaper, the Thresher, the Vintager* (θεριστής, ἀλωνάρης, τρυγητής), peculiar to the Ionian Islands. These names remind us of the ancient English and the Slavonian sets of names. Γούλης for Γιούλης (Ἰούλιος), if not a misprint, exhibits the Rhodian and Cyprian peculiarity of hardening a y sound after liquids before a, o, u, as καμμγὰ σαρανταργὰ for καμμιὰ σαρανταριὰ, *une quarantaine, a lot of forty*.

ρέμπεται. It is impossible to say whether this means "it is raised," or "it is seized," owing to the author's use of high polite Greek instead of real Greek. Ἐπαίρεται is good ancient Greek in the former sense. Παίρνεται, its legitimate derivative, is good modern Greek in the latter sense. No such word as ἐπαίρεται exists in the modern Greek language, properly speaking. But it has become, as I have said before, a point of honour to revive ancient forms, letting them take their chance as regards embodying modern idiom; and the confusion thus occasioned to philological work is great. So, below, χάρακας (λίθος) may be stone or may be marble; we cannot tell which, because the author uses an ambiguous and dead word instead of his own living words, πέτρα in the one case, μάρμαρον in the other. So, above, μύρμιγξ, explaining μελίτακας. Μυρμήκι or -μῆγκι is good modern Greek for "an ant," and μύρμηξ is good ancient Greek for the same; but μύρμιγξ is a jumble of a misspelling and a dead and withered case-ending. In the present case, moreover, it is most important to know which is which. If the word be παίρνεται ("it is seized"), ῥέμπεται must be one

ON CRETAN AND MODERN GREEK. 383

of two things—either a very old vernacular cognate of the Indo-European word which we possess in the form *rob*, or else the Albanian "remb" (rembéñ, "I seize") which has passed over into Crete.

ρούκουνας. Arabic *rukna*; as this word is not used in ordinary Turkish, the Cretan must be from Arabic direct—a very rare occurrence.

σιμοσάτωρας. Probably for ἡμισάτωρας, or from εἰς+ἥμισυ+-άτωρας. This last form, which is from the Latin -*ator*, is common in Byzantine and modern Greek. Compare βλεπάτωρας above.

σκοράρω. Apparently from It. *scorrere*.

ταγή. Properly "a ration" or "allowance" (from τάσσω), thence specially one of horse-provender, thence oats generally. In this sense it is used by Byzantine writers. From it, further, comes the modern verb ταγίζω, "I feed" (active). Compare the converse process in the Latin *cibus* becoming limited in the Spanish *cebada* to the meaning of *barley*.

ταυτέρου. Can this contain the lost ἕτερος in any way?

τουπιά. Perhaps from τύπος, with the common retention of the old sound of υ: *types, moulds*.

ὑστεροβύζης. Hence the family name of Sterovízi.

φθαρμός is probably to be referred to ὀφθαλμός, elsewhere lost.

χαροκόπος. The common word for "a spendthrift" or "free-liver."

II.—THE CAPTURE OF A PROTESTANT DIVINE, BY AN ALGERINE CORSAIR, IN THE SEVENTEENTH CENTURY.

THE following is an extract from the Journal of the Rev. Devereux Spratt, my direct ancestor, who was taken by an Algerine corsair, in sight of the coast of Ireland, near Youghal.

" May the first, An. Dom. 1620, I was borne in a parrish called Stratton-upon-the-Vosse, in the county of Somersett, where I was religeously educated by my parents Mr. Thomas Spratt and Elizabeth his wife; my father being a reverend godly divine, whome God made instrumental in the conversion of many a soule. When I was 14 years old, my father died. Afterwards I was sent to Maudling Hall, in ye University of Oxford, where I tooke my degree. After which I removed for Ireland, my mother Elizabeth being called thither by her father, Mr. Robert Cooke, a reverend divine, pastor of ye parish called the Island of Kerry, in the county of Kerry, where I remayned not long; but was called to ye head towne of ye county named Tralee, where I was tutor to Sir Edward Dennys's 3 sons. After, by the persuasion of friends, I entered into the functions of the ministry . . . . . October 23, 1640, the horrid rebellion of Ireland brake forth, and in it God's severe judgments upon the English Protestants, there being not less than 150,000* murdered, as by publique records appears. In Feb. 1641 it reached us, the whole country being

---

* N.B.—The above is in the handwriting of the said Devereux Spratt.

up in rebellion, and two companyes beseiging us in two small castles, where I saw ye miserable destruction of 120 men, women, and children by sword, famine, and many diseases, amongst whome fell my mother Elyzabeth and my youngest brother Joseph, booth which lyes interred there. This was a sad affliction; yet I was comforted by the good end Joseph made, being but 8 years old, yet beged of me to pray for him, and gave good assurance of dying in the Lord. After two months' seige, booth castles were surrendered, upon artikles, into ye hands of the Irish rebbells. Then ye Lord removed me to Ballybegg garrison, where I preached to the poor stript Protestants there; and passing thence to Ballingary, an island of the Shannon, I fell sicke of a feaver, out of which the Lord delivered me. Then haveing an opportunity, I returned to Ballybegg, Captaine Ferreter being my convoy, where I remained in the discharge of my calling untill the English army came to carry us off: at which time the enemy burned booth ye castle and towne of Tralee, and twice set upon us in o^r march to Corke, but with ye power of God wee still beat them. Then at Corke, I petitioned the Lord Inchaquon, who gave me a pass for England; and coming to Yougholl in a boate, I embarked in one John Filmer's vessell, which set sayle with aboute sixscore passengers; but before wee were out of sight of land, wee were all taken by an Algire piratt, who putt the men in chaines and storkes. This thing was soe greivious that I began to question Providence, and accused Him of injustice in His dealeings with me, untill ye Lord made it appear otherwise, by ensueing mercye: upon my arrivall in Algires I found pious Christians, which changed my former thoughts of God, which was that He dealt more hard with me than with other of his servents. God was pleased to guide for me, and those relations of mine taken with me, in a providentiall ordering of civil patrons for us, who gave me more

VOL. I. 2 C

liberty than ordinary, especially to me, who preached the gospel to my poor countrymen, amongst whom it pleased God to make me an instrument of much good. I had not stayed long there, but I was like to be freed by one Captaine Wilde, a pious Christian; but on a sudden I was sould and delivered to a Mussleman dwelling with his family in ye towne, upon which change and sudden disappointment I was very sad; my patron asked me the reason, and withall uttered these comfortable words, 'God is great!' which took such impression as strengthened my faith in God, considering thus with myself, Shall this Turkish Mahumitan teach me, who ame a Christian, my duty of faith and dependence upon God.

"After this a bond of £1000, preserved in my pockett at sea, where all else was lost, was now like to be lost, the chest wherein it lay being broken up by theives.

"After this, God stirred up ye heart of Captaine Wilde to be an active instrument for me at Leagourno in Ittaly, amongst the merchants there, to contribute liberally towards my randsome, especially a Mr. John Collier. After the captaine returned to Algires, he paid my randsome, which amounted to 200 cobs. Upon this a petition was presented by the English captives for my staying amongst them; y^t he showed me, and asked what I would do in ye case. I tould him he was an instrument under God of my liberty, and I would be at his disposeing. He answered noe, I was a free man, and should be at my own disposeing. Then I replyed, 'I will stay,' considereing that I might be more servisable to my country by my continuing in enduring afflictions with the people of God than to enjoy liberty at home.

"Two years afterwards a proclamation ishued, that all free men must begone. I then gott my free card, which cost 50 cobes, and departed with several of my countrymen to Provence, where I found the English merchants very civil to me.

At T—— I embarked in a vessell bound to London. Wee touched at Malaga, where I went ashore to refresh myselfe. From thence wee put to sea againe; and comeing upon ye coast of Cornewall, the Vice-Admirall Battin invited me aboard his ship, and keept me a time as chaplaine to his squadron; and goeing to ye Downes I parted from him and went to London, thence to a kinsman, one Mr. Thomas Spratt, minister of Greenwitch. . . . . After a time the Lord opened a doore of settillment for me, in a place in the county of Corke, called Mitchaellstowne."

END OF THE FIRST VOLUME.

www.ingramcontent.com/pod-product-compliance
Lightning Source LLC
Chambersburg PA
CBHW050848300426
44111CB00010B/1173